Leavenworth Papers Number 15

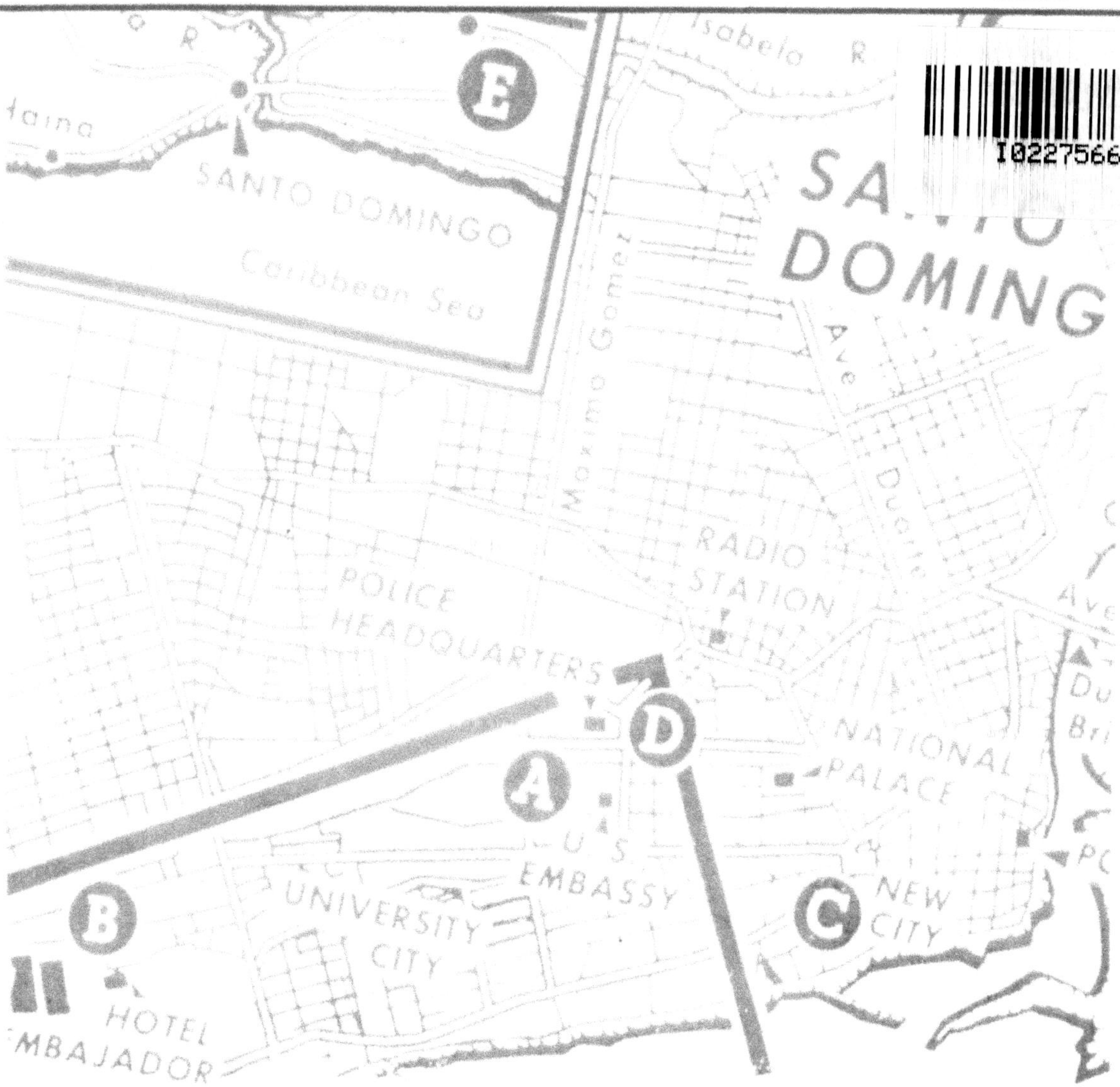

Power Pack:
U.S. Intervention in the Dominican Republic, 1965-1966

by Lawrence A. Yates

Combat Studies Institute
U.S. Army Command and General Staff College
Fort Leavenworth, Kansas 66027-6900

Library of Congress Cataloging-in-Publication Data

Yates, Lawrence A., 1945—
    Power pack : U.S. intervention in the Dominican Republic, 1965-1966 / by Lawrence A. Yates.
        p. cm.—(Leavenworth papers, ISSN 0195-3451 ; no. 15)
    Bibliography: p.
    1. United States—Military relations—Dominican Republic.
2. Dominican Republic—Military relations—United States.
3. Dominican Republic—History—Revolution, 1965. 4. United States—Foreign relations—1963-1969. I. Title. II. Series.
E183.8.D6Y68 1988   88-19209
972.93′054—dc19   CIP

For sale by the Superintendent of Documents, U.S. Government Printing Office, Washington, D.C. 20402

Contents

Illustrations v
Preface vii
Chapter
    1. Prelude 1
    2. Coup, Civil War, and Crisis Management 19
    3. To Protect American Citizens 37
    4. Intervention 55
    5. Stability Operations I: Confusion and Cross-Purposes 73
    6. Stability Operations II: Adjustments 97
    7. Stability Operations III: Peacekeeping 119
    8. The IAPF and the Peace Settlement 145
    9. Conclusions 171
Appendix. Chronology of Crisis Events 181
Notes 187
Glossary 213
Bibliography 217

Illustrations

Figures
1. Relationship of CONARC and TAC to STRICOM and LANTCOM 58
2. U.S. command relationships, 30 April 1965 109
3. U.S. command relationships, 1 May 1965 109
4. U.S. command relationships, 4–6 May 1965 111
5. U.S. command relationships, 7 May 1965 112
6. U.S. and OAS relationships, Dominican Republic, May–June 1965 151
7. Headquarters, IAPF 153
8. Organization, IAPF 154

Maps
1. The Caribbean region 3
2. The Dominican Republic 8
3. Santo Domingo and vicinity 26
4. Santo Domingo and San Isidro airfield 63
5. Movement of units of the 3d Brigade, 82d Airborne Division, 30 April 1965 80
6. U.S. marines establish International Security Zone, 30 April 1965 83
7. Linkup of U.S. Marine and 82d Airborne Division patrols, 1 May 1965 89
8. Final disposition of the International Security Zone and line of communication 95

Preface

The Combat Studies Institute's previously published Leavenworth Papers addressed, to a degree, joint and combined military operations. Leavenworth Paper No. 15, *Power Pack: U.S. Intervention in the Dominican Republic, 1965—1966*, by Lawrence A. Yates, describes a military operation characterized by multiple-service participation. Professor Yates' contribution provides an important analysis of the interplay between statecraft and military operational planning and execution. Based extensively upon recently declassified official documents and direct interviews with several key participants, *Power Pack* addresses not only questions of planning and deployment but the course of the intervention from the landing of marines to evacuate American citizens, through the commitment of the 82d Airborne Division to separate the combatants in the Dominican civil war, to the establishment of the ad hoc Inter-American Peace Force, the first hemispheric military organization of its kind.

The United States intervention in the Dominican Republic was successful. It accomplished the mission of preventing a Communist takeover and providing the military presence to make a political settlement possible. Nevertheless, Power Pack experienced its share of problems associated with outdated operations plans, poor communications and coordination, hasty planning, and inadequate staff and facilities. This study's true value lies in the identification of these problems in an effort to understand why they occurred and to prevent their recurrence.

While the J-7 Directorate works daily to resolve such problems by promoting material interoperability actions; joint professional military education (PME); joint doctrine and tactics, techniques, and procedures (JTTP) development; joint training exercises; and plans formulation, all military professionals are responsible for anticipating and preparing those joint and combined actions necessary for their successful execution. Dr. Yates' case study provides insight into the causes of these problems and the need for flexibility, innovation, and common sense in resolving them.

The Dominican Republic case study thus testifies to the value of military history for officers coming to grips with the kinds of joint and combined military operations most likely to occur in today's world.

FREDERICK M. FRANKS, JR.
Major General, U.S. Army
Director, Operational Plans and
 Interoperability Directorate (J-7)
Joint Chiefs of Staff

Author's Preface

In proposing a major research project to be sponsored by the Combat Studies Institute, my criteria were simple. The subject had to be useful to the Army and, with luck, of interest to myself as well. Ideally, the topic would combine my specialized training in cold war history and my current preoccupation with military operations at the low-intensity level. In selecting my subject, several topics came to mind but were discarded for one reason or another: the U.S. intervention in Lebanon in 1958 had already been covered in a Leavenworth Paper, Vietnam was too broad a subject to treat adequately in monograph form, and Army activities in preparation for an invasion of Cuba during the missile crisis remained too sensitive and highly classified to receive more than brief consideration.

One case study, however, showed considerable potential: the U.S. intervention in the Dominican Republic in 1965. The utilitarian value of studying the Dominican crisis was obvious for several reasons. To begin with, it presented a logical sequel to Leavenworth Paper No. 3—Dr. Roger Spiller's *"Not War But Like War": The American Intervention in Lebanon*.[1] Both case studies, in today's terminology, meet the criteria of peacetime contingency and peacekeeping operations. As with Lebanon in 1958, the Dominican intervention was a joint operation. In general terms, many of the deficiencies revealed in joint planning, command and control, coordination, intelligence, communications, and deployment for Lebanon plagued the Dominican venture as well, despite U.S. efforts to remove the causes of these problems during the interval between the two interventions. Many of these problems have yet to be resolved satisfactorily and, for this reason alone, deserve further analysis.

There is another similarity between the two operations. Dr. Spiller, in his Lebanon study, emphasizes the discrepancy between "operational military plans" and "the realities of operational practice."[2] The same discrepancy certainly affected the marines and paratroopers who entered the Dominican Republic. Hurried planning, poor intelligence, inadequate briefings, and unfounded rumors created in the combat soldiers' minds a simplistic perception of what would confront them once they arrived in the objective area. When the complex reality of the Dominican civil war became apparent to the soldiers and their superiors, they had to demonstrate flexibility and common sense in adapting to the situation. Most soldiers retained their initial convictions as to who constituted the "good guys" and the "bad guys." Adaptation came more in the realm of what duties the soldiers would be called on to perform. Except for the frequent firefights with snipers, combat was rare. Instead, combat units found themselves distributing food, performing a variety of civic action programs, and, within weeks after their arrival, trying to maintain peace between warring Dominican factions until diplomats could arrange a political settlement. Ultimately, the marines and paratroopers made the necessary accommodations to reality. They were, after all, professionals with a mission to accomplish. Still, many of them, in command and on the line, never fully understood why they could not effect a military solution to the crisis, and all resented the avalanche of politically motivated restrictions that flew in the face of military tradition and, in some cases, made it difficult for them to defend themselves.

Thus, another reason for writing a paper on the Dominican crisis was to explore in more detail the causes and implications of the often inescapable incompatibility between political objectives and military considerations. Much of what would become associated in the public mind with the Vietnam War originated, or first became a source of controversy, during the Dominican crisis. Limited war theories, spawned by the Korean conflict, dictated that policymakers in Washington determine the nature, scope, and acceptable limits for military operations in the field—operations traditionally left to a theater commander's discretion. The strict application of limited war theories during the Dominican intervention undermined civilian-military relations well before the controversy became a cause célèbre in Vietnam (and the basis for many "stab-in-the-back" theories of that war).

In another area, the "credibility gap" with which President Lyndon Johnson had to contend and the souring of what had been a close, in many ways symbiotic, relationship between the military and the news media had their origins in the Dominican Republic—although they would be exacerbated in Vietnam. The Vietnam War overshadowed the Dominican intervention, and as a result, many of the controversies surrounding the latter crisis have been largely forgotten. The purpose of this monograph is not to resurrect these controversies just to prove that they existed before Vietnam became America's foreign policy obsession but, rather, to probe the causes of this friction with an eye to ameliorating instances of it in the future.

Finally, I selected the Dominican crisis because it offers insight into a basic dilemma the United States faces in Latin America today. Maintaining friends and allies in the hemisphere depends in no small part on U.S. adherence to its pledge of nonintervention in the internal affairs of Latin American countries. Since the mid-1930s, U.S. presidents have largely honored that pledge, at least in terms of military intervention. The dilemma arises when the United States perceives that threats to its vital interests in Latin America can be countered only by recourse to military action. While such action may remove the security threat, it is almost certain to create a crisis in U.S.-Latin American relations. In a given crisis, many Latin American governments may be sympathetic to the U.S. concerns that might prompt intervention, but the sympathy of those governments in most cases will not be as strong as their aversion to Washington sending troops on a combat mission into a sovereign nation. The historical specter of U.S. gunboat diplomacy and interventionism in the hemisphere still casts a dark and pervasive shadow. This study will examine how, in the Dominican crisis, the Johnson administration tried a number of expedients to escape this dilemma, including the formation of a hemispheric police force.

After CSI accepted my proposal to write on the Dominican crisis, I pursued research at the Lyndon B. Johnson Presidential Library in Austin, Texas, and at other archival repositories. These quests revealed that sufficient unclassified material existed to warrant further research. An excellent dissertation by Herbert Garrettson Schoonmaker and a subsequent monograph by Major Lawrence Greenberg proved invaluable to the project,[3] as did interviews with several participants in the crisis. The assistance rendered both by General Bruce Palmer, Jr. (USA, Retired), the commander of U.S. forces in the Dominican Republic in 1965, and by Colonel Steven Butler, currently at USACGSC, deserve special mention. The list of others to whom I am indebted is extensive, and my deepest thanks go out to all of them. Their names and institutions can be found in the notes and bibliography. As the research continued, several documents were declassified. I am especially grateful to Mr. Randall Rakers of the Military History Institute at Carlisle Barracks, Pennsylvania, for keeping me abreast of these developments. I would also like to express my gratitude to the Joint Chiefs of Staff for making publication of this Leavenworth Paper possible. Finally, I cannot praise enough the expertise and, perhaps more important, the patience that Mr. Don Gilmore brought to editing this manuscript. The work of Elizabeth Snoke on my notes and bibliography was also indispensable.

The resulting monograph seeks to analyze the Dominican intervention within a chronological framework. I have examined U.S. involvement in the crisis at various levels, from the national command authority down to the soldiers in the streets of Santo Domingo, and have demonstrated how statesmen and soldiers acted and interacted within each level of command and between one level and another. Although the Dominican intervention was a political-military operation, the study emphasizes the military role. The political dimension is discussed extensively, but only as a vehicle for continuity or for demonstrating the political-diplomatic impact on military activities.

By way of previewing the study that follows, the first two chapters assess the history of U.S. interventionism in the Caribbean area, U.S. policy toward the Dominican Republic, the origins of the Dominican crisis, and the U.S. system for monitoring and managing the crisis. Chapters three and four treat the decision to land the marines and paratroopers and the preparations that went into the effort. Chapters five and six focus on the initial military actions by American soldiers in the country and the adjustments they had to make during the first days and weeks of the intervention. Chapter seven analyzes the activities of U.S. units once the stability operation acquired the characteristics of a peacekeeping mission. Chapter eight explores the way in which peacekeeping became a multinational operation and a political solution to the crisis finally took shape. My general findings are presented in chapter nine.

Prelude

In late April 1965, President Lyndon B. Johnson ordered U.S. marines and Army paratroopers into the Dominican Republic in America's first armed intervention in a Latin American country in three decades. LBJ insisted that the operation was necessary to prevent the establishment of another Communist country, a "second Cuba," in the Western Hemisphere. The president's justification quickly became known (and almost as quickly forgotten once Vietnam captured the headlines) as the Johnson Doctrine. In the controversy generated by the intervention, critics accused LBJ of displaying an "arrogance of power" that, in effect, repudiated the solemn pledges made by his predecessors since the 1930s not to interfere in the internal affairs of sovereign countries within the hemisphere. The Johnson Doctrine, the president's detractors charged, arrogated to the United States the right to intervene unilaterally in any Latin American country that Washington judged imperiled by the threat of an imminent Communist takeover. As one protest song proclaimed, American soldiers had become "Cops of the World."

Sticklers for historical consistency might suggest that the so-called Johnson Doctrine be more appropriately labeled the Johnson Corollary, in that, like Teddy Roosevelt's earlier edict claiming for the United States a hemispheric "police power," it was but yet another twist to the tenets of the venerable Monroe Doctrine. In 1823, President James Monroe had informed the European powers that the Western Hemisphere was closed to their colonial ambitions and "alien" political systems. Over the next 140 years, American* statesmen would define U.S. interests in Latin America in terms of security, economics, politics, and regional unity, with circumstances dictating the specific issue or emphasis of the moment. But however issues and policies might shift, there remained constant the principle that no foreign power should be allowed to establish a permanent presence or acquire preponderant influence in what many Americans regarded as their back yard.

---

*As a rule, the term "American" is used in this study as an adjective referring to the United States and *not* to other countries in the Western Hemisphere. The exceptions to this rule are few and obvious. For example, the Organization of American States clearly refers to an agency composed of various countries in the Western Hemisphere.

Few American presidents found need to enforce the principle until the United States expelled Spain from Cuba and Puerto Rico in 1898 and acquired, a few years later, the right to build and control an isthmian canal across Panama. The strategic importance of the canal and the advent of modern navies capable of launching major amphibious operations from military bases far from their home ports underscored America's need, by the turn of the century, to establish hegemony in the Caribbean area (see map 1). To remove any pretext or temptation for outside powers to intervene militarily in Latin America, the United States sought to impose stability on Central American and Caribbean countries suffering from chronic political and financial upheaval. The means for achieving this goal included diplomacy, economic leverage, and, when necessary, the deployment of American troops. In the most noteworthy interventions between 1898 and 1934, U.S. forces occupied Cuba, Haiti, the Dominican Republic, and Nicaragua to restore order and counter what Washington perceived as external threats to U.S. security. The devastation World War I visited upon Europe also served America's hemispheric interests by further reducing foreign influence in Latin America.

By the time Franklin D. Roosevelt entered the White House in 1933, the dominant position the United States had built up in the Caribbean region enabled the president to eschew gunboat diplomacy and inaugurate the Good Neighbor Policy. U.S. troops withdrew from Nicaragua and Haiti, and American statesmen formally renounced the "right" to intervene militarily in the affairs of Latin American countries. The consequent improvement in U.S.-Latin American relations enabled North and South America to stand virtually united against the emerging Fascist threat to world peace and hemispheric security. In various ways, World War II reinforced in Washington's eyes the advantages of working through a multilateral, inter-American system.[1]

When world war gave way to cold war, the paramount goal of U.S. policy in the hemisphere became that of insulating Latin America from Soviet-Communist penetration. So as not to antagonize potential allies to the south, Roosevelt's successor, President Harry S. Truman, reaffirmed America's adherence to the Good Neighbor Policy and the principle of nonintervention. U.S. statesmen also worked with their Latin American counterparts to create a regional mechanism for countering the Communist threat. The thrust of this cooperative effort was decidedly military. The Rio Treaty of 1947 declared that an attack on one American republic would be regarded by the signatories as an attack on them all. The Charter of the Organization of American States (OAS), approved the following year, strengthened hemispheric solidarity and provided an instrument for the enactment of military measures under the collective security clauses of the Rio Treaty. Truman's appeals for a U.S. program to standardize weapons and equip and train the military of Latin America met with little success until the Korean War prompted Congress to pass the Mutual Security Act of 1951. Title IV of this act extended the existing Military Assistance Program (MAP) to Latin America. A series of bilateral treaties between the

Map 1. The Caribbean region

United States and the nations receiving this assistance helped transform what had been a meager effort involving sales from existing military stocks into a comprehensive program that would better protect the hemisphere from outside attack.

These regional defense measures integrated Latin America into Truman's policy of containing communism. Latin American heads of government endorsed the arrangements, partly because they, too, shared Washington's concern over Communist expansion. More important, as leaders of underdeveloped nations, they hoped that their cooperation on security matters would prompt a grateful ally to approve large-scale economic aid and commodity agreements that would help to diversify and expand the industrial base of Latin American economies. Hopes were quickly dashed; there would be no quid pro quo. While acknowledging that economic conditions in Latin America provided a tempting target for Communist agitators, American officials bluntly told Latin American leaders that limited U.S. resources and more pressing commitments elsewhere precluded a replication within the inter-American system of the Marshall Plan of massive economic aid to Europe. Instead, Latin American governments would have to attract private investment and rely on internal market forces to stimulate economic development.[2]

Although Truman's Republican opponents often criticized his policies toward Latin America as inadequate, little changed in 1953 when Dwight D. Eisenhower became the first GOP president in twenty years.[3] The new administration eloquently proclaimed its determination to help southern neighbors solve their problems, but the rhetorical fanfare heralded few new initiatives. Advocates of greater economic aid to Latin America saw their case collapse in the face of the administration's fiscal conservatism and infatuation with private enterprise as the cure for underdevelopment. When Eisenhower and his advisers discussed Latin America in 1953 and 1954, they were troubled most by the situation in Guatemala, where a Left-leaning—some U.S. officials said Communist—government triggered the hemisphere's first cold war crisis. Preoccupied as was his predecessor with events in Europe and Asia, Eisenhower sought to end the crisis expeditiously by having the Central Intelligence Agency (CIA) engineer the downfall of the offending regime.[4] After the success of the CIA-sponsored coup, Latin American affairs reverted to their traditional place low on America's cold war agenda, there to remain barring new hemispheric crises that would accord them a higher priority.

A series of crises erupted during Eisenhower's second term that ultimately forced the president to reassess his policy toward Latin America. The first hint of impending trouble appeared in the mid-1950s, when the Kremlin launched an economic offensive calculated to win the allegiance of the world's underdeveloped countries. Eisenhower and his advisers worried that Soviet offers of aid and technical assistance might prove irresistible to Latin American republics struggling to remain solvent. Concern deepened when Vice President Richard M. Nixon, during a tour of several South American countries in 1958, encountered hostile, anti-American crowds, including one in Caracas from which he barely escaped with his life. Concern finally turned to alarm during 1959 and 1960, when Fidel Castro, having overthrown the dictatorship of Fulgencio Batista in Cuba, employed harsh measures and increasingly anti-American rhetoric to consolidate his power.

While Castro's advocacy of radical economic and social change troubled Washington, it was his pledge to export revolution throughout Latin America and his apparent willingness to open his country to Soviet influence

Fidel Castro leads a group of guerrillas in the Sierra Maestra

that convinced several State Department and CIA officials that Cuba would become a Communist state aligned with the USSR. Eisenhower was not convinced that Castro was himself a Communist, but that hardly mattered. From Washington's perspective, the Russians, without recourse to force but in violation of the Monroe Doctrine, were establishing a foothold in Cuba from which they could more easily promote internal subversion in an area where one of the most stable commodities was instability. Something had to be done to shore up Latin America and to eliminate the Cuban threat.

Eisenhower's response to these developments took several forms during his last two years in office. Largely because of Nixon's harrowing experience in South America, the administration conceded that private investment alone could not stimulate the level of economic growth needed to steel Latin Americans against Communist violence and subversion. Accordingly, the United States acquiesced in the establishment of the Inter-American Development Bank, a regional agency that would provide greater assistance to the hemisphere's underdeveloped countries. After Castro entered Havana, the National Security Council updated policy statements that, while reaffirming America's nonintervention pledge, indicated that in certain circumstances the United States would take whatever "political, economic, or military actions [it] deemed appropriate" to sever close ties between a Latin American state and the Soviet Union.[5]

The president certainly deemed covert operations an appropriate form of action for dealing with the situation, and in the spring of 1960, his patience with Castro exhausted, Eisenhower approved a CIA plan to train Cuban exiles for paramilitary operations against the Castro regime.[6] He also struck at Cuba's sugar quota in the United States and, through diplomatic channels, sought Latin American support for further sanctions against Castro. Most governments resisted the request: their commitment to the principle of nonintervention, or their reluctance to challenge Castro's charismatic appeal, overrode Washington's entreaties. The few leaders who heeded the call tended to set conditions on the scope and application of the proposed sanctions. The conditions served to intensify a debate already underway within the American government concerning the most vulnerable aspect of U.S. policy toward Latin America: the support of right-wing dictatorships.

Although U.S. and Latin American leaders often spoke of democracy as if it were the prevailing political system in the hemisphere, in too many instances, democratic trappings provided only the flimsiest cover for the authoritarian rule of strongmen and military juntas. During the formative years of the cold war, these regimes tended to be right wing and repressive, causing more than a few U.S. officials to squirm over Washington's attachment to this dictator or that. But democracy, it could be rationalized, while certainly the preferred system of government for the hemisphere, simply lacked deep roots in Latin America's political tradition. The United States had, in times past, challenged that authoritarian tradition, but by and large, efforts to teach southern neighbors "to elect good men" had generated more anti-Americanism than enduring commitments to popular government. Because Communists could exploit the tenuous nature of both democracy and progressive change in Latin America, the safe course for an American administration, by this reasoning, was to support right-wing regimes so long as they posed no threat to U.S. security and economic interests, remained dependable allies, and established barriers to Communist totalitarianism.

Washington's acceptance of this uncomfortable but convenient relationship could not easily survive the regional turbulence of the late fifties. Chronic economic woes, growing social unrest, and rising expectations in Latin America intensified demands for change that regimes committed to the status quo could not easily meet without undermining the foundations of their own power. As the rigidity inherent in the right-wing systems became apparent, there arose the unsettling prospect that, instead of erecting bulwarks to communism, U.S.-supported dictatorships might be paving a pathway to power for left-of-center movements.

Authoritarian regimes in Columbia, Peru, and Venezuela were the first to succumb to reformist groups, the political complexion of which caused some distress among conservative officials in Washington. But it was Nixon's ordeal in South America and, more important, the excitement generated throughout Latin America by Castro's charisma and revolutionary rhetoric that forced the Eisenhower administration to reassess its policies toward right-wing dictators. In 1958, Eisenhower imposed an arms embargo on Batista—a protest against the increasing brutality of the Cuban regime, but a gesture diluted by the continuation of U.S. military training programs and other visible signs of American support.

Not until confronted with Batista's defeat and Castro's call for revolution did Ike truly realize that his hopes for preventing the spread of communism in the hemisphere hinged on the willingness of his administration to support reform movements in Latin America—even those to the left of center—and to distance itself from allies on the extreme right.[7] Suddenly, progressive leaders such as Rómulo Betancourt in Venezuela and José Figueres in Costa Rica found that they had influence in Washington and that they could use it as leverage to exact a price for their support of U.S.-sponsored sanctions against Castro. The United States, they insisted, must condemn all dictatorial regimes in Latin America, both of the Left and of the Right, not just the government of Cuba. Of the remaining right-wing candidates for censure, the one that came most readily to mind was the malevolent dictatorship of Rafael Leoñidas Trujillo Molina, the strongman of the Dominican Republic (see map 2).

*   *   *

Trujillo seemed but the latest testament to the sad commentary that Dominican history comprises a succession of foreign occupations, domestic tyrants, coups, countercoups, dictatorships, and revolutions—broken occasionally by unsuccessful experiments in democracy. By one count, the Dominican Republic had 123 rulers, mostly military men, from its discovery in 1492 until Trujillo. Chaos, political factionalism, corruption, and economic instability continuously wracked the country, contributing to the sense of resignation, fatalism, and low self-esteem that engulfed large segments of the population.[8]

The United States played but a small role in Dominican affairs until the early twentieth century, when changing security interests rendered Hispaniola strategically important.[9] Lodged between Cuba to the west and Puerto Rico to the east, the island occupied a position along the Atlantic approach to the Panama Canal. In 1905, the fear that Santo Domingo's chronic financial crises would provoke European intervention led U.S. and Dominican officials to establish, by mutual agreement, a U.S. receivership over Dominican customs. This arrangement brought only temporary stability, and a decade later, against the backdrop of the war in Europe, President Woodrow Wilson ordered U.S. marines into the country in 1916 to impose order and counter German influence. The American military occupation of the Dominican Republic lasted eight years. During most of that time, U.S. military governors tried to reshape Dominican politics, economic relationships, and society in such a way as to institutionalize peace and stabil-

Map 2. The Dominican Republic

ity. Drawing on and elaborating military experience in similar situations, the marines initiated public works programs together with reforms affecting health and sanitation, education, government administration, the judicial and revenue systems, tax laws, land titles, and agriculture. The occupation policy was comprehensive and well intentioned but obtained mostly transitory results. When the marines withdrew in 1924, the country's political, economic, and social structure remained fundamentally unchanged and as potentially unstable as ever.[10]

Although the occupation failed to impose stability on the country, it left behind a vehicle that would accomplish that goal, though not in the way intended by Washington or the marines. To maintain order and democracy after their departure, the marines had organized and trained a native national guard and had tried to imbue it with the professional and apolitical standards to which U.S. soldiers conformed. But Trujillo controlled the *guardia* and turned it into a partisan instrument that, together with the secret police and an army he created from the National Police in 1928, allowed him to take control of the country in 1930. "Thus began," according to one account, "the reign of one of the earliest—and longest surviving—totalitarian dictators of the 20th century," a reign characterized by nepotism, terror, murder, malfeasance, torture, concentration camps, repression, corruption, commercial monopolies, and the financial aggrandizement of the Trujillo family.[11]

Dominicans, then as now, regarded Trujillo with ambivalence: they feared his methods and resented the pain he inflicted on many of his countrymen, but they admired the economic development, the prosperity, the political stability, and the national discipline and prestige his rule fostered. U.S. policymakers shared the ambivalence. Franklin Roosevelt allegedly referred to Trujillo as a son of a bitch, but "our son of a bitch." One of Truman's secretaries of state, James F. Byrnes, described Trujillo to the president as "the most ruthless, unprincipled, and efficent dictator in this hemisphere," the head of a "completely unsavory" regime. Byrnes advised Truman to "avoid even the appearance of lending him any support." The U.S. Embassy in Ciudad Trujillo (Santo Domingo) echoed this sentiment early in the Eisenhower years in a message that referred to "Trujillo's psychosis" and urged "greater efforts to prevent identification of the United States with Trujillo in the minds of the Dominican people in light of his growing excesses and the likelihood that he has only a few more years."[12] Yet Trujillo clung to power. He proclaimed himself the hemisphere's leading anti-Communist and placated the skeptics in Washington by ensuring domestic stability. He also cultivated (some would say bribed)[13] U.S. congressmen, hired lobbyists in the United States, and flaunted U.S. military and economic assistance and the laudatory public statements of prominent Americans as endorsements of his personal rule.

Trujillo's deftness in soliciting American support could not continue indefinitely. By the late 1950s, he had become too much of an international embarrassment for Washington to tolerate. In 1956, the dictator's henchmen kidnapped a Spanish scholar teaching in the United States. The scholar had written a scathing biography of Trujillo, a "crime" for which he and two unwitting pawns paid with their lives. Revelations regarding the affair outraged many Americans. Trujillo's continued military assistance to Batista after the United States had terminated arms shipments to the Cuban dictator further antagonized the Eisenhower administration. But it was Trujillo's intrigues against the Betancourt government, including an attempt to assassinate the Venezuelan president, that led to OAS and U.S. sanctions against the Dominican dictator in 1960. As signs of its displeasure, the United States cut economic aid and broke diplomatic relations with the Dominican Republic. An even stronger measure went unannounced, as President Eisenhower once again turned to the CIA, in this case authorizing it to assist Dominican opposition groups conspiring to overthrow the Trujillo dictatorship. As these groups made clear, the regime could not be toppled unless the dictator himself were assassinated. "If you recall Dracula," one conspirator emphasized, "you will remember it was necessary to drive a stake through his heart to prevent a continuation of his crimes."[14]

Thus, as the Eisenhower administration came to a close, it was engaged, through of variety of overt and covert tactics, in trying to rid the hemisphere of extremism on the right and left, as personified by Trujillo and Castro, respectively. As the president informed a small group of advisers, he would "like to see them both sawed off."[15]

*   *   *

Eisenhower's tentative reassessment of U.S. policy toward Latin America gave way to major initiatives in the region under his successor, John F. Kennedy. By the time Kennedy became president in January 1961, the main battlefield in the cold war had clearly shifted from Europe—where only the anomaly of Berlin threatened a superpower crisis—to the world's underdeveloped countries, most of which were engaged in the process of gaining or adjusting to independence from Western colonial powers. Although Latin American republics had been independent for some time, they shared certain characteristics with the newly emerging nations: economic backwardness, social fragmentation, political instability, a maldistribution of wealth and power, rising expectations, and an increasingly militant nationalism. Politically active labor unions and student associations and an emerging middle class were more apparent in Latin America than elsewhere in the underdeveloped world, but their existence did not guarantee the kind of stability Washington desired. As Nixon's tour of South America had demonstrated, militant nationalism as espoused by elements of these groups could exhibit anticapitalistic, anti-American overtones by fixing on such themes as Latin America's neocolonial dependency on the United States.

The "sweep of nationalism," the new president believed, was "the most potent factor in foreign affairs today." Long before entering the White House, Kennedy had expressed fears about the Communists exploiting Third World nationalism to further their own universalist programs. These fears were reinforced just two weeks before his inauguration when Soviet Premier Nikita Khrushchev proclaimed Russian support for "wars of national liberation" in Asia, Africa, and Latin America. Confronted by Khrushchev's challenge and Castro's revolutionary fervor, New Frontiersmen surpassed Eisenhower in raising Latin America from the mire of U.S. neglect. As Kennedy was noted to have observed, "the most critical spot on the globe nowadays was Latin America, where the situation seemed made-to-order for the communists."[16]

Kennedy christened his vessel for Latin American stability the "Alliance for Progress." Conceptually, the Alliance differed little from U.S. programs designed for other parts of the Third World, where, according to foreign policy experts, demands for change—defined as modernization—were inevitable, and right-wing regimes that opposed change, atavistic. Support for the status quo portended dangerous consequences, but so, too, from Washington's standpoint, did the Communist alternative of forcing change through violent revolution. The role of the United States was to promote change through peaceful evolution—the "middle way" between reaction and revolution.

This was hardly a novel idea in American foreign policy, but Kennedy differed from its previous proponents in the amount of U.S. assistance he was willing to countenance in the form of foreign aid and in the ideological latitude he was willing to tolerate on the part of recipient countries. In the Alliance for Progress, Latin America would at last have its Marshall Plan. Through a cooperative venture entailing massive economic aid from public and private sources and the enactment of fundamental social and economic reforms by aid recipients—preferably democratic, nationalistic governments of the center and non-Communist Left—*La Alianza* promised to promote economic development, social stability, and, where it did not exist, political democracy. Planners optimistically (and naively) projected that Latin American economies could be placed on a self-sustaining basis within a decade. The peaceful transformation to modernity would bring stability to Latin America, and stability would insulate the hemisphere from communism.

The emphasis on *gradual* change meant that developing countries had to be protected in the short term from right-wing procrastination and from Communist-inspired sabotage, guerrilla warfare, and coups d'état. U.S. diplomatic, economic, and military leverage seemed ample for overcoming the Right's resistance, while the strategic doctrine of Flexible Response devised by the Kennedy administration offered several options for countering the full range of Communist tactics.

In the president's opinion, the most effective method for checking Communist subversion and guerrilla warfare in Latin America was counterinsurgency.[17] In its broadest sense, counterinsurgency encompassed a variety of economic, social, political, psychological, and military activities that required the expertise and interaction of various U.S. government agencies. The Agency for International Development (AID), for example, would oversee economic assistance to Latin American countries, while its Office of Public Safety would train indigenous police in interrogation techniques and riot control. The United States Information Agency (USIA) would counteract

Communist propaganda by assisting host governments in improving their image at home and abroad, while the CIA would gather intelligence and engage in covert and paramilitary activities.

The Latin American armed forces had the key role to play in counterinsurgency. Many of President Kennedy's advisers propounded the then-popular thesis that the younger and midlevel officers within the Latin American military represented a new breed of technically skilled professionals who were not only receptive to civilian democracy but also ready to serve as willing agents of the Alliance for Progress. Specifically, these officers would engage in civic action and counterguerrilla activities designed to win popular support for their governments and to defeat hard-core rebels for whom reformist programs were anathema.

Latin American officers who lacked sufficient training and experience in counterinsurgency could receive it in service schools in the United States or at the School of the Americas in the Panama Canal Zone. In most cases, Military Assistance Advisory Groups (MAAGs) operating in eighteen Latin American countries under MAP-authorized bilateral treaties would provide the necessary training. (The original rationale for MAP had been hemispheric defense, but a 1959 study of the program recommended a greater emphasis on internal security. The Kennedy administration accepted this shift in emphasis because it reflected the president's predilection for counterinsurgency.) To enhance the training provided by regular U.S. military advisers, small Mobile Training Teams (MTTs) of U.S. Special Forces (Green Berets) could be dispatched, on request of a host country, to provide more specialized instruction in civil affairs, psychological operations, engineering and construction, medical assistance, intelligence and interrogation, riot control, electronic security, civic action, and counterguerrilla tactics and techniques. Kennedy had resuscitated, upgraded, reoriented, and expanded the Special Forces so that by 1963, Green Berets specifically designated for MTT or other duties in Latin America were located with the 7th Special Forces Group at Fort Bragg, North Carolina, and with the Special Action Force, consisting of the 1,500-man 8th Special Forces Group augmented by specialized detachments, located in the Canal Zone.[18]

Should unconventional methods fail to eliminate the Communist threat to peaceful development in Latin America, Kennedy had the ability to conduct within the hemisphere a variety of conventional military operations ranging from a show of force to all-out U.S. intervention. Two unified (more than one service) commands had planning responsibilities for such contingencies: the newly activated United States Southern Command (USSOUTHCOM or SOUTHCOM), located in the Canal Zone, had Central and South America as its area of operations; the older United States Atlantic Command (USLANTCOM or LANTCOM) had the Caribbean as one of its areas of operations. A third unified command activated in 1962 acquired operational control over combat-ready army and tactical air forces within the United States. Known as the United States Strike Command (USSTRICOM or STRICOM), it was responsible for providing a rapidly deployable force for use in emergencies anywhere in the world, including Latin

Civic action at work: a training class in Bolivia during the early 1960s

America. STRICOM had operational control over two Army corps, the III Armored and XVIII Airborne, and the Air Force's Tactical Air Command (TAC). Selected units from these groups could be employed in a crisis either to reinforce other unified commands or to carry out contingency operations assigned by the Joint Chiefs of Staff (JCS) to STRICOM itself.[19] Also available for deployment in Latin America were U.S. Navy and Marine Corps units.

The array of U.S. conventional and unconventional military power available for use in Latin America presented a sobering backdrop to Kennedy's pledge to support democracy and to fight communism in the hemisphere. During his three years in office, the president would not hesitate to employ the military option in his attempt to honor that pledge.

* * *

President Kennedy at Fort Bragg greeting paratroops during a combat readiness demonstration

On taking office, Kennedy inherited from Eisenhower the two covert operations aimed at ridding the Caribbean of Castro and Trujillo. The Cuban venture turned into a fiasco at the Bay of Pigs in April 1961. Although Kennedy recouped some of his spent credibility the following year by imposing a naval blockade that forced the Soviet Union to withdraw nuclear missiles from Cuba, Castro remained in power. Trujillo was not so fortunate. Scarcely a month after the Bay of Pigs, Dominican gunmen ambushed and killed the dictator.[20] All but two of the conspirators forfeited their lives, as the military and the Trujillo family took an exceptionally grisly revenge. Killing the assassins might have had a therapeutic effect on the family, but it could not guarantee that the political void left by the dictator's death would be filled by his followers. Anything seemed possible, especially if the United States should become involved in the succession crisis. In Washington, Kennedy was determined to do just that. His enumeration of the political possibilities in the Dominican Republic has become a classic statement of the cold war dilemma facing American foreign policy toward the Third World. "There are three possibilities in descending order of preference," the president calculated, "a decent democratic regime, a continuation of the Trujillo regime or a Castro regime. We ought to aim at the first, but we really can't renounce the second until we are sure that we can avoid the third."[21]

Soon after the Bay of Pigs, Kennedy—to avoid the third possibility—approved contingency plans for U.S. intervention in the Dominican Republic should the Communists attempt a coup d'état. Then, in the days and weeks following Trujillo's assassination, JFK put pressure on the country's nominal president, Joaquín Balaguer; the late dictator's son, Rafael ("Ramfis"); and the Dominican armed forces to liberalize their policies and prepare the country for elections. Continued economic sanctions and the presence of U.S. naval units and a Marine brigade (later reduced to a battalion) in Dominican waters conveyed the seriousness of Kennedy's intentions. The Balaguer regime responded with token reforms and promises of more to come, but these tentative movements were placed in jeopardy when two of Trujillo's brothers, after receiving an urgent summons from Ramfis, returned to the country in mid-November determined to restore the family to power. Kennedy's secretary of state, Dean Rusk, issued a public warning that the United States would not "remain idle" in the face of such defiance. Kennedy again deployed a large naval task force off the Dominican coast in plain sight of Santo Domingo. As U.S. jets flew overhead and the ships broadcast warnings that the task force's marines were ready to intervene, diplomats served an ultimatum to the Trujillos and their military followers not to initiate armed action. Dominican officers backing Balaguer supported U.S. goals by bombing Trujillist troops designated to spearhead the coup. Realizing that the situation was hopeless, Ramfis left the country, followed soon thereafter by the "wicked uncles."[22]

With the Trujillos gone, Balaguer began to retreat from his democratic pledges. In this, he fared no better than the family he had once served. Washington helped to force his resignation and then blocked a military attempt to restore him to power. Finally, in early 1962, Kennedy regarded the prospects for turning the Dominican Republic into a "showcase of democracy" under the Alliance for Progress as promising enough to warrant U.S. recognition of a Dominican Council of State that had promised elections for the country. He also resumed U.S. economic and other assistance. To enhance the chances for democracy and order, the administration attempted to build up the Dominican police force and to reduce the size and pro-Trujillo sympathies of the regular armed forces. The MAAG for the Dominican Republic was reopened, and a new military assistance agreement signed. The president, according to one source, perceived the Dominican Republic as a "testing ground between the revolutionary ideology of Cuba and [the] democratic ideals of open societies."[23]

The major obstacle to meaningful democratic elections was posed not by Trujillo loyalists—U.S. threats could hold them in check—but by the late dictator's political legacy. His thirty-year reign had left the country bereft of an organized and responsible political opposition. In 1962, no fewer than eight major parties emerged in contention for the presidential and national assembly elections. The parties spanned the political spectrum from conservative to Communist, but the two with the largest following were the right of center *Unión Cívica Nacional* and the left of center *Partido Revolucionario Dominicano (PRD)*—the latter founded by Juan Bosch, an idealist, poet, and reformer. To the surprise of American officials, Bosch won the presidency by a convincing 2 to 1 margin. His inauguration took place in January 1963.

Juan Bosch campaigning for the presidency of the Dominican Republic

At first, Washington lavished Bosch with economic, technical, and military aid (the latter included increasing the MAAG from five to forty-five advisers). Bosch, for his part, published a constitution—a seemingly propitious beginning for an experiment in U.S.-style democracy. But Washington's optimism soon waned as the Dominican president proved an inept politician and administrator. Having spent the twenty-four years before the election in exile, Bosch had lost touch with the realities of his country's predicament. Few in the Kennedy administration would have quarreled with George Ball's recollection of Bosch as "unrealistic, arrogant, and erratic. I thought him incapable of running even a small social club, much less a country in turmoil. He did not seem to me a Communist... but merely a muddle-headed, anti-American pedant committed to unattainable social reforms."[24] After only a few months in office, Bosch had managed to alienate American officials and most groups within his own country. His 1963 constitution failed to guarantee privileges to the Catholic church and contained a clause prohibiting the expulsion of Dominicans from the country—a technique, according to one author, that "had come to be regarded as an inalienable right of the party in power for getting rid of national troublemakers."[25] In addition, Bosch's reform program foundered—to the dismay of the Left—while his refusal to take a strong stand against radicals alarmed

W. Tapley Bennett, Jr., the new U.S. ambassador to the Dominican Republic

Washington, conservative elements in Dominican society, and anti-Communists within the armed forces. With the government degenerating into chaos, an archconservative segment of the Dominican military led by Colonel Elías Wessin y Wessin overthrew Bosch in September 1963.

The coup leaders promised free elections, banned Communist activities, declared Bosch's constitution "nonexistent," and replaced Bosch with a civilian Triumvirate. The new government played on American fears of continued chaos in the Dominican Republic. As one Dominican general put it, "If the United States refused assistance, the regime would go it alone. If this meant terror and civil war and Castro/Communist guerrilla warfare, the regime would do its best. With the United States' help, it might win; without it, it might lose."[26] Despite these attempts to manipulate Washington, the United States severed diplomatic relations, suspended aid, and recalled most of its official personnel. But the displeasure expressed by U.S. officials was halfhearted and short lived. Few bemoaned Bosch's forced exile, and Kennedy, by now disillusioned with the prospects for democracy and the progress of the Alliance—not only in the Dominican Republic but throughout much of Latin America—decided to recognize the new government.[27] Before the decision could be implemented, though, President Kennedy was assassinated.

Lyndon Johnson, Kennedy's successor, waited a month before recognizing the Triumvirate and dispatching a new ambassador, W. Tapley Bennett, Jr., to Santo Domingo. The pause was intended to deflect speculation that, by recognizing a government that had come to power through a military coup, the new president was deviating from the course Kennedy had charted toward Latin America. Not that such speculation would have been idle. The decision to recognize the latest Dominican regime might have been Kennedy's, but whereas JFK had acted out of disillusionment, LBJ acted more out of indifference, as would become apparent early in his administration. Preoccupied with the Great Society at home and the growing war in Vietnam, Johnson left hemispheric affairs to the State Department's assistant secretary of inter-American affairs, Thomas Mann, a conservative and fellow Texan. Under Mann, the emphasis the Kennedy people had placed on structural reform and political democracy in Latin America gave way to a different set of priorities: economic development and the protection of American business and security interests. One commitment survived the transition intact: LBJ, like his predecessor, had no intention of allowing a "second Cuba" to be established in the hemisphere, and to that end, he would employ military force if necessary. In time, the unhappy course of events in the Dominican Republic presented him with the opportunity to demonstrate his determination on this point.

Coup, Civil War, and Crisis Management 2

During 1964, Donald Reid Cabral, an automobile distributor and member of a powerful Dominican family, emerged as the central political figure in the post-Bosch period.[1] A resignation resulted in Reid being appointed president of what within six months became a two-man "Triumvirate." In this position, he wielded considerable, but not absolute, power. Like Bosch before him, he could prescribe treatments to cure the country's deep-seated ills, but he could not force the patient to take the medicine. Low prices for agricultural exports had created a severe economic crisis that Reid tried to relieve by imposing an austerity program on the country. The program's stringent measures, together with Reid's toleration of corruption and contraband, alienated labor, business, consumers, and many professional groups. Similarly, the triumvir's well-intentioned efforts to eliminate the excessive military privileges and corruption of the Trujillo era succeeded mainly in angering senior officers who faced dismissal or at least financial hardship and junior officers who, appalled by the venality of their superiors or simply anxious to see openings on the promotion lists, criticized what they regarded as the slow pace and narrow scope of the reforms. Under these conditions, Reid's ascendancy to the Triumvirate heralded no "golden age" in Dominican politics.

Few Dominicans seriously thought that it would. Even a more cunning and charismatic politician than Reid would likely have succumbed to what one American scholar, Abraham Lowenthal, has dubbed the "politics of chaos." According to Lowenthal, the post-Trujillo period in the Dominican Republic acquired an exceptionally byzantine character as contending groups engaged in "direct confrontations," employing "undisguised and unrefined displays of power, directed more often at replacing the government than at forcing it to take specific actions":

> Political parties, labor unions, student groups, and military factions have formed, split, realigned, and split again.... Shifting groups of "outs" have arrayed against equally temporary alignments of "ins" in a continuous political kaleidoscope. There has been almost no institutional continuity, very little consistency by political leaders with regard to program or ideology, and not even much loyalty to personal caudillos.[2]

In this unstable ferment of conspiracy, intrigue, and incessant plotting, expediency often overpowered principle but never quite subdued it. Virtually all opposition groups acted from a mixture of the two on what quickly became the central issue in Dominican politics, the legitimacy of Reid's government. On the extreme Left, the country's three Communist parties—the Moscow-oriented *Partido Socialista Popular*, the Maoist *Movimiento Popular Dominicano*, and the Castroite 14th of June movement (the largest and most militant of the three)—denounced the "illegal" Triumvirate in an effort to discredit the regime and regain the freedom of action they had enjoyed under the 1963 constitution. While the three parties sought mass support by demanding Bosch's reinstatement as president, they bickered among themselves over tactics and, despite propagandistic appeals for a united front, shunned cooperation with more moderate, "imperialistic" parties also seeking Bosch's return.[3]

The more moderate supporters of Bosch could be found within the deposed president's own *PRD*—or at least a goodly portion of it—and among a number of colonels, junior officers, and enlisted men within the Dominican Army, Air Force, and the Navy's elite frogman unit. Some within the armed forces sincerely deplored the coup against Bosch and the demise of electoral government; others acted to advance their stagnating careers. Whatever the motive, a sizable faction within the military plotted with several *PRD* leaders to overthrow Reid and restore Bosch to the presidency. Because Bosch had not been allowed to serve out his elected term, the military-*PRD* conspirators argued that his reinstatement need not be predicated on new elections.

The pro-Bosch military would play a critical role in events to come, thanks largely to their ability to keep much of their plotting a secret and their success at replenishing their ranks with fellow conspirators following government purges of officers suspected of disloyalty. An example of their recoupable power occurred soon after the coup against Bosch in September 1963, when the Triumvirate dismissed eighteen pro-Bosch lieutenants and captains who had taught at a military academy near the city. The director of these *académicos*, Lieutenant Colonel Rafael Fernández Domínguez, received an appointment to Spain. Even so, Fernández and the teachers continued to conspire and enlisted Lieutenant Colonel Miguel Angel Hernando Ramírez, a close friend of Fernández, as the new leader of the military dissidents. At no time during the Triumvirate's rule did Reid or the U.S. Embassy personnel ever fully grasp the extent to which Bosch supporters permeated the middle and lower ranks of the military, especially the army.

Of greater concern to Reid were the senior army officers assigned to the military base at San Cristóbal. Their dissatisfaction with his anticorruption program was no secret, nor was the fact that several among their ranks were conspiring with Balaguer supporters to bring that former president out of exile. The question of whether Balaguer would claim the presidency by right or whether he would campaign for election (during which time a military junta would rule in place of Reid) divided the generals. Those who favored the junta-election approach found sympathizers both within Balaguer's *Partido Reformista (PR)* and, surprisingly, among many members of Bosch's *PRD*. To complicate the picture further, some of the

San Cristóbal generals were plotting to establish an independent military junta aligned neither with Bosch nor with Balaguer.

With large portions of the regular military and practically every political or interest group in the Dominican Republic bent on overthrowing Reid, it is a wonder that he survived his first year in office. That he did suggests that he was not completely without a power base. In fact, his regime rested on two supporting pillars. One was the United States. Washington had hailed Reid's appointment to the Triumvirate and had lavished him with economic and military aid. American officials remembered the triumvir's participation in the anti-Trujillo movement and the post-Trujillo Council of State, praised his businesslike qualities, and applauded his enthusiasm for "civic action" projects promoted by U.S. military advisers (an enthusiasm not shared by the Dominican military).[4] These same diplomats also energetically backed his efforts to restore economic stability and to end military corruption.

Such endorsements, however well intended, did not always redound to the president's advantage. While Reid's political survival might depend in part on U.S. support, that support, when it extended to unpopular programs, could prove counterproductive. Furthermore, the close personal and working relationship Reid established with Ambassador Bennett offended Dominican nationalists and earned Reid the sobriquet *el americano*, while Bennett, who personally maintained only minimal ties with opposition groups, came to be known as *el otro triunviro*. Despite mounting criticism of his relationship with the Americans, Reid could not wean himself from reliance on U.S. assistance. As Bennett later recalled, "My problem was keeping the little president from coming over and sitting in my lap everyday."[5] The more Reid sought to bolster his political authority by deliberately identifying his regime with the United States, the more precarious that authority became.

For public relations purposes, Bennett in late 1964 tried to dispel the image of unqualified U.S. support for Reid. The effort convinced few among Reid's opponents, although those who conspired against him were betting that the United States would acquiesce in the return of Bosch or Balaguer rather than send in troops to prop up an unpopular regime. But Bennett considered Balaguer too closely identified with Trujillo and dismissed Bosch as an ineffectual Leftist. Reid, in the ambassador's view, was still the best hope for a stable, prosperous, and democratic Dominican Republic. Consequently, the ambassador urged his government to purchase more Dominican sugar, and he secured additional U.S. economic assistance in hopes of strengthening Reid's position. Bennett also began to explore ways in which the Embassy might quietly assist the triumvir to win elections scheduled for the fall. Just how far Washington or the Embassy would or could go to guarantee Reid's political longevity remained to be seen. It would take a political crisis to find out.

Alongside the United States, standing as the second pillar supporting the Reid regime, was the person of Elías Wessin y Wessin, newly promoted to general following his role in the coup against Bosch. Wessin commanded the Armed Forces Training Center (*Centro de Entrenamiento de las Fuerzas*

Elías Wessin y Wessin

Armadas, or *CEFA*), an elite group of nearly 2,000 specially trained infantry that, unlike regular units, possessed tanks, recoilless cannon, and artillery. Trujillo, in creating *CEFA*, had made it an independent organization that would protect the dynasty and serve as a watchdog over the army, navy, and air force. Officers in these three services commanded forces that outnumbered *CEFA*, but their troops were scattered throughout the country and, with the exception of three army battalions and a naval frogman unit, were poorly trained and equipped.[6] The regular military, therefore, had reason to resent the *CEFA* force and fear the power Wessin y Wessin wielded as its commander. Based at San Isidro, less than ten miles east of Santo Domingo, *CEFA* was collocated with the 19th of November air base. Taken together, this "all powerful *conjunto* (ensemble)" concentrated at San Isidro 4,000 armed men, all the tanks in the armed forces, and most of the country's air power. "Everyone in the Dominican Republic knew," one analyst has written, "that whoever controlled San Isidro controlled the country."[7]

A competent officer and rabid anti-Communist, Wessin controlled San Isidro and was therefore regarded as the power behind the throne. He saw himself as the guarantor of order and the principal bulwark against Leftist ideology in the country. He answered only to the president, who, in the case of Reid, initially spared little effort or inducements in the way of better housing and food to keep the general and his men placated. They had, after all, paved the way for his political ascendancy. They could as easily remove him from power, even over American protests. As time passed, however, Reid apparently began to take Wessin's support for granted. In a move calculated to mute criticism from the regular military concerning favoritism toward *CEFA*, the president of the Triumvirate let it be known that he regarded his alliance with Wessin as temporary. Wessin noted Reid's rebuff but continued to help the government remove what enemies it could uncover in the military.

Reid had made a potentially costly blunder. In the event of an attempted coup d'état, would Wessin readily support a regime that had deliberately slighted him? The conspirators bet that he would not, but as with their predictions regarding U.S. behavior, they were uncertain as to what he would do. Having been instrumental in forcing Balaguer's resignation, Wessin could not easily sanction the former president's return. Bosch, whom Wessin had personally overthrown, was in the general's opinion a Communist. Some pro-Bosch conspirators believed that Wessin—confronted with a fait accompli and wholesale defections from the military—would have to acquiesce in Bosch's return. Others knew better. If he abandoned Reid, Wessin would most likely side with those generals advocating an independent military junta.

As rumors of an imminent coup attempt mounted, Ambassador Bennett and General Wessin continued to support Reid. Each had his own reasons for doing so, including a common conviction that Reid, despite his shortcomings, was preferable to Balaguer or Bosch, the only two Dominican politicians who could command a large enough following to unseat the government, either in a coup or in free elections. As it turned out, the promise of the latter hastened an attempt to precipitate the former. When Reid scheduled elections for September 1965, the U.S. Embassy applauded the move, anticipating that the current "temporary" government would prevail at the polls. But in pursuit of that end, Reid proved to be his own worst enemy. The chaotic political scene and the worsening economic crisis had left him highly vulnerable. As he gradually realized the extreme precariousness of his political position, he began hinting that the elections might have to be postponed or that certain "destabilizing" individuals, namely Bosch and Balaguer, might be barred from standing as candidates. Such rhetoric, as Lowenthal has observed, "far from exploiting the latent divisions among his opponents . . . drove his enemies closer together. . . ."[8] The pro-Bosch element among the anti-Triumvirate conspirators hoped without much conviction that the United States would guarantee an open election. This group also decided that if American assurances were not forthcoming by 1 June, the opening day of the campaign, it would take action to overthrow the government.

By April, the American Embassy had yet to reveal whether it would insist on elections. A CIA poll indicated that Reid would capture no more than 5 percent of the vote in a free election, while Balaguer would likely receive 50 percent to Bosch's 25. What to do in light of this unsettling news divided the Embassy's political officers. Some, including Bennett, favored exploring nonelectoral alternatives that would keep Reid in power;

others advocated easing Reid out and finding a basis for accommodation with Balaguer.[9] The debate would have to be resolved in Washington. All parties realized the risks of delaying a decision. As rumors of a coup d'état mounted, Bennett warned Washington that "little foxes, some of them red, are chewing at the grapes."[10]

Just as it seemed that time was running out, Reid, on 22 April, dismissed seven junior officers involved in the plot to restore Bosch as president. Embassy officials now believed they had time to maneuver and deliberate before the United States decided how to handle the situation. The day after the dismissals, Bennett felt confident enough to leave the Dominican Republic to visit his sick mother in Georgia and then present his case in Washington for further U.S. assistance for Reid. In the ambassador's absence, Deputy Chief of Mission William Connett, Jr., who had been in the Dominican Republic fewer than six months, would be in charge. The U.S. military mission stationed in Santo Domingo also relaxed its vigil, sending eleven of its thirteen members to a conference in Panama. The AID mission director and the public safety adviser assigned to the Embassy were in Washington, and the U.S. naval attaché, a Marine lieutenant colonel, took to the country for a weekend of duck hunting with General Antonio Imbert Barrera, one of only two survivors among Trujillo's assassins. Imbert was also one of the few general officers not actively engaged in any conspiracy against the government, perhaps because his rank was honorary and his association with the regular military strained.

That Ambassador Bennett, most of the U.S. military advisers, and other key officials were out of Santo Domingo as the last weekend in April began stands as vivid testimony to the ability of the pro-Bosch conspirators to retain a high degree of secrecy (even after suffering the loss of seven of their members) and to the failure of U.S. officials charged with gathering intelligence to penetrate opposition groups. It soon became clear, in the starkest of terms, that the officer dismissals of 22 April, far from providing the government with a political respite, foreclosed what time it had left to extricate itself from the mounting political crisis. Fearful that further delay might place the entire plot in jeopardy, the conspirators moved the date for the coup forward from 1 June to 26 April. They also decided that any move by Reid against their ranks before the 26th would trigger immediate action against his regime. It was a prescient decision.

On Saturday, 24 April, the chief of staff of the Dominican Army, General Marcos A. Rivera Cuesta, informed Reid that four more officers had been discovered plotting against the government. Reid, still unaware of the magnitude of pro-Bosch sentiment within the military, ordered Rivera to dismiss the officers involved. When the chief of staff, without armed escort—a move Reid later decried as "stupid"—arrived at army headquarters, the conspirators arrested him. The long-anticipated coup was under way, albeit two days ahead of schedule. Most of the conspirators were taken by surprise as they were called away from their lunches or back to their posts to be informed of the morning's events. Until units involved in the plot could be assembled and others persuaded to join them, Colonel Hernando could not implement his plan for military operations against the government. As one analyst has noted, "The telephone, far more than the machine gun, was the weapon of the first hour—really of the first half day—of the constitutionalist revolt."[11] Military officers were notified first, civilian plotters thereafter. By Saturday afternoon, between 1,000 and 1,500 disaffected military personnel, mostly from an army battalion at the 16th of August camp and the 250-man unit at the 6 1/2 Artillery camp (both located northwest of the city) had joined the effort to topple Reid. Another battalion from the 27th of February camp, also northwest of the city, would join the revolt that evening, while the Mella Battalion at San Cristóbal pledged its support. The *PRD* and other anti-Reid civilian organizations, including the Communists, were also mobilizing their resources.

By chance, José Francisco Peña Gómez, a civilian leader of the conspiracy, received word of the revolt while delivering a radio speech. He quickly announced that the government had been toppled and urged all sympathizers to take to the streets. Thousands turned out in celebration. Caught by surprise, the Dominican police made no effort to stop the demonstrations. This inaction added to the general feeling that Peña's radio report was accurate. It was not. Reid had not capitulated but was frantically trying to determine what was happening. So, too, were American Embassy personnel, who began receiving often conflicting reports from their network of local contacts. The political picture that emerged was blurred and confusing but alarming enough to prompt Connett to dispatch to Washington a cable marked CRITIC ONE, which began, "Santo Domingo rife with rumors of coup."[12]

By the time Connett sent the cable, the *CEFA* unit attached to the Palace guard was moving toward Radio Santo Domingo, which had fallen to the conspirators earlier that afternoon (see map 3). The military forces in revolt had yet to enter the city, and the unarmed populace could not defy *CEFA* tanks. Government forces recaptured the radio station and arrested several agitators, after which Reid went on television and radio to assure the country that he was in control. In an appeal for calm, he explained the nature of the military revolt and the moves being taken to quell it, gave the rebels until 0600 to surrender, and announced a curfew. Connett dutifully reported the speech to Washington but could offer little more concrete information concerning the situation. U.S. Embassy officials could not identify any one organization or political group responsible for the uprising, but they singled out the presence of Leftist labor leaders and "hotheads" of the "leftist PRD ilk" among the demonstrators. More important, the cables warned that Communists seemed to be involved.[13] On the first day of the crisis, therefore, the Embassy raised the ideological issue that would dominate the deliberations of U.S. policymakers in the days to come and the public controversy over American intervention for years thereafter.

*   *   *

The events in Santo Domingo on late Saturday, culminating in Reid's public appeal, conveyed an impression that the Triumvirate had restored

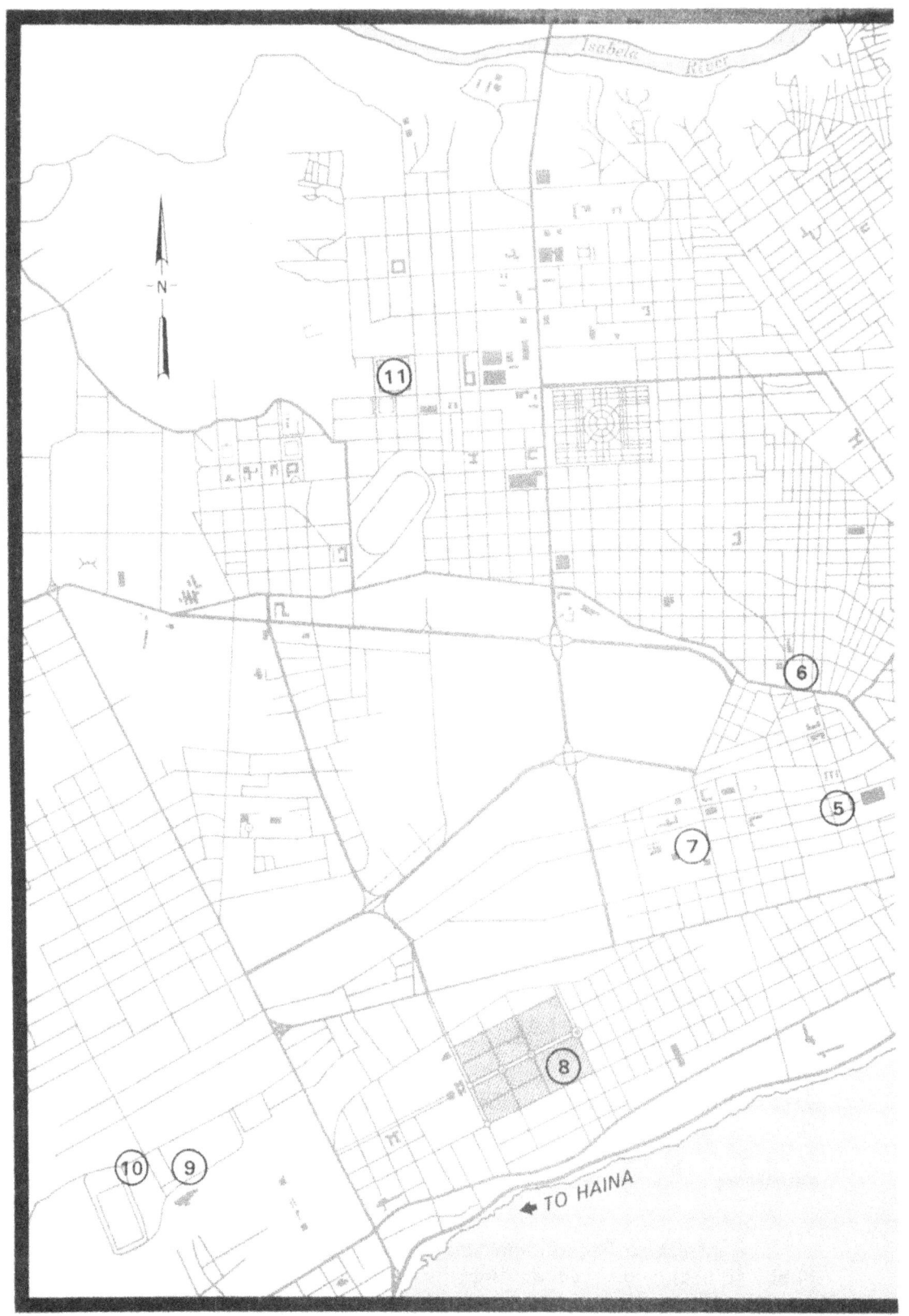

Map 3. Santo Domingo and vicinity

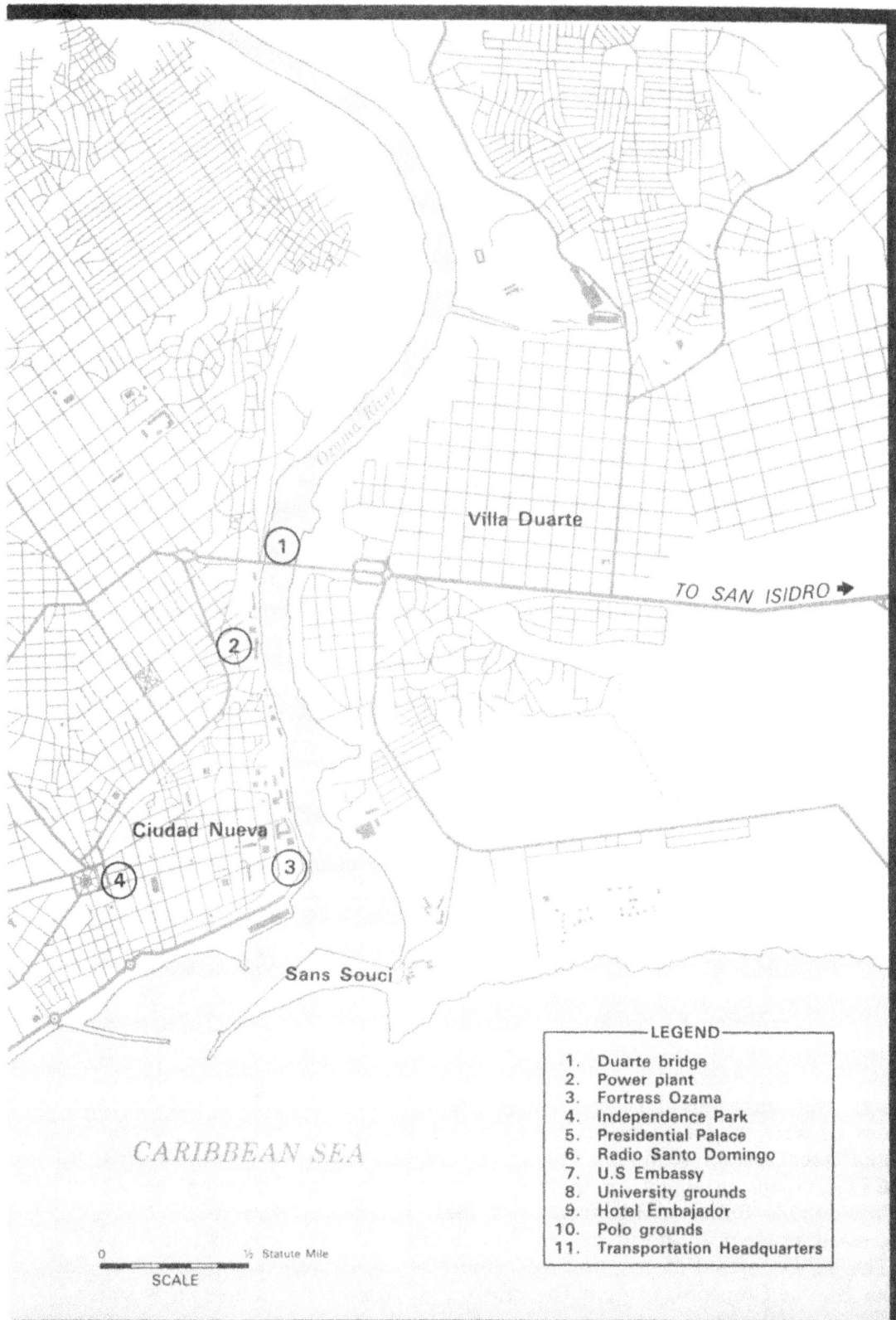

its authority and that the revolt was near collapse. This notion was reinforced by erroneous reports from the Embassy on Saturday that Wessin and other key military leaders were standing fast in support of Reid. Just how deceptive this impression was became apparent on Sunday when what had begun as an attempted coup d'état accompanied by antigovernment demonstrations turned into civil war in the streets of the capital.

According to intelligence reaching the U.S. Embassy by Sunday morning, up to two-thirds of the army stationed in or around Santo Domingo was in revolt and arming sympathetic civilians. During the night of 24–25 April, rebel forces had entered the capital, captured a fire station, set up defensive positions at key locations, and continued to hand out weapons to the civilian population. Leftist extremists now seemed to be out in force, setting up command posts, distributing arms gathered at military arsenals, and inciting crowds to violence. *PRD* and military spokesmen for the rebels demanded Reid's downfall and a return to constitutional government, the latter demand resulting in the rebels adopting the label "Constitutionalist" to designate their movement. Constitutionalist forces retook Radio Santo Domingo and moved on Fortress Ozama, one of the main armories in the city. Local police, now outgunned by the rebels, made no attempt to interfere. As Piero Gleijeses wryly notes, the police chief, General Hernán Despradel Brache, anxious not to be aligned with the losing side, whichever it might be, discovered with "unsuspected mental agility...the concept of an 'apolitical' police force." The "neutrality" of the police, however, did not guarantee their safety. Memories of their repressive tactics ("beating a little common sense into the opposition") were still vivid. Thus, policemen shed their uniforms as rumors spread that many of their comrades had been summarily executed by undisciplined groups of armed civilians, especially young toughs calling themselves *Los Tigres*.[14]

Once Reid realized that the rebels had entered Santo Domingo proper, he redoubled efforts he had begun Saturday afternoon to ensure the support of top military leaders. The naval chief of staff pledged his support as did General Wessin. Both men talked to Reid and U.S. military attachés about imminent military action, but neither officer made any effort to protect the government, even after Reid, in the early hours of Sunday morning, named Wessin secretary of state for armed forces. Despite the honor, Wessin now repaid Reid for the president's earlier disparagement of the Triumvirate-*CEFA* connection by adopting a cautious approach in which opportunism overrode duty to an unpopular regime. Unlike the previous coups in which he had participated, Wessin this time faced an armed force of uncertain size. His tanks might be capable of overwhelming the rebels, but he could not be sure, and to lose his tanks meant losing his power. Moreover, he had good reason to doubt the loyalty of the air force at San Isidro. If *CEFA* troops marched on the city and the *conjunto* fell apart, he would face hostile forces to his front and rear. Based on these calculations, it seemed prudent to stand pat at San Isidro and let the situation develop. The public refusal of the air force chief of staff, Brigadier General Juan de los Santos Céspedes, to fight the rebels gave Wessin an excuse for inaction.

Armed rebels in the streets of Santo Domingo

He denounced the air force for its decision and, in a conversation with Reid Sunday morning, explained that tanks from San Isidro could not be sent against the rebels without air cover.[15]

Finally realizing that Reid could not count on support from his military, Connett called Washington and conferred with Kennedy M. Crockett, the State Department's Caribbean country director, about what courses of action the United States might follow. Both men at this time ruled out U.S. intervention to save Reid; they agreed, instead, that the best means of avoiding further bloodshed and preventing a Communist takeover was to encourage military leaders on both sides to establish a temporary junta that would promise elections in the fall. In discussing this option, Connett and Crockett miscalculated on two points. They both envisaged popular support for a junta and assumed that rebel officers would be amenable to such an appeal now that Communist participation had contaminated their movement. A formal message from State instructing Connett to encourage negotiations for a military junta soon followed, although it did not reach the deputy chief until after his midmorning meeting with Reid, during which the latter evinced little interest in the junta formula. Not that Reid's reservations mattered at this point. U.S. military attachés were already discussing the formation of a junta with Dominican military leaders, thus making it less likely that their units would come to Reid's defense. Nor would the United States, as Connett informed *el americano*. Once Reid grasped the hopelessness of his situation, he gave in to the inevitable. Shortly after his meeting with Connett, he called the U.S. Embassy and announced his intention to resign in favor of a military junta. The gesture went for naught. Within the hour, Constitutionalist troops under Colonel Francisco Caamaño Deño seized the Presidential Palace and placed Reid under arrest. The junta, to which Reid said he would turn over power, did not yet exist.[16]

Who and what would fill the political vacuum became the principal concern of all interested parties. The junta solution advanced by the United States was well received by so-called Loyalist military officers who had not joined the revolt, while even rebel officers indicated they were willing to discuss the subject. But as the day progressed, Connett began to hold out little hope for these negotiations: the rebels were clearly in charge and had little reason to compromise. Furthermore, CIA reports indicated that Communist leaders, whose influence in the streets seemed to be increasing by the hour, would never agree to the establishment of a military government. Finally, the most vocal civilian and military spokesmen among the rebels had already declared their intention to restore Bosch and constitutional government. Plans were already well under way to bring the former president home from exile in Puerto Rico. Meanwhile, Bosch had given his supporters permission to set up a provisional government under a prominent *PRD* politician, José Rafael Molina Ureña.

The inauguration of Molina and the attempt to bring Bosch to Santo Domingo had fateful consequences in that both moves irreparably split the anti-Reid coalition. Several military leaders who had joined the revolt on

Molina Ureña at his swearing-in ceremony as the Constitutionalist "president"

behalf of Balaguer, or in hopes of establishing a military junta, found the prospect of Bosch's return anathema. Even before Molina was sworn in as provisional president Sunday afternoon, General de los Santos dissociated himself from the rebel cause and informed the U.S. air attaché that the Dominican Air Force, together with Wessin y Wessin's elite troops, would fight to prevent Bosch's elevation to the presidency. The Loyalist officers, Connett reported, had agreed that the "return of Bosch would mean surrendering the country to communists."[17]

Late Sunday afternoon, the Loyalists made good their threat, as air force F-51s attacked the Presidential Palace, the two rebel military camps, and rebel positions on the west side of the Duarte bridge. The attacks turned a coup d'état into a civil war. Negotiations on the formation of a military junta, never likely to succeed, collapsed immediately. More civilians from the lower and middle classes in Santo Domingo poured into the streets in support of the revolt. Some rebels took the families of Loyalist air force pilots hostage and threatened over television to transport them to targets being attacked by government forces. The Loyalists' use of force and the rebel response deepened divisions on both sides and ruled out, under existing circumstances, anything other than a military solution to the crisis.[18]

The Loyalist attacks on the Palace and other targets were initiated with the knowledge and "reluctant" support of the U.S. Embassy. As Connett explained to Washington prior to the attack, the Embassy's Country Team* was unanimous in opposing Bosch's return "in view [of] extremist participation in [the] coup and announced communist advocacy of Bosch's return as favorable to their long-term interests." The plan of the Loyalists to attack rebel headquarters was, in the Country Team's opinion, the "only course of action having any real possibility of preventing Bosch's return and containing growing disorders and mob violence." "We recognize," Connett continued, "that such [a] course of action may mean further bloodshed, but we think we should be prepared to take this risk," with the Embassy doing what it could to minimize the violence. Connett concluded by saying "Our attachés have already stressed to [the] three military leaders concerned our strong feeling that everything possible should be done to prevent a communist takeover in this country and to maintain public order." As the Dominican Republic stood minutes away from civil war, American Embassy officials had in effect defined for themselves and Washington the opposing sides, together with what side the United States should support.[19]

* * *

By the time Connett's grim assessment reached Washington Sunday afternoon, enough message traffic had passed between the Embassy and the State Department to awaken the administration to the fact that it might

---

*The Country Team is a formal organization chaired by the U.S. ambassador to a country and composed of the heads of all U.S. government agencies represented in the country. A typical Country Team would include the top officials of AID, USIA, and the CIA; the military attachés; and, at the ambassador's discretion, the deputy chief of mission, the political officer, and others.

have a serious crisis on its hands and to prompt various midlevel officials to enact measures for better monitoring events in the Dominican Republic and for managing the U.S. response. In doing so, one problem surfaced immediately: as was the case in Santo Domingo, key officials were out of town or new to their positions. The president was at Camp David, where on Saturday evening, he was notified of developments by Thomas Mann, the undersecretary of state for economic affairs and former overseer of American activities in Latin America. Mann's replacement as assistant secretary of state for inter-American affairs, Jack Vaughn, was attending a conference in Mexico City. His deputy, Robert Sayre, Jr., had acquired all of one week's experience at his post; the same was true of William Bowdler, the White House's specialist on Latin America. Ambassador Bennett had yet to arrive in Washington; he heard about the coup against Reid over his car radio while in Georgia. Other Dominican specialists were out of town for the weekend. Further complicating matters was an imminent personnel changeover in two important positions. On 28 April, Director of Central Intelligence John McCone would retire, to be replaced by Admiral William Raborn, a neophyte in the world of intelligence who knew little about the CIA's capabilities or modus operandi. On 30 April, Admiral Thomas Moorer would replace Admiral H. Page Smith as Commander in Chief, Atlantic Command (CINCLANT).[20]

President Johnson did not leave Camp David until late Sunday afternoon. Throughout the day, he kept in touch by telephone with his top foreign policy advisers on the situation in Santo Domingo and scheduled a meeting with them upon his return. Despite the numerous phone calls, the president seemed in an "extremely good mood" during his trip to Washington.[21] The sense of urgency felt in the U.S. Embassy in Santo Domingo had yet to percolate to the highest authorities at home. It had begun to be felt among Latin Americanists at the State Department, however. Even before the president had arisen on Sunday morning, officials at State, after receiving a message from Connett that the situation was "rapidly deteriorating," had set up an ad hoc Dominican task force in the department's Operations Center. As the crisis developed, this task force, composed of State, Defense, and CIA personnel, would work a twenty-hour command post, collecting, processing, and disseminating information; planning; and making decisions not requiring LBJ's authorization. The command post provided a direct link with Santo Domingo, as most cables and telephone calls to and from the Embassy went through the task force, which usually operated under the supervision of Undersecretary Mann.[22]

To enhance diplomatic-military coordination, task force members would frequently change places with officers and civilians at the National Military Command Center (NMCC), the facility at the Pentagon that provided communication channels to all military commands and bases, the White House, and other Washington agencies. In the collection and dissemination of military information, the NMCC functioned much like State's Operations Center. It differed in one important feature. Whereas State, as a matter of procedure, maintained a direct link with American embassies around the

Thomas Mann

world, standard procedure on the military side dictated that in most cases orders issued by the secretary of defense, or the JCS acting on his behalf, pass through the NMCC to a unified command with regional or functional responsibilities before being sent to the commander of any U.S. combat troops within a specific country. The existence of the unified command as an intermediary agency between the Pentagon and a local commander made sense in theory, but, as the Dominican crisis would reveal, could become the source of much confusion in practice.

The CIA, besides providing people to help staff the Dominican task force at State, also spent Sunday the 25th setting up its own command post—dubbed "the Pit"—for monitoring the situation. Technicians quickly installed teletype machines and a battery of telephones capable of receiving messages from the CIA chief of station in Santo Domingo, copies of diplomatic and military traffic, foreign radio and press comments, and a variety of "sensitive and esoteric information."[23]

The special teams working at State, the NMCC, and the Pit exchanged information via liaison contacts, telephone, and information copies of cables and telephone calls. As for keeping the president informed, two formal channels existed: information could be passed from each crisis center to the White House Situation Room run by President Johnson's national security assistant, McGeorge Bundy; or the heads of each of the three organizations involved (that is, the secretaries of state and defense and the director of central intelligence) could brief the president personally.

The effectiveness of the formal crisis management system set up on 25 April depended on its usefulness to the president and on how the president chose to use it. To be useful to the president, the system had to provide accurate and timely information and a list of realistic courses of action. This required rapid and secure communications among all parties involved at each level of the crisis, efficient planning and intelligence gathering, and creative thinking. At times, the system performed well; at times, it did not. When it did not or could not, President Johnson did not hesitate to circumvent it. Throughout the crisis, LBJ relied heavily on his formal advisers, in particular Secretary of State Dean Rusk, Secretary of Defense Robert McNamara, Bundy, Mann, Vaughn, and Undersecretary of State George Ball. But he also tapped people outside this official circle, his friend Abe Fortas and former ambassador to the Dominican Republic John Bartlow Martin, for example, to serve as special advisers and emissaries. He also had no compunction about violating formal chains of command, both civilian and military, if he thought it would produce results.

Once Johnson returned to Washington on the 25th, he immediately began to make his presence felt in a flurry of telephone calls and meetings with his advisers on the situation in Santo Domingo. Although preoccupied with the American military buildup in Vietnam, he could not ignore U.S. interests in and around the Dominican Republic and the deteriorating situation in that country. The island of Hispaniola's strategic position in the Caribbean weighed on his and other policymakers' minds. So, too, did the realization that violence in the Dominican Republic could place American lives and property in jeopardy. But what the president and other U.S. officials feared most was a Communist takeover of the country. Castro, as Johnson later reminisced, "had his eye on the Dominican Republic" and, in Cuba, was training Dominican Leftists in guerrilla warfare and sabotage. Reports that over fifty Communist agents trained in Cuba, Russia, and China had entered the Dominican Republic during April reinforced this impression. A Communist takeover in the Dominican Republic would violate the "no second Cuba" policy, enhance Castro's revolutionary attraction within the hemisphere, open Latin America to further Soviet-Cuban penetration, and diminish U.S. credibility throughout the world as a faithful ally and a bulwark against Communist expansion. Johnson made this last point explicit when he asked his advisers early in the crisis, "What can we do in Vietnam if we can't clean up the Dominican Republic?" The latter country acquired a symbolic importance of global proportions in light of the fact that the American buildup in Vietnam was largely designed to convince friends and adversaries, especially in Europe, that the United States had the will and resolve to fulfill its worldwide commitments. An irresolute response to the Dominican crisis would undermine U.S. credibility in Vietnam, which in turn would damage U.S. credibility in Europe, the Middle East, and elsewhere.[24]

Given these linkages and what were perceived to be the high stakes involved, Johnson quickly made clear that he would assert his presidential prerogatives to the fullest in directing the U.S. response to the Dominican crisis. As George Ball later observed, Johnson became absorbed "to the point where he assumed the direction of day-to-day policy and became, in effect, the Dominican desk officer."[25] This was in character for the energetic Johnson; it also reflected, as the crisis increasingly took on a military character, the current theories of limited warfare that regarded war and peace as a continuum in which military capabilities served primarily as political and diplomatic instruments that could be orchestrated not so much to effect military victory as to affect the *intentions* of the combatants and make them amenable to *political* solutions. Adherents of limited war theories deemed centralized civilian control as essential—not only over policy determinations but over military operations as well. The military had to be kept on a tight leash lest the actions of a local commander jeopardize the political objectives sought by Washington, or worse, escalate a local crisis into a regional or global confrontation.

Limited war theories collided head-on with military tradition. Military professionals conceded policymaking and the formulation of political objectives to the civilian establishment, but they insisted on autonomy in the control of military operations and the tactics employed to achieve those objectives. That politicians lacked the expertise, competence, and understanding necessary to direct military forces in the field was accepted among the ranks as an article of faith. Political interference in military operations was counterproductive, unnecessarily restrictive, and invited disaster. The idea of a president or secretary of defense issuing orders directly to a local commander violated the basic tenets of sound military doctrine up and down the chain of command. It also diminished the role of uniformed officers in policy deliberations. During the Dominican crisis, as in Vietnam, LBJ relied more often on McNamara than the JCS—by statute the president's military advisers—for military advice. Although McNamara provided a conduit between the JCS and the White House, this hardly compensated for the infrequency with which the chiefs could present their professional advice directly to the president. This shortcoming was brought home during the first week of the crisis, when Johnson did not meet face-to-face with General Earle "Bus" Wheeler, chairman of the JCS, until Thursday, 29 April, after the initial contingent of U.S. troops had already landed in Santo Domingo.[26]

The divisive issues surrounding the political management of military operations had not yet surfaced on 25 April, the second day of the crisis, for one simple reason: as Johnson turned his attention to Santo Domingo, neither he nor any of his close advisers thought U.S. military intervention a likely prospect. But even before the president left Camp David that day, the first step toward U.S. military involvement in the crisis had been taken. A naval task force was heading toward Dominican waters. It was only a precautionary step, but, ironically, in light of LBJ's determination to take charge of the situation, it was ordered without his direct authorization. On the 25th, the crisis management system still contained some latitude for midlevel officials to initiate military movements. In the ensuing days, that latitude, together with hopes for an early negotiated settlement to the crisis, would become casualties of time, as events in Santo Domingo moved the United States closer to intervention.

To Protect American Citizens 3

When Deputy Chief of Mission Connett informed Washington of Loyalist plans to attack the Presidential Palace and other rebel targets Sunday afternoon, he and other members of the Country Team contemplated not the outbreak of civil war but the early restoration of order within Santo Domingo. For that reason, they recommended against a U.S. "show of force or other military support." But Connett also warned that if the Loyalists failed to end the "present conditions bordering on anarchy," the Embassy might have to reconsider its position on U.S. military activity. Should that happen, he advised, the Country Team might "wish later to make some use, in this connection, of naval units now en route to waters outside" the Dominican Republic.[1]

The naval units to which Connett referred had been dispatched that morning at the request of State's Director of Carribbean Affairs Kennedy Crockett. Acting on a "contingency basis"—that is, without notifying the president but in accordance with established procedures—he had asked the Defense Department to send ships into Dominican waters in case American citizens should have to be evacuated. The proposed move was purely precautionary; as Connett made clear during the day, U.S. citizens and American property in Santo Domingo had not become targets of rebel violence. Yet both the Embassy and Washington expressed concern should that condition change. At 1032 Washington time, following Crockett's initiative, the JCS sent CINCLANT a message requesting that the "minimum number of vessels" needed to evacuate up to 1,200 Americans proceed to the vicinity of Santo Domingo, there to "remain out of sight [of] land until further orders issued."[2]

Admiral H. Page Smith, serving his last week as CINCLANT, had been receiving reports on the Dominican Republic since Saturday evening. Informed of State's request one-half hour before the JCS sent their formal message Sunday, he had already ordered Task Group 44.9, also known as the Caribbean Ready Group, to proceed from its position off Vieques Island, Puerto Rico, toward the troubled country to the west. The task group, with its assigned units rotating every three months, operated on a year-round

A U.S. Marine Corps ONTOS

basis in Caribbean waters, conducting exercises and supporting contingency operations. The group at sea in April was designated Carib 2-65 and consisted of six naval vessels and the 6th Marine Expeditionary Unit (MEU). The MEU numbered 131 officers and 1,571 marines, was organized around the 3d Battalion of the 6th Marines, 2d Marine Division, and was equipped with small arms, helicopters, tanks, ONTOS, LVTs, and artillery.* Although it would require only a portion of Task Group 44.9 to evacuate 1,200 Americans, CINCLANT sent the entire Caribbean Ready Group just in case other measures, including the use of military force, should be required. Prudence dictated such a decision, given the sketchy but increasingly alarming information available to the admiral.[3]

En route to their destination, Commodore James A. Dare, commander of the task group (TG 44.9), and Colonel George W. Daughtry, commander of the 6th MEU, devised an evacuation plan. Neither man wanted a confrontation with the rebels, whose composition and location were unknown to both officers. To avoid an unnecessary provocation, the two decided that on receipt of an evacuation order, they would send ashore a control element

---

*ONTOS are weapon systems wielding six 106-mm recoilless rifles on tracked carriages. LVTs are tracked landing vehicles.

of unarmed marines dressed in fatigues, who would supervise the loading of buses, ships, and helicopters. As a precaution, a company of armed marines wearing body armor would stand by offshore, ready to go to the control element's assistance should that group encounter rebel resistance. With the details of the plan worked out, Daughtry issued a warning order to the marines for possible evacuation operations.[4]

Early Monday morning, the task group arrived on station thirty miles off the Dominican coast, where, in another precautionary measure, Dare positioned his ships so that if called on, they could launch air strikes or amphibious operations. One problem surfaced immediately: neither TG 44.9 nor the U.S. Embassy in Santo Domingo had equipment adequate for communicating with one another. The marines offered to provide the Embassy with what communication equipment they could spare, but until the transfer could be made, the Embassy and the task group conducted business via TG 44.9's helicopters and by employing the services of Fred Lann, a U.S. Embassy official who was also an amateur radio operator. Only the radio in Lann's home proved capable of reaching Dare's flagship, the *Boxer*. As middle man, Lann relayed messages between the *Boxer* and the Embassy, keeping in touch with the Embassy by telephone and walkie-talkie until rebel movements forced him to take his radio to the Embassy's courtyard, where he operated it out of his car. The Marine communication equipment arrived at the Embassy on Wednesday, but "to the amazement of all concerned," it was not powerful enough to be received aboard the *Boxer*. Consequently, Lann continued to transmit messages for another four days, a time during which the marines became increasingly involved in the Dominican crisis.[5]

As the communication problem added to the difficulties the naval task force and the Embassy staff experienced in trying to coordinate plans for the possible evacuation of American nationals, the bloodletting in Santo Domingo continued. On Monday, 26 April, the Dominican Air Force renewed its attacks against rebel positions, and Wessin prepared to move his forces from San Isidro into the city. The *CEFA* commander and General de los Santos asked the Embassy for U.S. troops to help suppress the revolt, but

The *Boxer*, Commodore Dare's flagship

Rebels filling Molotov cocktails at a local gas station

their request was denied. Embassy officials warned State that there existed "a serious threat of a Communist takeover in this country, and very little time remains in which to act," but they agreed with Washington that the situation did not require U.S. military intervention, especially in light of the adverse consequences such a move would have on U.S.-Latin American relations. To head off the Communists, the Embassy proposed instead a continuation of diplomatic efforts to encourage the military leaders on both sides to join in a junta pledged to free elections. Assuming that the rebels would be the more reluctant of the contending parties to accept this solution, the Embassy requested authorization to make the proposal to Molina and rebel officers in strong terms, backed if necessary by an American show of force.[6]

As it turned out, the Loyalist air strikes caused some Constitutionalist officers to approach the U.S. Embassy Monday with a request to arrange talks with the officers at San Isidro. During the course of the day, U.S. military attachés arranged four cease-fires but could not bring the two sides together. A renewal of the negotiations that had collapsed Sunday after the strafing of the Palace foundered for one simple reason that would surface repeatedly in the days ahead: whichever side thought itself to have the military advantage showed little inclination to negotiate with the other side. In their inability to arrange negotiations, Embassy officials glossed over this problem and blamed the impasse on the rebels, accusing them of using the brief cease-fires solely for the purpose of regrouping militarily.[7] In the meantime, as each successive cease-fire broke down, the civil war gained in intensity, taking a high toll in Dominican lives.

With the streets of Santo Domingo becoming increasingly dangerous, Embassy personnel advised Americans in the country to prepare for evacuation. Mann, over Rusk's signature, instructed Connett to contact leaders on both sides of the civil war to obtain their cooperation in an immediate evacuation of American and foreign citizens. Monday afternoon, Connett met with rebel political leaders, while U.S. military attaches talked with officers on both sides. By evening, everyone had agreed to the Embassy's plan for evacuation. In brief, persons desiring to leave would congregate at the Hotel Embajador, a luxury accommodation in the suburbs of western Santo Domingo. From there, they would be taken by helicopter to U.S. naval vessels that would be allowed access to Haina, a port eight miles west of the city. In reporting the agreement to Washington, Connett recommended that the evacuation begin at daybreak, but State, citing JCS opposition to an immediate evacuation, suggested that the operation not begin until around noon. The Embassy countered by urging a midmorning operation. Connett also proposed another change in the evacuation plan: because of possible small-arms fire from rebel civilians in the area of the hotel, he recommended that helicopters not be used without first obtaining the Embassy's permission. State made no objection to the latter request but again insisted on beginning the operation at noon so that "developments next six to eight hours can be assessed."[8]

The debate over the timing of the evacuation reflected a difference in perspective between Washington decision makers and American officials in the field, a difference that is normally exacerbated during a crisis. To be sure, both groups were extremely concerned about the possibility of a Communist takeover in the Dominican Republic, and both were reluctant to countenance any overt American military intervention that would strain U.S.-Latin American relations and cast the United States in opposition to what was widely perceived as a democratic revolution. But officials in Santo Domingo, within earshot of the shooting and inundated with information (some substantiated, some not) of atrocities and Leftist machinations, perceived the situation in much more alarmist terms than did their counterparts in State, the JCS, and the White House—all far removed from the chaos and action. Washington demonstrated its relatively greater detachment by wanting to buy time in order to collect additional evidence and to give Loyalist forces a chance either to force cease-fire negotiations and the establishment of a temporary military government or to defeat the rebel movement and set up an exclusively Loyalist junta. Prior to his return to Santo Domingo, Ambassador Bennett met with the president, who reiterated that another Communist regime in the Caribbean was unacceptable and that the Embassy should promote a cease-fire and negotiations in order to prevent a second Cuba. The atmosphere in the White House appeared calm, with Johnson only mildly concerned with the prospects for a Communist takeover in the Dominican Republic. In Santo Domingo, Embassy personnel followed the president's instructions, although they were beginning to see little merit in a negotiated settlement. Given their perception of the increasingly Leftist composition of the Constitutionalist movement, they believed that negotiations would accomplish little except provide the rebels with a

American citizens line up to be evacuated from the Dominican Republic

respite during which they could consolidate their forces for the main battle to come.⁹

In the cable traffic between the Embassy and State's Operations Center, only the timing of an evacuation, not whether to conduct one, had been subject to debate. Foreign nationals wishing to leave the country began to assemble at the Hotel Embajador at daybreak Tuesday. That morning, TG 44.9 moved to within five miles of the Dominican coast, and the 6th MEU assumed a fifteen-minute alert status for evacuation operations. Before the operation could begin, though, a group of about fifty armed rebels, most of them young civilians, entered the hotel lobby about midmorning in search of an anti-Communist Dominican newsman. The journalist was not in the hotel, and the youths, before departing, took out their frustration by firing shots over the heads of the assembled Americans and by threatening some with execution. For the Americans at the Embajador, the episode was unnerving; in the eyes of U.S. officials, including President Johnson, it provided strong evidence that the rebel movement was getting out of control and raised again the ominous prospect that U.S. troops would have to be deployed to protect American lives.¹⁰

The evacuation began soon after the incident at the hotel. The JCS directed CINCLANT to order ships from TG 44.9 into Haina. The order moved down the chain of command, and two ships designated by Dare arrived at the harbor shortly after noon. A caravan of buses had already started carrying foreign nationals to the port, where a U.S. Marine control element supervised the evacuation. By early evening, over 1,000 foreign nationals were on their way to safety in San Juan, Puerto Rico.[11] The evacuation went without a hitch: neither side in the civil war interfered, and of the Americans who arrived at Haina, none had been physically harmed.

*   *   *

While many foreigners were preparing to leave the Dominican Republic, Ambassador Bennett arrived back in the country. At the Santo Domingo airport, he was met by Colonel Daughtry, a fellow Georgian, and taken by helicopter to the *Boxer* for a brief conference with Dare. From this meeting, Bennett made his way to the Embassy via Haina. The briefing he received from his staff indicated that a military solution to the crisis might be at hand. The Mella Battalion at San Cristóbal, unwilling to accept the return of Bosch, had switched its support to the Loyalists and, under the command of General Salvador Augusto Montás Guerrero, was advancing on Santo Domingo from the west. Meanwhile, the strafing and naval bombardment of rebel positions in the capital had been followed by the long-awaited attack by Wessin's tanks, armored personnel carriers, and infantry from San Isidro. Moving under heavy fire across the Duarte bridge, the *CEFA* units engaged the enemy in what one chronicler has called "the bloodiest single battle in Dominican history," an action in which hundreds were killed or wounded. After Wessin's elite troops advanced several blocks into the city, rebel resis-

Rebels blocking the Duarte bridge to prevent Wessin's forces from entering the city

tance seemed on the verge of collapse, a prospect not in the least repugnant to Embassy officials who had probably approved the Loyalist plan.[12]

Loyalist military pressure prompted several rebel officers to visit the U.S. Embassy three times on Tuesday to request, as they had the previous day, American help in arranging cease-fire talks. During the first visit, the Embassy's military attachés contacted the Loyalists by radio and conveyed to each side the other's position. When a stalemate ensued over where to hold the proposed talks, the attachés refused to effect a compromise. Their instructions allowed them to encourage negotiations but not to enter the negotiating process. When the rebels returned to the Embassy early Tuesday afternoon, Bennett met with the officers. He told them directly that they bore responsibility for the "senseless slaughter" now taking place and that the "extreme left" was "taking full advantage of [the] situation." He reiterated that Washington preferred a cease-fire and the formation of an effective government and indicated that he was talking to both sides "in the same vein" to achieve those goals. Bennett concluded by citing the Loyalists' clear military advantage and urging the rebels "to capitulate and make [an] announcement so that [the] work of reconstruction could begin." At least one of the officers seemed receptive to this appeal. There followed a third visit by rebel military leaders in midafternoon, after which Molina Ureña agreed to come to the Embassy and confer with Bennett in person. The Constitutionalists were clearly desperate to negotiate a settlement.[13]

Following his return to the Embassy and prior to his meeting with Molina Ureña, Bennett informed State of his talk with the rebel officers, Wessin's military fortunes, and the Embassy's belief that Communists were calling the shots on the rebel side. Later, he also notified Washington that he had requested the *Boxer* and another ship to move within sight of land in order to demonstrate the U.S. presence and, by allowing the populace to see that the ships were not engaged in hostile activities, to quell rumors that the U.S. Navy was supporting the Loyalists. In carrying out the ambassador's instructions, Commodore Dare's subordinates had to maneuver their vessels through several Dominican corvettes, gunboats, and merchant ships. It was a precarious situation. "This show of force," Dare later wrote, "was conducted under circumstances which would turn any skipper's hair grey." He added that during the maneuver, "it seemed almost as though the Ambassador had the conn."[14]

By late afternoon, it appeared as though U.S. military measures, aside from the evacuation and show of force, would not be necessary. At 1600, "a nervous and dejected" Molina Ureña entered the American Embassy with fifteen to twenty of his political and military advisers. Bennett met for an hour with the group, whose main purpose was to have the ambassador serve as a mediator in arranging a negotiated settlement. Bennett told the Constitutionalist leaders that it was their action on Saturday that had "initiated this fratricide" and that the "senseless shedding of blood must end." The ambassador blamed the *PRD* for allowing the Communists to take advantage of the party's "legitimate movement" and denounced a variety of rebel activities including the incident at the Embajador. Citing evidence of the Embassy's good faith, he reminded Molina Ureña that on Monday the staff had persuaded the Dominican Air Force on four different occasions not to bomb the rebels. What Bennett perhaps did not know was that the Constitutionalists had monitored telephone conversations between the Loyalists and the U.S. military attachés in which the Loyalists' plans for attacking rebel positions on Tuesday were discussed and at least tacitly approved by the attaches. When Connett later told rebel leaders that Embassy personnel knew nothing of such plans, he had unwittingly compromised the Embassy's credibility insofar as U.S. officials claimed to be neutral and evenhanded. Thus, Molina Ureña might have been disappointed, but could hardly have been surprised, when Bennett refused a request to use the Embassy's good offices to get negotiations under way. Bennett maintained that he lacked the authority to mediate, which was technically true,[15] and that any "accord should be reached by Dominicans talking to Dominicans." President Johnson later wrote that Bennett's refusal to help negotiate was the ambassador's own decision but one in keeping with the general guidance he had received from State and with the U.S. policy of nonintervention.[16]

The meeting at the Embassy Tuesday afternoon has been the subject of much controversy, with Bennett being accused of deliberately scuttling a chance to end the civil war on terms short of a complete Loyalist victory, thus preventing further bloodshed or U.S. intervention. Possibly the meeting did represent a missed opportunity. But at the time, the absence of trust between U.S. officials and the rebels, the apparent lack of an acceptable middle ground between the warring sides, and the shared perception that Loyalist troops would soon defeat an increasingly Leftist-dominated force militated against an American diplomatic initiative, other than to suggest for the record that the two sides get together. Furthermore, even if Bennett had agreed to mediate, he would have had great difficulty in getting the Loyalists to agree to negotiate. With their offensive on the verge of success, there seemed little to talk about except a rebel surrender.

Facing imminent military defeat and dejected by Bennett's refusal to intercede on their behalf, Hernando Ramírez, Molina Ureña, and other "moderate" rebel leaders sought political asylum upon leaving the U.S. Embassy. When Bennett learned of this development, he concluded that the extreme Left would now seize complete control of the revolt. He would report to Washington the next morning that the fighting had become a "straight Communist and non-Communist struggle." In the days and weeks to come, the Johnson administration adhered undeviatingly to the line that Tuesday, 27 April, represented a critical turning point in the crisis, the point at which the Constitutionalist cause came under Communist domination. On Tuesday night, however, Bennett did not immediately perceive this as cause for undue alarm. In his report to State, he expressed the opinion that mopping-up operations by the Loyalists would soon end the radical threat. Responding to this optimistic assessment, State asked the Embassy to do what it could to prevent reprisals and atrocities by Loyalist forces. The department then sent a briefing paper to the White House predicting that Santo Domingo would soon be in Wessin's hands. After discussing the report, LBJ and John McCone, who was serving his last day as director of the CIA, agreed that U.S. military intervention to restore order in the city would not be necessary. To American officials in Santo Domingo and Washington, the Dominican crisis seemed to be subsiding.[17]

*   *   *

The optimism of Tuesday night was short lived, as the emotional roller coaster American officials had been riding since the outbreak of the revolt again took another downward plunge on Wednesday. The change in mood this time could be traced largely to one man, Colonel Francisco Caamaño Deño, the rebel officer who had arrested Reid on Sunday only to seek asylum himself later that day after the civil war broke out. His time in hiding was brief, and by Tuesday, he was in a position to accompany Molina to the meeting at the Embassy. Caamaño claimed later to have been insulted by what he considered to be Bennett's patronizing lecture. When Hernando, Molina, and other rebel leaders asked for asylum, Caamaño became the pro forma leader of the Constitutionalist forces. Few, if any, U.S. officials thought Caamaño a Communist, although there existed from the outset speculation—soon to become conviction—that his newfound leadership within the Constitutionalist movement was more nominal than real, given the restrictions placed on him by the radicals now seen to be in control of the revolt.

Caamaño did not have time for such speculation. Following the Embassy meeting, he had hastened to the rebel stronghold in Ciudad Nueva in southeast Santo Domingo, where, during the night of 27—28 April, he undertook the enormous tasks of regrouping rebel troops and planning a counterattack against Wessin's Loyalist forces. Additional weapons for the counterattack came from two police stations captured by the rebels on Wednesday morning. Caamaño participated in the attack on the first station; at the second, his followers executed the policemen captured when the station fell, an incident that would fuel doubts regarding Caamaño's actual control over the variety of armed groups in the city. A major counterattack

Rebels using captured cannons firing on government forces

against the Loyalists got under way soon thereafter. Wessin took the brunt of the attack and quickly discovered that his tanks worked to little advantage in the narrow streets of Ciudad Nueva.[18]

Embassy officials had yet to realize the full import of this turn of events when, on Wednesday morning, Bennett, acting on an "urgent request" from General de los Santos, asked State to seek immediate authorization for providing Loyalist forces with fifty U.S. walkie-talkies, then in storage at Ramey Air Force Base, Puerto Rico. The Loyalists needed the communications equipment to expedite what the ambassador called a "mopping up" operation. If Bennett did not yet grasp the magnitude of the rebel counterattack, he was aware that the Loyalist offensive had stalled of its own accord after its initial gains on Tuesday. Wessin had established positions on the west bank of the Ozama River but showed little inclination to expand his area of control. General Montás Guerrero, who had led the Mella Battalion into the fairgrounds in western Santo Domingo and had recaptured the Presidential Palace,[19] had stopped his advance on Tuesday afternoon and had broken his force into small units, now scattered in unknown locations. Neither Wessin nor Montás had any clear idea of the opposition he faced, and neither man fully trusted the other. (One account suggests that Montás, a *Balaguerista*, stopped his drive because he "was suspicious of the course Wessin might follow, if victorious," and therefore wanted the *CEFA* commander to bear the brunt of the fighting.)[20] Prior to the rebel counterattack, the main problem facing Wessin and Montás, besides personal rivalry, was one of coordination and communication. Not only were their two forces out of touch, but they had no direct communications with Loyalist air and naval units either. When Bennett tried to resolve the problem, Washington turned him down. Mann directed only that walkie-talkies be sent to the *Boxer*, "just in case" the situation should deteriorate.[21]

That Caamaño's counterattack had caused the situation to deteriorate would not be fully appreciated in Washington until early Wednesday afternoon. In the meantime, Bennett reported that the Loyalists had announced formation of a military junta led by a Dominican Air Force officer, Colonel Pedro Bartolomé Benoit. In keeping with American wishes, the junta declared that its "principal purpose" was to prepare for elections and the return of a constitutional government.[22]

Within minutes after reporting this development, Bennett cabled State with news that the two police stations had fallen. Two other messages followed within the hour. The second of the two reported that Ciudad Nueva was in rebel hands, although it did not elaborate the extent to which small houses had been turned into tiny fortresses, barricades were appearing at critical intersections, essential utilities had fallen under rebel control, and rebel patrols dominated the streets. The first and more detailed message again raised the walkie-talkie issue. Bennett now tried to impress upon Washington the seriousness of Loyalist reversals that morning. "It is our combined judgment that communications equipment is most critical lack in current situation" and "could well mean difference in results of present confrontation," he warned. The Loyalists, the ambassador continued after he

Aerial view of Ciudad Nueva

had outlined the military situation, "are not asking for offensive weapons, merely [the] means to talk." Bennett expressed regret that "once again we have to rely on [a] military solution for political crisis engendered by the confused democratic left," but he hastened to add that the "plain fact of situation is that ... issue here now is fight between Castro-type elements and those who oppose it [sic]." In closing, Bennett indicated that he did not "wish to be over-dramatic, but if we deny simple communications equipment and [the] opposition to leftist takeover here loses ..., we may very well be asking in near future for landing of Marines to protect U.S. citizens and possibly for other purposes. Which would Washington prefer?"[23]

What the ambassador in good faith posed as a choice between troops or equipment soon became a package deal when, shortly before 1500, Colonel Benoit phoned the Embassy to request the landing of 1,200 marines "to help restore order to this country." In a cable to State, Bennett did not endorse Benoit's appeal; he agreed, instead, with the naval attaché's caution that "Marines should not be used in any street-cleaning operations." But the ambassador did indicate that Washington, still relying perhaps on the Embassy's earlier, more optimistic, reports of that morning, might not have grasped the full gravity of the situation. A "severe test of nerves" was in progress, he reported, and the military attachés considered the outcome "still in doubt." Bennett now suggested that State "may want to do some contingency planning in case situation should break apart and deteriorate rapidly to extent we should need Marines in a hurry to protect American citizens."[24]

On receiving Bennett's message, Bundy telephoned Mann to discuss the possibility of U.S. intervention. Although both stated their aversion to sending marines into the country, they based their view, as Bennett feared, on the erroneous belief that the military edge still belonged to the Loyalist junta. Mann found the Embassy's pessimistic assessment of Loyalist chances difficult to believe, but he agreed with Bundy that the president needed to be briefed that afternoon on the changing situation. As a result of their conversation, Bundy authorized providing Loyalist forces the walkie-talkies, whereupon Mann requested that General Wheeler arrange for the equipment to be airlifted to Santo Domingo.[25] Meanwhile, Washington officials monitoring the crisis waited apprehensively for further word from Santo Domingo.

Their fears proved well founded. As President Johnson and his advisers met late Wednesday afternoon to discuss the U.S. buildup in Vietnam and the Dominican crisis, two cables, CRITIC FOUR and CRITIC FIVE, arrived from Bennett within half an hour of each other. The first telegram simply relayed the junta's plea for "unlimited and immediate military assistance" from the United States to keep the Dominican Republic from becoming another Cuba. In the second cable, which reached the White House at 1715, Bennett reported that the situation was "deteriorating rapidly." The MAAG chief, who had that day returned from Panama and visited San Isidro, had informed him that the general atmosphere among the Loyalist leaders was "dejected and emotional, with [a] number of officers weeping" and Benoit claiming that without U.S. help, the officers would "have to quit." In view of these developments, the Country Team had reached the unanimous conclusion that the "time has come to land the Marines." Bennett's final sentence was unequivocal: "I recommend immediate landing."[26]

The desperate situation depicted by Bennett left the president and his advisers little choice but to accede to the ambassador's wishes. Johnson told McNamara to alert the forces in the area for possible landing. Mann also telephoned Wheeler with news of LBJ's instructions to "go ahead." At 1746, both Dare and the commander of Caribbean Sea Frontier (COMCARIBSEAFRON), who had operational control over TG 44.9, received instructions to alert the marines for possible landing and to await further word. At 1800, after McNamara informed Johnson that the troops were ready to move, the president authorized the landing of 500 marines for defensive operations. He also instructed specific advisers to notify the OAS regarding U.S. intentions, to arrange a meeting with congressional leaders, and to draft a statement he could read to the American people.[27]

The content of the presidential statement became the subject of some debate. Secretary Rusk wanted to make at least passing reference to the Communist threat as a rationale for the troop movement. Other advisers, including Bundy and UN Ambassador Adlai Stevenson, argued that the president should not go beyond the need to protect American lives in explaining his decision. An intervention to safeguard U.S. citizens could be justified as a limited operation that would in no way compromise the claim to neutrality the United States had staked out for public consumption; intervention "to restore order" and prevent a Communist victory would almost certainly involve the United States in openly pro-Loyalist activities likely to be condemned throughout the hemisphere as a return to gunboat diplomacy in support of a military regime. The Bundy-Stevenson view prevailed in drafting the statement but created certain problems. To provide a legal justification for intervention, the president's advisers wanted Benoit, whose junta Washington virtually regarded as the acting government of the Dominican Republic, to state explicitly that his request for intervention was based on the danger to Americans, a threat to which Benoit had made no reference in his original request for U.S. troops. Bennett had already assured Mann that Benoit had raised the issue of American lives in oral communications with Embassy personnel, but Mann told the ambassador that only a written statement from the junta leader would satisfy Washington's requirements. Presumably, Benoit would be given to understand that the debarkation of marines would be conditional on receiving such a statement.[28]

At 1929, just minutes after Johnson, McNamara, Rusk, Ball, Bundy, Stevenson, and the new director of central intelligence, William Raborn, began briefing congressional leaders, an Embassy cable, CRITIC SIX, arrived in Washington. In the message, Bennett indicated that the Dominican police chief had informed the Embassy that "he can no longer guarantee safety [of] Americans en route [to] evacuation area." Bennett went on to explain that Benoit was sixteen miles away at San Isidro and could not be contacted except over an "open channel." For that reason, the ambassador was sending the Embassy's air attaché to obtain the statement required by Washington. "I have no doubt whatever he will give it," Bennett asserted. Benoit made good the ambassador's prediction. "Regarding my earlier request," he wrote, "I wish to add that American lives are in danger and conditions of public disorder make it impossible to provide adequate protection. I therefore ask you for temporary intervention and assistance to restore public order in this country." The air attaché returned to the Embassy with the statement at midnight, hours after Johnson had met with congressional leaders and addressed the American people.[29]

At the time these presidential actions were taking place, over 500 combat marines had already landed in the Dominican Republic. For most of the Leathernecks, the trip from the *Boxer* to the polo field near the Hotel Embajador had been made by helicopters at dusk or in the pitch black of a rainy night. It was an impressive transit, in contrast to the confusion that characterized the coordination and control of the troop commitment all along the chain of command.

The landing of marines on the 28th took place in two phases. The first involved bringing several small units ashore to establish a landing zone in the polo field, to help evacuate Americans still gathering at the hotel, and

President Johnson briefs congressional leaders on the Dominican Crisis, 28 April 1965

to reinforce the Embassy security guard consisting of seven marines and thirty-six Dominican policemen who had sought refuge at the compound from armed mobs. A pathfinder element, military police, and a platoon of unarmed marines would be used for the polo field and hotel operations; a platoon of armed marines, reinforced by two squads, would follow for use at the Embassy. The request for these initial units went directly from Bennett to Dare, the commodore being contacted at some time between 1722 and 1745, that is, before President Johnson had authorized the large-scale landing of combat troops. The available evidence does not indicate whether Bennett or Dare required or received authorization to commit these initial units—which included the armed platoon—prior to being notified of the president's decision to commit the much larger force. Dare apparently assumed the ambassador had received such authorization, although a draft Defense Department statement indicates that Bennett's request was a "local initiative." Bennett no doubt believed that his actions were in keeping with the evacuation procedures still under way and that reports reaching him that the evacuation area and the Embassy compound were under sniper fire required him to dictate emergency measures on his own authority.

Just when Washington found out about the initial landing is uncertain. Embassy officials, in an hour-long teleconference with key State Department officials that began at 1830, referred to the landing of marines at the polo field and to the arrival of the armed platoon at the Embassy in terms that indicated State had prior knowledge of these movements. Yet Bennett's CRITIC SIX, which was dispatched at 1902, made no mention of his request to Dare. The first mention the ambassador made of the request came in a Flash cable sent to State at 1915 in which he said, in part, "I have *just* asked Boxer to provide helicopter evacuation" and Embassy security. (Italics mine.) In explaining his reasons for doing so, Bennett stated that "I hope this action will give some heart to loyal forces." That this telegram was dispatched over an hour after the request had been made and granted can perhaps be attributed to the overloaded communications network at the Embassy, which delayed even the transmission of Flash messages.[30]

As the evacuation and security units requested by Bennett were en route to the polo field, Dare received a directive from CINCLANT through COMCARIBSEAFRON that instructed him to land whatever marines Bennett requested. This directive stemmed from Johnson's decision concerning the 500 marines, and Colonel Daughtry immediately contacted Bennett to discuss what measures to implement. Having already asked for immediate intervention in CRITIC FIVE, Bennett took only three minutes to decide in favor of landing more combat troops. Daughtry conferred with Dare, after which two rifle companies of the 3d Battalion, 6th Marines, and an advance echelon of the battalion headquarters began moving ashore. By 1900, over 100 marines in this second phase had landed; more would follow.[31]

The timing here is again revealing in terms of coordination and communication. At 1921, well after the second phase of the landing was under way, the JCS directed that Dare *prepare* to land marines should the ambassador so request. Apparently, having alerted the marines to the possibility of intervention as Johnson was deciding the issue, the JCS had not been informed later that the operation was under way. Once they learned that several hundred armed marines were in fact landing at the polo field, the Joint Chiefs tried to get what information they could. Again, for reasons that cannot be fully documented, when they informed the president, presumably through McNamara, of the number of marines ashore, their count was inaccurate. When the president addressed the nation shortly before 2100, he stated that 400, not the actual 536, marines had landed. The Department of Defense daily report for the Dominican Republic for 28 April also lists only 400 marines on land in and around Santo Domingo.[32]

The significance of the problems surrounding the landing of combat troops in the Dominican Republic should not be exaggerated. The confusion caused by inadequate communications, poor coordination, and the frenzied activities of key decision makers under stressful conditions had little impact on events of the 28th: the president had decided that armed marines would go ashore, and before midnight, they had. But the confusion revealed some shortcomings in the administration's crisis management system. How could the president and his principal advisers in Washington exert tight control over the situation if they could not receive timely and accurate information from the field? For their part, the JCS, in future directives to the unified commands and other military elements connected with the crisis, insisted that no action be taken without an appropriate execution order and that all deployments be reported to the Pentagon immediately.

The administration soon confronted another problem that called into question its ability to manage the crisis. To avoid antagonizing Latin American allies and to maintain the pretext of U.S. neutrality, the president, as noted previously, justified the Marine landings solely in terms of "protecting American lives." Reporters arriving in Dominican waters the next day soon had reason to challenge the official position on the crisis and the landings. Aboard the *Wood County*, they overheard radio conversations between Bennett and Benoit in which the Embassy seemed to be promising the junta communications equipment, food, and other supplies, despite the proclaimed neutrality of the United States. At one point, Bennett was reported to have told Benoit, "Do you need more aid?" and "Believe that with determination your plans will succeed." When the reporters went aboard the *Boxer* to be briefed by Dare, the commodore told them that marines would stay ashore as long as necessary to "keep this a non-Communist government." For many in the audience, this was the first hint that in sending troops ashore, the administration had motives other than the safety of U.S. nationals.[33] From these early discrepancies between official pronouncements and military behavior, there emerged a "credibility gap" that would set much of the media against the administration for the duration of the Dominican crisis—and beyond. It was inevitable that at some point the military would become a part of that confrontation.

Of more immediate concern to the military were the implications implicit in the problems encountered in command, control, and communications procedures during the Marine landings. If that much confusion surrounded the task of putting 536 marines ashore, what would happen if those troops had to be reinforced, not only by the remaining marines in the 6th MEU but by U.S. Army and Air Force units as well? In short, could the military mount an effective joint operation should the situation warrant it? To this question, anyone taking part in the planning then under way for just such a contingency would have been hard pressed to give an affirmative reply.

Intervention

4

Few U.S. officials believed sending 536 marines into Santo Domingo constituted military intervention in the Dominican Republic. The troops were too few in number and their mission too passive for the landing to have much more than a psychological influence on the contending parties in the country's civil war. The presence of the marines might boost Loyalist morale, but it could not stave off the junta's seemingly imminent defeat. Realizing this, Bennett recommended during the evening of the 28th that "serious thought be given in Washington to armed intervention which would go beyond the mere protection of Americans and seek to establish order in this strife-ridden country" and "to prevent another Cuba from arising out of the ashes of this uncontrollable situation."[1] Although the cable did not mention it, preparations to send U.S. Army units into Santo Domingo, if needed, were already well under way.

Those preparations had begun on Monday, 26 April, when the JCS issued an alert to place two airborne battalion combat teams (BCTs) with airlift, tactical air units, and command-support forces on defense readiness condition (DEFCON) 3 status (which, in the case of the airborne BCTs, meant being combat ready and prepared to board aircraft for which all mission-essential loads had been rigged for an airdrop). The two battalions would come from the 82d Airborne Division, the "fire brigade" in America's strategic reserve. Collocated with its parent headquarters, the XVIII Airborne Corps at Fort Bragg, North Carolina, the 82d Airborne Division had recently been reorganized in line with the Reorganization Objectives Army Division (ROAD) concept. In the changeover from the pentomic division configuration of the late 1950s and early 1960s, five cumbersome battle groups gave way to nine airborne infantry battalions that could be shifted among three brigade headquarters and, thus, tailored to meet a variety of contingency operations. On 26 April, the 3d Brigade's 1st Battalion (Airborne), 508th Infantry, was serving as the division ready force (DRF), a unit maintained in a high state of alert for a one-week period, ready to load and launch within hours of receiving an execution order. The 3d Brigade's commanding officer designated the 1st Battalion (Airborne), 505th Infantry, as the second BCT called for in the JCS alert.[2]

The 82d, as a whole, was well prepared for any contingency that might arise, up to and including military intervention in a crisis such as that in the Dominican Republic. Each of the three brigades had undergone extensive training and had been involved in a variety of field exercises. That the two BCTs from the 3d Brigade were designated to be the first Army forces into the Dominican Republic, should the need arise, was the result of the DRF assignment of one and the availability of the other. At the time of the alert, battalions from the 1st Brigade were on stand-down status performing routine details, while battalions from the 2d Brigade, together with other divisional elements, were participating in Blue Chip V, a joint Army-Air Force demonstration conducted at Fort Bragg under the auspices of USSTRICOM. The availability of the 3d Brigade was a matter of timing, not design. It was, however, fortuitous from one standpoint. In early April, the brigade had finished Quick Kick VII, a joint, CINCLANT-directed exercise involving all the services in an airborne-amphibious surface-heliborne assault on Vieques Island, an isle with many geographical similarities to the Dominican Republic. As a result of the exercise, certain problems in coordination, communication, and intelligence were identified (although not necessarily resolved), valuable joint training was received, and many of the joint staff who would later work together in the Dominican Republic came to know one another on a first-name basis. Also, because of its participation in Quick Kick VII, the 3d Brigade was, in the 82d's own assessment, "combat ready."[3]

No matter how well trained the paratroopers, before any of the 82d's units could be committed to a crisis, the troops had to be alerted, marshaled, provided airlift, and launched; equipment had to be rigged; and missions had to be formulated and their execution planned. One could not hope to meet these requirements by simply following routine procedures. Unanticipated problems would invariably arise, some unique to the situation at hand, some recurrent in the history of joint operations.

One of the first problems encountered in the preparation of Army and Air Force units concerned messages sent through and outside the formal chains of command. LANTCOM would exercise operational command over military activities in the Dominican Republic. But LANTCOM had no Army or Air Force units assigned to it on a permanent basis. Those units would come from strategic forces based in the United States, in this case primarily from the XVIII Airborne Corps, a key Army contingency planning agency, and the Tactical Air Command (TAC), the primary air arm for use in small wars). When not engaged in joint undertakings, the XVIII Airborne Corps and TAC answered to the Commanding General, U.S. Continental Army Command (USCONARC), and the commander of TAC, respectively. When a unified command, in this case LANTCOM, required augmentation forces from these strategic reserves, operational command for the alerting, marshaling, loading, and launching of the designated units fell to STRICOM. STRICOM, in this sense, acted as a "packaging and delivery service," in which its planners drew the designated forces from their component commands, " 'packaged' them with a command element and 'delivered' them to the theater."[4] Two parallel alert channels existed to set these procedures in motion. One ran from the JCS to the Commander in Chief, U.S. Strike

Command (CINCSTRIKE), to STRICOM's Army and Air Force components. The other ran from the service departments to CONARC and TAC and, then, to the designated units. Once STRICOM had the Army and Air Force units ready to launch, operational command of those forces would be passed ("chopped") to CINCLANT.

Some confusion marked the initial alerting process during the evening of the 26th, when an information copy of the JCS alert order reached the XVIII Airborne Corps and 82d well before notification arrived through formal command channels. According to one source, General Wheeler further complicated matters by telephoning Major General Robert York, the commander of the 82d, to notify him personally of the impending alert. Although these premature warnings allowed the corps and the 82d to assemble key staff personnel in anticipation of formal notification, the deviations from standard alerting procedures also resulted in the assembled staff at Bragg receiving sometimes conflicting information from different sources, a situation that took hours to straighten out.[5]

A more persistent communication problem surfaced between the two unified commands involved—LANTCOM, located at Norfolk, Virginia, and STRICOM, located at MacDill AFB, Florida. The difficulty stemmed from the dual role assigned CONARC's commanding general, General Paul Freeman, and TAC's commander, General Walter Sweeney, in the event that LANTCOM required augmentation forces from the strategic reserves under their commands. When this happened, as in the case of the Dominican crisis, Freeman and Sweeney became component commanders under both CINCSTRIKE and CINCLANT, as the two unified commanders carried out their separate missions (see figure 1). As Commander in Chief, U.S. Army Forces, Strike Command (CINCARSTRIKE), and Commander in Chief, U.S. Air Forces, Strike Command (CINCAFSTRIKE), respectively, Freeman and Sweeney would assist CINCSTRIKE, General Paul D. Adams, in alerting, marshaling, and preparing elements of the 82d and TAC prior to their being chopped to CINCLANT. As Commander in Chief, U.S. Army Forces, Atlantic Command (CINCARLANT), and Commander in Chief, U.S. Air Forces, Atlantic Command (CINCAFLANT), these same two officers would assist CINCLANT in matters pertaining to the operational needs of the Army and Air Force units deployed under CINCLANT's operational command, that is, after the units had been chopped from CINCSTRIKE to CINCLANT. Because Freeman and Sweeney originally controlled the units required by LANTCOM and were involved under Adams in preparing them for LANTCOM's use, CINCLANT often found it more convenient to talk directly to his component commanders and their subordinates regarding troop requirements and preparations. The result was to bypass CINCSTRIKE at the very time Adams exercised operational command over the augmentation forces prior to deployment. According to Adams, "The communications from CINCLANT . . . were practically zero except through CINCLANT to Bragg. . . ." So as not to be cut out of the chain of command entirely, Adams sent several of his J3 (operations) staff to Bragg and Pope to help "guide this thing on its way and get it going, get it untangled, . . ." The

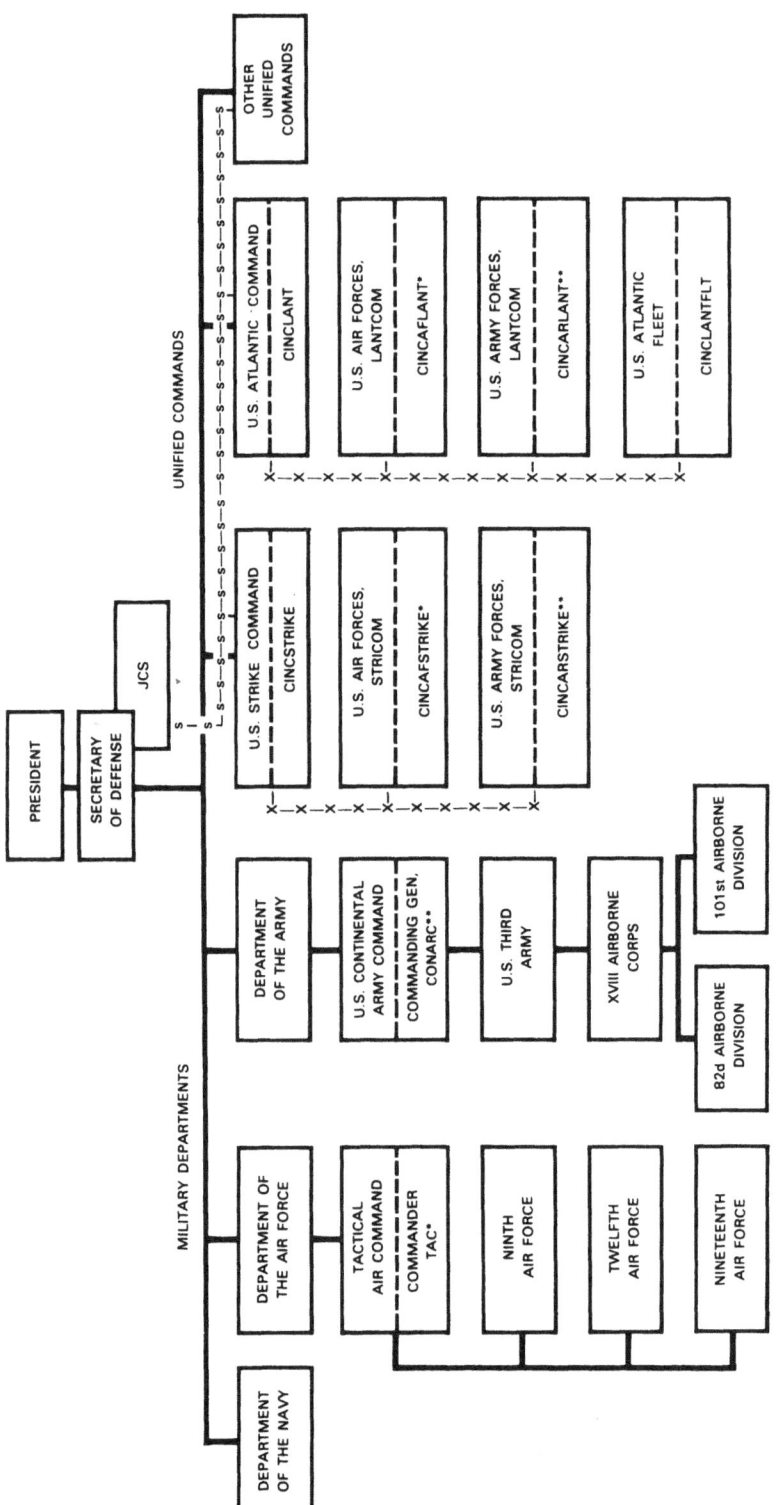

Figure 1. Relationship of CONARC and TAC to STRICOM and LANTCOM

discord between STRICOM and LANTCOM, however, continued throughout various phases of the Dominican crisis, with no attempt to resolve the jurisdictional conflict until the intervention was over.[6]

Communications outside formal command channels were not the only problem to surface as the military prepared for possible intervention. Once XVIII Airborne Corps, the 82d, and TAC received the alert notification on the 26th, planning for deployment began immediately. Because the Dominican Republic fell within LANTCOM's area of operations, CINCLANT was responsible for having ready an operation plan (OPLAN) covering the spectrum of contingencies that might involve U.S. military activity directed toward that country. In early 1965, LANTCOM had cleared with the JCS and had published an updated plan for the Dominican Republic, OPLAN 310/2-65, the provisions of which covered such contingencies as a show of force, blockade, the protection and evacuation of American nationals, and all-out intervention. In the event of the last contingency, the plan called for the deployment of up to six airborne infantry battalions and four U.S. Marine battalion landing teams, together with other special and supporting units. When the crisis in Santo Domingo raised the possibility of intervention, the JCS designated the specific forces to be alerted, but they did not order the execution of OPLAN 310/2-65. In accordance with a warning included in the plan, units on alert were to regard it only as basic guidance and to expect inevitable deviations.[7]

When the first alert to the Army and Air Force went out on 26 April, neither service had updated contingency plans based on OPLAN 310/2-65. The XVIII Airborne Corps and the 82d had not received copies of LANTCOM's newly published plan, while the Nineteenth Air Force, TAC's planning agency, had not published the airlift portion of its component plan. The result was that staff officers from both services approached their tasks with woefully outdated plans in hand. The XVIII Airborne Corps' OPLAN 310/2L did not have up-to-date troop lists, while the 82d's OPLAN 310/2L-63 did not even reflect the current ROAD configuration of the division but called for deployment of two or three battle groups, the main combat element of the discarded pentomic division. Because of the "fire brigade" status of the 82d, the division had dozens of OPLANs in its inventory and little time for updating them. Thus, the table of organization and equipment (TOE) attached to the plan was inaccurate. TAC's working plan was also geared to the deployment of two or three battle groups. Finally, none of the plans, from LANTCOM on down, allowed for the possibility that an entire division might have to deploy to the Dominican Republic.[8]

For Army and Air Force staffs at Fort Bragg and Pope AFB, the period 27–29 April entailed some frantic activity, as they labored to revise outdated plans, tend to routine tasks, and keep abreast of changing conditions and requirements. It was frustrating work, given the numerous obstructions they faced.[9] Most of these obstacles were related directly to STRICOM's joint Army-Air Force Blue Chip V exercise taking place that week at Fort Bragg. Across the board, Blue Chip V had an adverse effect on preparations for possible intervention by the 82d in the Dominican Republic. The exercise tied up divisional staffs, the 2d Brigade headquarters, paratroopers of the 1st and 2d Brigades and other major units, available airlift, rigging lines, equipment, air field control units, parking and billeting facilities—the list goes on. As the two battalion combat teams of the 3d Brigade prepared for possible deployment, they encountered immediate delays in getting their equipment rigged for possible airdrop—first, because Blue Chip loads had to be derigged in order to make room on the rigging lines for the BCT loads, and later, on the 27th, because STRICOM's refusal to cancel a parachute assault demonstration necessitated the simultaneous rigging of Blue Chip and BCT loads. On Wednesday, 28 April, when the JCS directed that the two BCTs achieve DEFCON 2 status (meaning that all designated airlift had to assemble at Pope AFB so that the loading of equipment could begin as the paratroopers staged nearby), the unloading and repositioning of Blue Chip aircraft required four hours before loading BCT-rigged equipment could begin.

Once under way, the loading process took nearly fourteen hours, as it encountered further delays caused by inadequate lighting, too few loadmasters and inspectors, and a shortage of loading equipment. Consequently,

A 2½-ton truck being rigged and loaded for airdrop aboard a C-130 transport

the 3d Brigade did not reach DEFCON 2 until the afternoon of the 29th, just hours before it received the order to deploy. As a TAC after-action assessment conceded, "The long delay in reaching the advanced condition of readiness was excessive for this type of airlift operation."

Although CINCSTRIKE was at Bragg observing the exercise—and was therefore fully aware of its disruptive effect in terms of the Dominican crisis—he refused to cancel Blue Chip V until the last minute on the 28th. Until then, General Adams did not believe it likely that the Army would actually intervene. He was not the only officer at Bragg to hold that view. The distraction caused by Blue Chip, when combined with the constantly shifting assessment of events in the Dominican Republic prior to the 28th, made it difficult for planners to sustain their concentration and sense of urgency with respect to the foreign crisis. There was, the 82d reported afterwards, a "decreased unity of effort and singleness of purpose so necessary for rapid response." On the evening of 28 April, just hours before receiving the JCS message to put the 3d Brigade on DEFCON 2 status, General York provided evidence for this observation when he sent his staff home because no one anticipated a combat deployment.[10]

Despite the confusion, division of effort, and delays, the personnel and resources required to prepare a two-battalion brigade for deployment strained, but did not exceed, the capabilities possessed by TAC and the 82d. Messages from "higher headquarters," though, had already made it clear by the 28th that additional BCTs, together with headquarters and supporting units, might be committed as well. Speculation on this matter ended that evening. As the first wave of armed marines was landing in the Dominican Republic and the 3d Brigade was ordered to attain DEFCON 2, the JCS directed that the four additional BCTs, command elements, TAC airlift and tactical air units, and the required support groups called for under OPLAN 310/2 be placed on DEFCON 3. This escalation placed enormous burdens on an already overtaxed system. Locating additional airlift, scheduling their timely arrival at Pope, devising a parking plan for an overcrowded facility, computing systematic loading plans and finding enough men qualified to implement them, locating billeting for the hundreds of flight crews and other personnel that would soon arrive at the airfield, and working out flight plans should the additional BCTs be deployed were but the more onerous of the myriad tasks that now confronted planners already weary from long hours of work. Exhaustion also plagued the paratroopers of the 2d Brigade, the designated follow-on force, who, having just completed their grueling Blue Chip assignment, had little or, in some cases, no chance to rest before beginning the alert procedures. Some soldiers that eventually deployed to the Dominican Republic had gone without sleep for seventy-two hours. Despite the indefatigable efforts of all concerned, not all of the problems inherent in the escalation to a larger assault force could be solved in a timely way.[11]

As staff officers labored to prepare aircraft and combat units for possible intervention, General York had to determine what the 82d's mission would be in the event of deployment. Neither LANTCOM's OPLAN nor the JCS-

Maj. Gen. Robert York, commanding general of the 82d Airborne Division

originated alerting message had contained a hint of what specific action the 82d would be expected to perform in the Dominican crisis. York, in effect, would have to devise a plan for the initial assault force. Staff officers working through the night of 26–27 April had a proposal to place before the general in an 0400 briefing. The plan—"deduced" from available information—called for the two BCTs to airdrop near San Isidro, seize and secure the airfield, expand the airhead westward to the Duarte bridge, and stand ready to assist in the evacuation of American personnel (see map 4). York approved the plan at 0500; Brigadier General Robert L. Delashaw, vice commander of the Nineteenth Air Force, soon added his concurrence. On the basis of these decisions, the staff prepared a "concept of operations" statement for publication, but York delayed disseminating his "tentative" plan "pending clarification of the mission and receipt of a directive from higher headquarters."[12]

In determining the mission that elements of the 82d would perform if sent into the Dominican Republic, commanders and their staffs, from York and Delashaw on down, required up-to-date, accurate intelligence, especially on the identity, status, and location of friendly and unfriendly forces and the location of key facilities in Santo Domingo. The information they received did not fulfill these requirements. York and his staff argued later that "a critical intelligence vacuum existed during the vital early stages of the operation." As is usually the case, given the shortage of intelligence officers and the easily overlooked duty of keeping plans updated, the

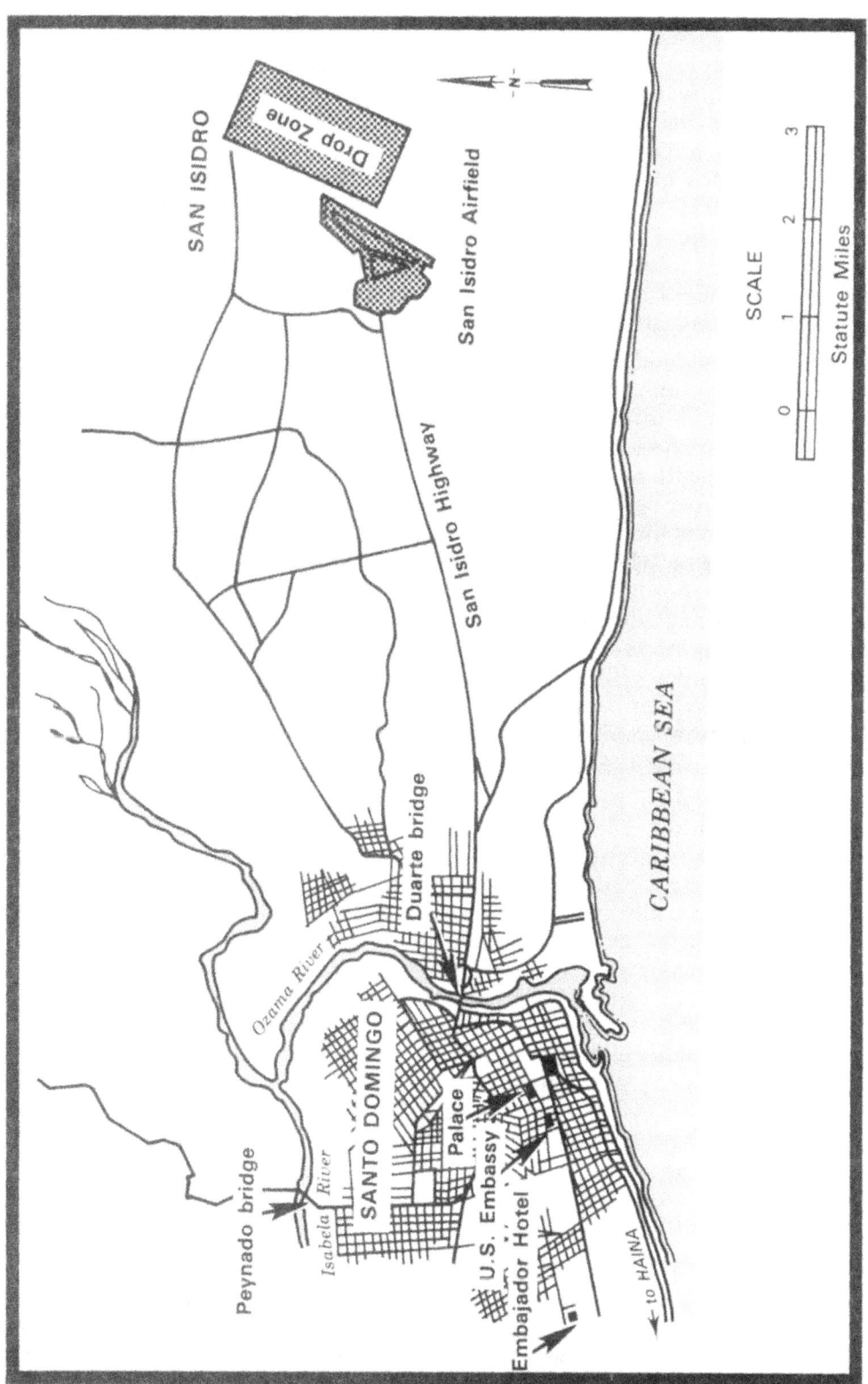

Map 4. Santo Domingo and San Isidro airfield

LANTCOM OPLAN offered little to an airborne commander in the way of useful information or analysis, either political or military, strategic or tactical. Nor, at first, was there a clear and secure channel through which the 82d could receive timely information from Norfolk or higher headquarters. CINCLANT was having his own problems in divining JCS intentions, and because of the lack of secure communications, the 82d could get little information from LANTCOM until the 29th, when a liaison officer sent to Norfolk on the 27th was able to see that intelligence available to CINCLANT was forwarded on a regular basis to Fort Bragg. Prior to that, of the only ten intelligence messages the division staff received, most were based on newspaper accounts, and all were outdated.

Some Embassy and CIA reports reached the 82d, but the staff regarded these messages as alarmist, unreliable, and because of their preoccupation with the Communist issue, virtually irrelevant in terms of military planning. Consequently, the twice-daily briefings for key 82d officers were based primarily on rough translations of Spanish-language television and radio transmissions and newspaper reports emanating from Santo Domingo and monitored in the corps' Emergency Operations Center at Bragg. That many military intelligence analysts who spoke Spanish had been sent to Vietnam did not help matters. When one throws in the lack of secure facilities at Bragg in which to gather and display classified material and the shortage of maps of Santo Domingo, it is little wonder that York later regretted not having sent one of his senior officers to the Dominican Republic for the purpose of gathering firsthand information for use in the division's planning phase. Instead, the general could only lament that "the division did not know friend from foe during the planning stage."[13]

The men of the 3d Brigade knew even less. Confined to their barracks after the alert of the 26th, most of their information came from radios, television, newspapers, and rumors. There was talk among them of "killing commies" or "kicking Red asses," but none of them had any idea of what he was to do specifically should he be deployed. Throughout the preparation phase, information of this kind was simply too highly classified. In the event of an execute order, there was a plan to brief the men during a scheduled stopover at Ramey AFB, Puerto Rico, prior to the planned airdrop. The layover at Ramey, according to one official history, was primarily for political and psychological reasons: there appears to have been some hope in Washington that the movement of U.S. airborne forces closer to the Dominican Republic would boost the morale of the Loyalists and perhaps turn the situation around, thereby obviating further U.S. intervention. When the situation in Santo Domingo continued to deteriorate on the 29th, the layover at Ramey would be canceled. So, too, would the much-needed briefings planned for the paratroopers.[14]

When evaluating the preparations that took place for the military intervention between the time Army and Air Force units received alert notifications on 26 April and the attainment of DEFCON 2 status by two airborne BCTs on the 29th, contemporary participants and later historians agree that what transpired hardly represented a textbook model for joint operational

Paratroopers ready to board C-130s

planning. Chain of command violations, conflicting priorities, escalating requirements, equipment and personnel shortages, coordination difficulties, outdated OPLANs, and inadequate and inaccurate intelligence: all presented problems with which commanders and their staffs had to contend. Long hours and diligent staff work overcame many of these obstacles; others persisted well into the intervention. Some of the general problems that the military encountered during the preparatory phase of the crisis continue to arise in joint contingency operations today.

*   *   *

While the 82d was preparing to move into the Dominican Republic, Ambassador Bennett was weighing the possibility of further U.S. military moves. Shortly after midnight on the 29th, a "clutch" platoon of marines had arrived at the Embassy bringing medical supplies requested by the ambassador for the Red Cross and providing additional forces for the protection of the Embassy. Marines had also expanded the polo field perimeter to include the Hotel Embajador (where a road block had been set up along the road leading to the hotel) and, at the ambassador's request, had used helicopters to deliver rations to Loyalist forces isolated at San Isidro. By then, Bennett had declared a moratorium on landing further troops until he could reassess the situation on Thursday. Having already suggested that Washington consider large-scale intervention, he informed the State Department before dawn that he was reluctant to recommend the actual execution of such a course because it would take the United States "down a tortuous path whose end we cannot see." He assured the department, though, that should the situation continue to deteriorate, he would not hesitate to recommend intervention.[15]

Information reaching the Embassy late Wednesday night and early Thursday—the veracity of which Embassy officials accepted without confirmation—depicted scenes of rebel atrocities and destruction of property. Armed bands reportedly filled the streets, and casualties of their violence filled the hospitals. By midmorning, however, Bennett was telling Washington that the fighting had tapered off and that the junta was preparing "Operation Clean Up," despite continuing problems with communications, coordination, and morale. Bennett noted that the Loyalists were passing word that U.S. marines would take part in the operation—a complete falsehood even in the unlikely event that the "clean-up" would be executed. Bennett, however, did not try to squelch the rumor because it might boost Loyalist morale, while having the opposite effect on the rebels. Both sides, he assumed, were tired and demoralized.

The accuracy of that assumption was called into question later in the day, as news coming into the Embassy again took on ominous overtones. The Constitutionalists, reports indicated, were attacking the Loyalist-held Transportation Headquarters in the northern part of the city, Fortress Ozama, and various police stations, where the defenders were allegedly murdered if captured. The U.S. MAAG offices in downtown Santo Domingo had been sacked, and there were widespread reports of looting and imminent danger to American property. To Embassy officials, it appeared that the rebels were on the move, the junta was stalled, and the situation was indeed deteriorating once again, despite the Marine landings of the previous day. In midafternoon, the Embassy came under sniper fire just as Bennett was holding a meeting in his office with Dare and Daughtry. From the perspective of American officials in Santo Domingo, the time for U.S. intervention had arrived.[16]

For once Washington was ahead of officials in the field. By midafternoon, President Johnson had already decided to land the remainder of the marines, which he thought were still aboard the *Boxer*, and to deploy two BCTs of the 82d to Ramey AFB. Washington had concluded that the United States could not accept the continuing instability in the Dominican Republic, thereby risking a Communist takeover. Furthermore, the president and his advisers had agreed that they should use overwhelming force to stabilize the situation. They recalled how, during the early phases of the 1958 crisis in Lebanon, President Eisenhower's deployment of large numbers of troops had created a climate of intimidation conducive to the reduction or cessation of hostilities. With the fiasco of the Bay of Pigs relatively fresh in his mind, Johnson needed only minimal prodding from McNamara and Wheeler to see the wisdom in Eisenhower's precedent.[17]

Bennett apparently knew of the president's decision to send in more marines even before the Embassy meeting with Dare and Daughtry (although he might have learned the information in telephone conversations during the meeting). What the ambassador said to the two officers is not exactly clear, but in a report to State, Bennett indicated that he had instructed Dare to bring ships carrying marines and heavy equipment closer to shore in preparation for a landing. As Bennett explained, "This will take two or three hours and gives us time to review situation again before finally committing troops to shore." Twenty minutes later, Bennett informed Washington that he had just instructed Dare to prepare to land the remaining 1,500 marines of the 6th MEU still aboard ship, together with their heavy equipment (tanks, ONTOS, LVTs, etc.). Lead time was estimated at three hours. The ambassador noted in passing that there were no marines left aboard the *Boxer*, contrary to what the president and his military advisers seemed to think.[18]

The substance of Bennett's message, a response to State's request for his estimate of the situation, dealt with how the marines should be deployed if they were ordered to land and the composition of the warring forces they would encounter. With respect to the first item, the ambassador favored establishing a security zone from the Hotel Embajador to the Presidential Palace, an area that would incorporate most American residences and foreign missions. Concerning the rebels, he wrote that "our best guesswork" indicated that about 1,500 were under Communist leadership, fewer than 1,000 were military regulars, and anywhere from 1,000 to 4,000 were "hangers-on." He estimated junta forces at about 1,700, scattered in various locations throughout the city, with the bulk of them located at San Isidro. (CINCLANT would pass these estimates on to his subordinate commanders, including York, who may or may not have received them prior to deployment.) In this same message, Bennett made reference to three U.S. Air Force MAAG officers already at San Isidro helping the Loyalists with communication work. In compliance with instructions received earlier that morning from Mann, the ambassador went on to state that he intended to have the three officers, together with an Army MAAG officer who had just been dispatched to the airfield, broaden their role to include advising the junta on operational planning. He chided the junta for accomplishing "literally nothing" of military significance and concluded with the observation that the Dominican Republic "has probably never in its history witnessed a battle of this magnitude and is totally unprepared for it."[19]

While Bennett was discussing troop movements with Washington, Dare was returning from the Embassy to the *Boxer* via helicopter. While airborne, he ordered the ships still containing marines and heavy equipment to approach shore. When he and Daughtry reached the *Boxer*, they were surprised to find Vice Admiral Kleber Masterson, commander of the Second Fleet. The day before, CINCLANT had activated Joint Task Force (JTF) 122, with Masterson as its commander. Under CINCLANT, Masterson would, for the time being, have responsibility for the conduct of all U.S. military operations in the Dominican Republic. That evening, the JCS selected the code name for these operations: Power Pack. Later, Masterson dissolved TG 44.9 and, in its place, activated a naval task force, TF 124. Dare became commander

Marine vehicles coming ashore at Red Beach

of TF 124, which assumed responsibility under JTF 122 for all U.S. naval units involved in the Dominican affair.

While Dare and Daughtry were briefing Masterson and his staff, the order came to execute Operation Barrel Bottom—the landing of the remaining marines and their heavy equipment. Masterson acknowledged the order, and marines began to move over Red Beach, a landing area near Haina that a beachmaster had discovered by chance during Tuesday's evacuation activities. Once ashore, the marines would wait for the tanks and other weaponry, then proceed in an armored column to the Embajador. The landing began at 1830, and the column reached the hotel an hour later.[20]

*   *   *

An hour or so after the marines had arrived at the hotel, Army units were also on the move. The initial assault force of the 82d was headed for Ramey, with General York in the lead transport of an air armada of 144 C-130s, 33 of which carried the 1,800 paratroopers involved, 111 their equipment.[21] Unknown to the troops, a debate was taking place in the United States over whether to divert the aircraft in midroute from Ramey to San Isidro, where the BCTs would airland instead of airdrop. McNamara and the JCS favored the San Isidro landing in view of a delayed departure by the 82d from Pope AFB and recent reports that the situation in Santo Domingo had reached a critical point.[22] "If we wait," Wheeler is reported to have said, "we may not have anything to support." CINCSTRIKE and CINCLANT opposed the change in plans, because they feared overcrowding at San Isidro and because the troops would have only their muscles and small tools for unloading heavy equipment rigged for airdrop. Besides, no one, not even the Embassy in Santo Domingo, seemed to know for sure whether the airfield was still in friendly—that is, Loyalist—hands. To clear up this latter point, Wheeler contacted Vice Admiral Masterson with instructions to find out who controlled the airfield and whether it was operational.[23]

Masterson had planned to send a Marine rifle company to San Isidro to secure the airfield, but after talking with Wheeler, he dispatched an officer and a Spanish-speaking sergeant by helicopter to find General Wessin and bring him back for an intelligence update. The men returned to the *Boxer* with General Imbert, instead. The general reported that the airfield was in friendly hands but that the control tower and runway lights had been shut down for the night. He also mentioned the possibility of armed rebel bands roaming the area. Masterson reported this information up the chain of command, after which Wheeler decided in favor of landing York's units at San Isidro that night. When CINCLANT informed Masterson of Wheeler's decision, the vice admiral ordered two marines and one Navy officer to go to the airfield, secure the tower, and get the runway working.[24]

York was two hours into his flight before he received word of the change in plans. Minutes later, he also learned that Wheeler had named him commander of land forces in the Dominican Republic. (The position was not designated in the LANTCOM OPLAN, even though an intervention implied an operation in which land, not naval, forces would play the predominant role.) Further information was sketchy. The airfield, York was told, was *assumed* to be in friendly hands. Although changing plans and incomplete information added to the uncertainty, there was one point about which the general had no doubt: it was pure lunacy under any circumstances to airland planes loaded with heavy equipment rigged for a parachute drop. From the C-130, he proposed to Washington that only the planes carrying troops airland and that the equipment be dropped as planned. Permission was denied. Apparently, the president and certain key advisers were convinced that parachutes opening in the night skies over Santo Domingo would appear far too "warlike"—more indicative of an invasion than an intervention.

When the paratroopers aboard the thirty-three C-130s learned that they would not have to jump, most cheered. Their enthusiasm would have reached even higher levels had they known that the designated landing zone near San Isidro (recommended by a U.S. officer in the Dominican Republic after he had reconnoitered what appeared to be a flat, grassy area from his car) was covered with coral. Had the original plan calling for an airdrop been carried out, the casualty rate among the two BCTs would have been enormously high.[25]

A TAC EC-135 airborne command post flying out of Ramey AFB established contact with the C-130s and guided them to San Isidro. At 0215 on 30 April, General York's plane touched down on the poorly lit airfield.[26] That the first C-130 to land carried General York and Colonel William L. Welch, USAF, the airlift task force (ALTF) advanced echelon commander, generated no controversy at the time but later caused some to question the wisdom of the move. While the commanding general needed to get on the ground as quickly as possible to provide leadership and exercise command, being the first to land entailed certain risks, particularly considering the poor intelligence with which the 82d had had to contend since the initial alert. The assumption that the airfield was in friendly hands, despite General Imbert's warning about bands of rebels in the vicinity, was put to the test immediately upon arrival. Imbert, who had flown by helicopter from the *Boxer* to see what was going on, met York but could offer no current information except to say that the situation was grave. To get to the control tower, York hitched a ride from a group of armed men in an automobile, not knowing whether they were junta or rebel forces. His worries ended when he arrived at the tower unharmed.[27]

The officers Masterson had sent to man the tower had the landing situation under control. The thirty-three C-130s carrying troops would land first, unload, and depart, after which as many of the aircraft loaded with equipment as the airfield could accommodate would land. Given the smallness of San Isidro and the absence of unloading facilities, 65 of the 111 C-130s carrying equipment were diverted to the SAC air base at Ramey, there to have the loads reconfigured for airlanding before the planes returned to San Isidro according to a hastily arranged schedule.

After satisfying himself that the tower was secure and functioning, York established a command post in a hangar nearby. In the meantime, paratroopers began to gather on the airfield as they waited for information regarding assembly points and instructions on what to do. The soldiers had no ammunition: the assumption that Loyalist troops controlled the airfield had led to a decision not to issue any ordnance while the paratroopers were airborne. A grenade pin pulled accidently aboard an aircraft full of troops could have fatal consequences. C-130s with equipment began landing about 0400, but a half-hour passed before groups of soldiers attached to the first wave made their way to the command post and received directions for unloading the aircraft. What followed was several hours of extremely hard work, during which the derigging and unloading of heavy equipment had

Initial 82d headquarters (HQ) in a hangar at San Isidro. The HQ was later moved to a military academy nearby.

to be accomplished by hand or with the most rudimentary of tools (for example, the use of axes for cutting through tough nylon webbing and lines). Some of the platforms were damaged in the process; all of the men who took part were exhausted. Nevertheless, by 0530, enough equipment had been unloaded and small-arms ammunition and grenades distributed to permit the assembly of task force personnel. By dawn, the two BCTs, together with Troop A of the 1st Squadron, 17th Cavalry, were ready to begin operations.[28] With combat marines already ashore and more airborne BCTs being readied at Bragg, the intervention that most American officials had hoped to avoid was now under way.

Stability Operations I: Confusion and Cross-Purposes

In keeping with the guidance of General Harold K. Johnson, chief of staff of the U.S. Army, military activities during the Dominican intervention acquired the generic label, "stability operations." In the fall of 1964, Johnson had expressed concern that the military demonstrated little understanding of counterinsurgency and other kinds of unconventional, nonnuclear warfare. The term then in vogue, "special warfare," proved the point. According to the general, there was nothing "special" about what he regarded as the Army's "major mission in the foreseeable future." "More so than ever before," he argued, "... overseas operations called for forces designed to safeguard or re-establish the peace and stability of areas threatened by guerrillas, insurrection, and other forms of local or foreign-inspired subversive pressure."[1]

By the spring of 1965, General Johnson's preferred terminology, "stability operations," was finding its way into the Army's lexicon. Lieutenant General Bruce Palmer, Jr., who came to command U.S. forces in the Dominican Republic not only employed the term in his periodic reports from Santo Domingo but elaborated its definition. The goal of stability operations, Palmer asserted, was neither "to maintain the status quo, ... nor to support any particular faction or political group, but rather to establish a climate of order in which political, psychological, economic, sociological and other forces can work in a peaceful environment. ..." Stability operations, according to Palmer, were "designed to help a country attain its legitimate aspirations in an atmosphere of tranquility,"[2] just as the Johnson administration said it was attempting to do in the Dominican Republic.

As articulated by Generals Johnson, Palmer, and others, the concept of stability operations dovetailed with the theories of limited war on one central issue: political considerations would dictate the focus of military operations to a much greater degree than experienced in such large-scale conventional conflicts as World War II. Recounting his experience in the Dominican intervention, General Palmer acknowledged that in a situation *"more* political than military," it "is inevitable that Washington is going to take direct control."[3]

Having conceded this point, however, the proponents of stability operations were reluctant to accept without qualification what the practitioners of limited-war theories regarded as the next logical step: policymakers in Washington, not commanders in the field, would determine the scope and nature of military activities at the operational and tactical levels. In coping with this inherent conflict between military tradition and civilian direction of military operations, the best one could expect was to mitigate its effects by establishing effective coordination among the parties involved on both sides of the issue.[4] The problem in the Dominican crisis was that during the first days of the intervention, political-military coordination suffered several breakdowns that aggravated the confusion and uncertainty attendant on any operation in its early phases and that, in one instance, led to the spectacle of U.S. officials working at cross-purposes when military necessity conflicted with political objectives.

Of the issues that surfaced between 30 April and 3 May where better political-military coordination might have diminished confusion or uncertainty, the one that generated the most controversy, then and later, was the discrepancy between the announced mission of U.S. military forces entering the Dominican Republic and the purpose for which many of those troops were used. Initially, the Johnson administration publicly justified military involvement in the crisis solely in terms of protecting American lives. Nothing was said to the American people on 28 or 29 April about preventing a "second Cuba." The president refrained from declaring the anti-Communist motive behind his decision until he could line up what support he could within the hemisphere for an action many Latin Americans were certain to regard as military intervention in the affairs of a sovereign nation.[5] In the meantime, all military operations in and around Santo Domingo would be explained, without exception, in terms of the announced mission of safeguarding American lives and property.

Where the marines were concerned, there existed little problem in defining military operations in terms of the administration's public statements. Elements of the 6th MEU were to establish control over the area between the Hotel Embajador and the U.S. Embassy, thus creating a neutral zone that would provide sanctuary for noncombatants and protection for the American residences and foreign embassies located therein. Bennett had suggested this operation on the afternoon of the 29th, and State and the White House had agreed. The JCS then included the mission as part of the guidelines it gave Vice Admiral Masterson in asking him, as commander of JTF 122, to develop an operations plan for the marines and the 82d. At the president's direction, the JCS later instructed Admiral Smith (on his last day as CINCLANT before Admiral Moorer took over) to delay the establishment of an International Security Zone (ISZ) pending the outcome of an OAS Council vote that Washington hoped would give multilateral sanction to the plan. After the OAS approved a resolution calling for a cease-fire and for "an urgent appeal" to all sides "to permit the immediate establishment of an international neutral zone," State informed Bennett that "authority is given to use necessary forces" to establish an ISZ.[6] The U.S. plan called for marines to sweep the area, after which the "urgent appeal" mandated by the OAS would be made to the rebels, in effect asking them to approve a fait accompli.

Using marines to establish an ISZ could be explained in terms of their acknowledged mission, even though policymakers understood the ulterior, anti-Communist reason for their actions. But how did the units from the 82d fit into this picture? Upon hearing that the 3d Brigade was to land at San Isidro, Bennett had queried the State Department, "Is it planned that these troops will immediately begin operations in view [of] statement [that] action continues to be based on need for protection US lives in DomRep?" State's reply was that the airborne forces could be used to help establish the neutral zone—a blatant fabrication considering the distance between the paratroopers and the marines, the lack of a feasible means for joining the two forces without risking a bloody engagement with the rebels who separated them, and the ability of the marines to carry out the ISZ mission by themselves. But Washington stuck to the fiction. As the JCS told Masterson, "Military commanders should respond to press queries relative to deployment of 82d Airborne troops that they are to reinforce Marines for purpose of protecting lives of Americans and other foreign nationals. No other response or conjecture should be offered."[7] These instructions arrived after surprised reporters had already heard Commodore Dare disclose the anti-Communist rationale behind the Marine landings. Dare's statement could not be retracted. But other officers, until notified to the contrary, found themselves in the position of having to mislead the press about what they knew to be the true objective of the 82d. The failure to square political pronouncements with military deployments produced confusion about U.S. intentions and marked the beginning of the military's confrontation with the theretofore friendly news media.

Adding uncertainty to confusion during the first days of the intervention were a series of ambivalent signals received by U.S. officials and military officers in the Dominican Republic concerning the manner in which Washington hoped to end the civil war on terms compatible with American interests. As the crisis neared the end of its first week, the overall goals of the Johnson administration remained the same: the prevention of a Communist takeover, the restoration of order, and the protection of American lives and property. The preferred method of achieving these goals was a negotiated settlement beginning with a cease-fire, although most in the administration would not have been dismayed had this option been canceled by a Loyalist victory.

Still not ready to give up on the Loyalist military, the State Department, during the night of the 29th, asked that Bennett "give urgent consideration to development of operational plans" by the junta, "with the quiet assistance of [a] few US officers[,] for the deliberate and systematic reduction of insurgent held parts of city." The next afternoon, however, after the OAS Council had called for a truce among the warring factions, State instructed Bennett to curtail U.S. participation in talks at San Isidro regarding immediate military action. Notably, the new position did not prohibit U.S. officers from assisting the Loyalists in making contingency plans for future operations. By the time the ambassador received this message, he had been notified on a "For Your Information Only" basis that Washington was considering "the feasiblity of interposing US armed forces between insurgents and Junta forces in order to bring about an effective cease fire and give the OAS time to address itself to and find solutions for [the] basic problems which we confront."[8]

To Bennett and to York, Masterson, and Dare—the American commanders in the field charged with planning operations in the Dominican Republic—the impression imparted by the messages emanating from State and the JCS was that a military solution to the crisis, in terms either of U.S. support for a Loyalist offensive or of a direct U.S. attack against the rebels, could not be ruled out. There existed little doubt in their minds that should the president's decision to intervene with overwhelming force fail to have the psychological impact necessary to stop the fighting and to force negotiations, U.S. Marine and Army units would be deployed militarily against the rebels. York, for one, saw no other alternative. Upon arriving at San Isidro, he had assessed the situation, the reality of which contradicted some of the information he had received at Bragg. With the exception of a few pockets of Loyalist resistance, the Constitutionalists controlled most of the city, not, as he had been told, just Ciudad Nueva in the southeast portion, although that was where the majority of rebels were concentrated because it constituted the economic heart of Santo Domingo. Most of what York saw and heard, however, confirmed what he had already been given to understand: the junta's forces were demoralized, plagued by desertions, hungry, and incapable of immediate combat. If Santo Domingo were to be cleared of rebels and order restored, the tasks would have to be accomplished by U.S. troops.[9]

Masterson agreed. The operations plan "deduced" by York on Tuesday and the plan developed independently by Masterson a few days later called for U.S. troops to move into areas bordering the rebel stronghold in Ciudad Nueva. Although the general and the admiral had not communicated prior to York's arrival at San Isidro, their separate plans were virtually identical. While the marines expanded the area they occupied into a neutral ISZ, the paratroopers would secure their airhead, move to the Ozama River, and relieve junta forces on both sides of the Duarte bridge. If successfully executed, these operations would secure the east bank of the Ozama, protect the junta at San Isidro from an anticipated rebel attack, and put the 3d Brigade in a position to enter Santo Domingo proper if need be. Masterson's plan contained an additional element: Loyalist forces, once relieved, would patrol the area between the marines and the paratroopers, that is, between the Duarte bridgehead and the U.S. Embassy. When Masterson and York met aboard the *Boxer* shortly after dawn on the 30th, the JTF commander told the general that he viewed the Loyalist patrol as a temporary expedient until enough U.S. reinforcements arrived to complete the encirclement of the rebels in Ciudad Nueva and to tighten the "noose" around them. If these operations did not produce a cease-fire, U.S. troops would be in ideal positions to launch an attack. Because York had already surmised that his troops might have to contain and destroy the rebels, he asked Masterson to request more troops, specifically the four additional airborne BCTs called for under OPLAN 310/2-65. Masterson forwarded the request directly to the JCS.[10]

Masterson, Dare, and York could contemplate combat operations to defeat the rebels, but they could not initiate them on their own authority. Washington had made clear to Bennett that "participation by US troops in offensive fighting against extremists is a major policy decision which should be made by highest authority here." Because of the hundreds, if not thousands, of Dominicans, including innocent bystanders, who would be killed and wounded in a direct U.S.-rebel confrontation, it was a decision LBJ hoped to avoid. Among his close advisers, there were those for whom the prospect of a frontal U.S. assault against rebel positions conjured up the unfavorable analogy of "another Hungary," a reference to the bloody suppression by Soviet troops of a popular uprising in Budapest in 1956. Counterbalancing that grim prospect was the equally unsettling possibility of a rebel victory.[11]

At midmorning on Friday, 30 April, the president met with his advisers amid reports that the junta was near collapse and that Fortress Ozama, a key arsenal manned by Loyalists, was about to fall into rebel hands. Johnson weighed a decision to send U.S. troops into Santo Domingo proper to engage the Constitutionalists militarily. It was a difficult decision, and he refused to make it, choosing instead to keep his options open. He would, he declared, continue for the time being to work through the OAS for a cease-fire. Through this and other initiatives involving Latin Americans, he hoped to make the intervention a hemispheric, multilateral affair. To assist Bennett and the papal nuncio—the ranking diplomat in the Dominican Republic—negotiate a cease-fire, the president directed John Barlow Martin, a former ambassador to that country and a well-known liberal, to go to Santo Domingo in order to establish contact with rebel leaders. (It was no secret that Bennett had little credibility within Consitutionalist circles; nor was he temperamentally inclined to negotiate with the rebels. There was also concern that the papal nuncio might make too many concessions to the rebels.) Should the cease-fire effort fail, Johnson wanted enough troops on hand to "take and hold" the troubled country. McNamara and Wheeler advised the president that one or two divisions would be necessary to perform the task, so Johnson authorized sending the rest of the 82d, the 4th Marine Expeditionary Brigade, and, if necessary, the 101st Airborne Division. LBJ went on to say that he would approve the use of whatever troops and measures necessary to prevent a Communist takeover. Having committed the entire 82d and having ordered the 101st placed on alert, the president decided to activate the Headquarters, XVIII Airborne Corps, and sent it to Santo Domingo. It was a busy morning in the Cabinet Room.[12]

Soon after the White House meeting ended, Bennett received word of the administration's position. Embassy personnel were to continue working for a cease-fire. They were also to discourage any rash military acts on the part of the Loyalists. The junta was the only organized Dominican force friendly to the United States and, thus, needed to be preserved as the basis for a new government. The White House did not want U.S. troops placed in a position of having to rescue the junta through military action. The president had also directed that American troops should use no more force than necessary and then only to carry out their previously assigned missions of establishing a neutral zone and securing the Duarte bridge and San Isidro. As of Friday morning, Washington was not ready to sanction U.S. attacks on rebel strongpoints.[13]

Not that policymakers had ruled out the employment of U.S. forces to secure a military decision. Until something happened to foreclose the possibility of a rebel victory, the administration could not dismiss any course of action. For this reason, the White House meeting on Friday did nothing to clear up the uncertainty in the minds of Bennett, Masterson, York, and Dare concerning the ultimate objective of military operations. All four thought a military showdown with Constitutionalist forces likely, and that conviction colored their approach to the deployment of Marine and Army units and to the attempts to arrange a cease-fire. As a result, the political and military measures taken by the United States over the next few days seemed at times to be working at cross-purposes. The extent to which this was the case was demonstrated vividly during the first week of the intervention.

*   *   *

In the early hours of Friday morning, while General York and his troops were landing and assembling at San Isidro, Vice Admiral Masterson relayed his operations plan to CINCLANT and within an hour received permission from the JCS to have the marines begin establishing the ISZ. Masterson chose to wait for the arrival of an additional company of the 6th MEU and for a chance to meet with York to coordinate marine-airborne operations. That meeting, as noted, took place aboard the *Boxer* shortly after York's arrival in the Dominican Republic. Because both men envisaged virtually the same mission for the paratroopers, the conversation was brief.[14] Afterwards, York, accompanied by Masterson's deputy, Major General R. McC. Tompkins, USMC, flew to the Embassy for what was to have been the final coordinating step before implementing the joint Army-Marine plan.

Bennett readily approved the proposed operations but requested that York, Tompkins, Connett, and the U.S. air attaché fly to San Isidro to explain the plan to the junta. Bennett wanted reassurances regarding Loyalist intentions. Thursday night, he had learned that the junta's leader, Colonel Benoit, was against using U.S. troops in combat operations. Any American military move against the rebels, the colonel feared, would play into Communist hands by arousing nationalistic and anti-American sentiments among the Dominican people. Benoit had urged, instead, that Loyalist forces be given one last chance to clean up the city by themselves, a position from which some of his generals dissented given the poor condition of the troops. Bennett, while not opposed to a combined U.S.-Loyalist operation to clear the city of rebels, objected to Benoit's proposal on two counts: the Loyalists were reportedly in no condition to fight, and more important, a unilateral Dominican clean-up operation would be "inconsistent with previous requests for US intervention"—requests based on the junta's admitted inability to restore order or protect American lives. The ambassador need not have been concerned. When York arrived at San Isidro, he quickly realized that Benoit's combative rhetoric exceeded his military capabilities. After a long and animated discussion, York persuaded the junta leader to accept the patrolling mission assigned his troops in the U.S. plan.[15]

Once the ambassador, the junta, and the U.S. commanders reached a consensus, the military operations commenced. At San Isidro, the 3d Brigade of the 82d began to move at daybreak (see map 5).[16] While the 1st Battalion, 505th Infantry, secured the airfield, the 1st Battalion, 508th Infantry, together with the cavalry troop and engineer attachments, moved in two columns toward the Duarte bridge. Intelligence provided no accurate estimate of rebel strength, although word circulated that the Constitutionalists were operating in groups of fifteen to twenty men with little central control and were incapable of offering resistance other than small-arms sniper fire. Because those Constitutionalists who had defected from the military wore uniforms identical to those of the Loyalists, a U.S. officer suggested that junta forces in the area wear their caps backwards to avoid accidentally coming under U.S. fire.

Within fifteen minutes, the lead elements of the 508th had made contact with junta forces on the eastern side of the bridge. An hour later, U.S. troops had secured the position. A patrol then crossed the bridge to contact Loyalists on the west side and to determine their positions. A larger U.S. force would follow but not until the east bank of the Ozama, especially the Villa Duarte area to the south from which increasing sniper fire was being received, had been cleared of rebel pockets. One company and a reconnaissance platoon cleared the area north of the eastern bridgehead, while another company and the cavalry troop moved against Villa Duarte. These were time-consuming operations, requiring house-to-house searches, but by midafternoon, the east bank was secure. Operating in accordance with an order to fire only when fired on, Company C of the 508th—flanked by the battalion's Company B and the 505th Battalion's Company C—crossed the bridge in force. Sniper fire and the remains of burned-out vehicles slowed their advance. Once on the west bank, they fanned out to secure the bridgehead, particularly the vital power plant to the south, which Company C of the 1st Battalion, 505th Infantry, seized under "withering fire." By late afternoon, U.S. forces had relieved all but a small number of Loyalists on the west bank. Besides the power plant, American troops controlled a semicircle with a six-block radius. On the east bank, units had moved all the way south into San Souci and had established positions atop an eight-story silo overlooking the rebel stronghold downtown. The entire operation had cost the paratroopers five casualties, none of them serious.

At this time, York expected the junta's troops to begin patrolling the area between the 82d and the marines. Instead, the Loyalists, with their equipment intact, returned to San Isidro. Until further U.S. troops arrived, the plan to isolate the bulk of the rebel force in Ciudad Nueva would have to be held in abeyance. Despite that, it had been a successful operation for the 82d, even if, by the division's own admission, "the current and planned

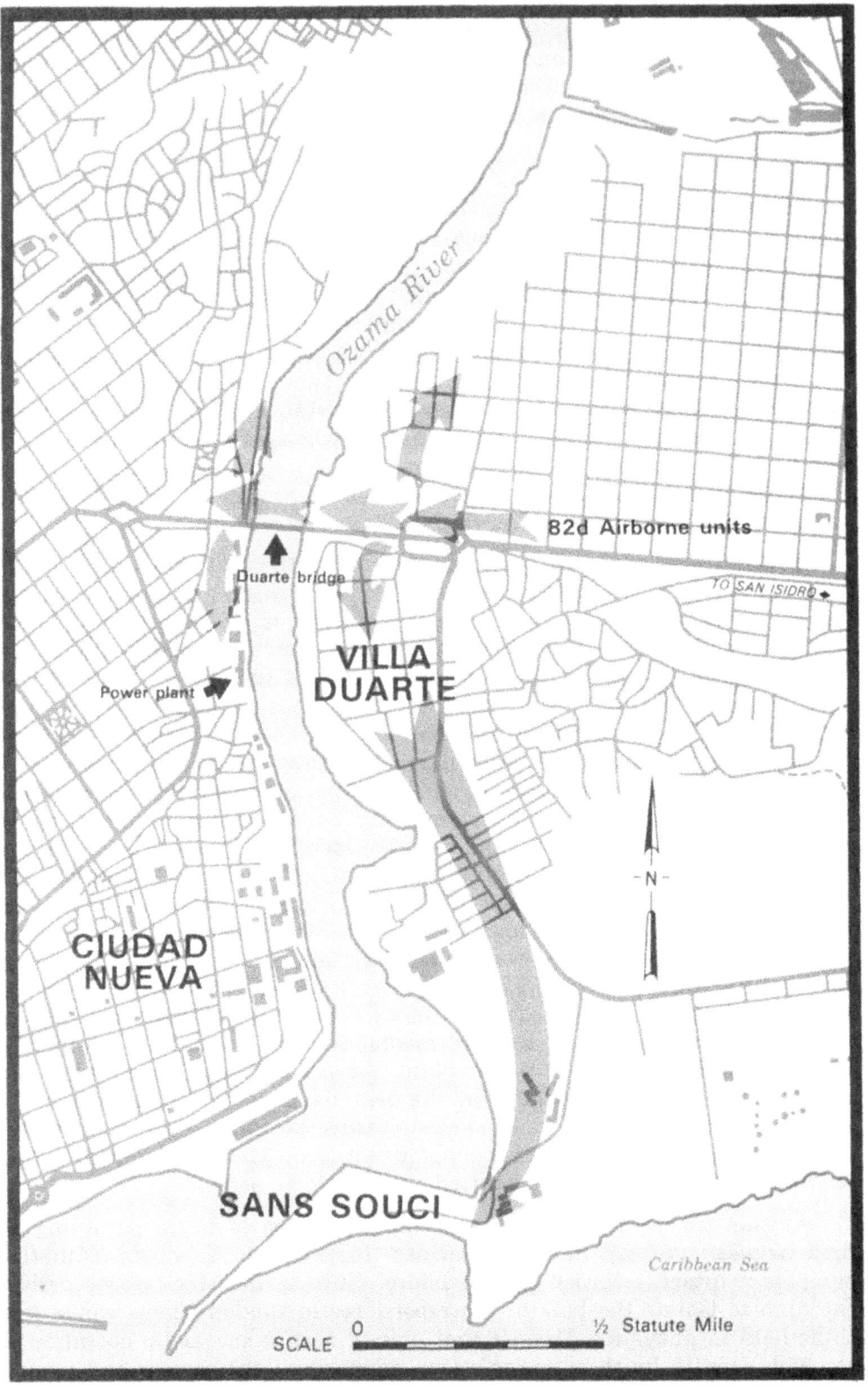

Map 5. Movement of units of the 3d Brigade, 82d Airborne Division, 30 April 1965

Aerial view looking north toward the Duarte bridge. The smokestacked building on the west bank (left) is the power plant.

disposition of ... [its] forces did not appear to substantiate the stated mission of protecting American and foreign nationals...." This discrepancy did not escape American reporters, who had only the previous day received

Marines move to line of departure in preparation for establishing the ISZ

Washington's permission to enter Santo Domingo. As one reporter noted, the 82d's move to the Ozama had nothing to do with evacuating Americans but was instead a political deployment designed "to prevent the collapse of the Benoit junta."[17]

On the western side of town, at the Hotel Embajador, the marines assembled on the morning of the 30th to begin the clearing operation that would establish the perimeter of the International Security Zone (see map 6).[18] While the battalion commander hovered overhead in an observation helicopter, the lead elements of the 3d Battalion, 6th Marines, began their advance from Avenida Abraham Lincoln, the north-south line of departure near the hotel, and moved eastward toward the Embassy. Expecting to encounter rebel sniper fire, the battalion's three companies moved in single file behind tanks, ONTOS, and LVTs, "hugging garden walls and moving from tree to tree and from telephone pole to telephone pole." Company K, advancing along Avenida Bolívar toward Point B at the intersection with Calle Socorro Sánchez, and Company L, moving along the right flank toward Point A at the intersection of Avenida Independencia and Calle Socorro Sánchez, reached their objectives without encountering opposition.

Company I, operating on the left flank, was not so fortunate. As it passed near the U.S. Embassy, newsmen and photographers who climbed aboard the vehicles wondered why the marines were being so cautious.[19] The answer came minutes later as the company approached its objective, Point C at the intersection of Avenida Francia and Calle Leopoldo Navarro, about a block and one-half north of the Embassy. Small-arms fire suddenly erupted from housing near the old Santo Domingo airport and from buildings along Avenida San Martín and Avenida Presidente Ríos, the latter an approach to the company's ultimate objective, Point D. The company commander, restricted to the use of small arms, sent a request up the chain of command to Masterson to use heavier caliber weapons to dislodge the snipers. While awaiting a response, the company commander proceeded to Point C, where he ordered his three platoons to silence the rebels through a series of squad- and fire-team rushes. The results were mixed, with the 1st and 3d Platoons taking casualties of one killed and eight wounded. That afternoon, the company received authorization to use 3.5-mm rockets

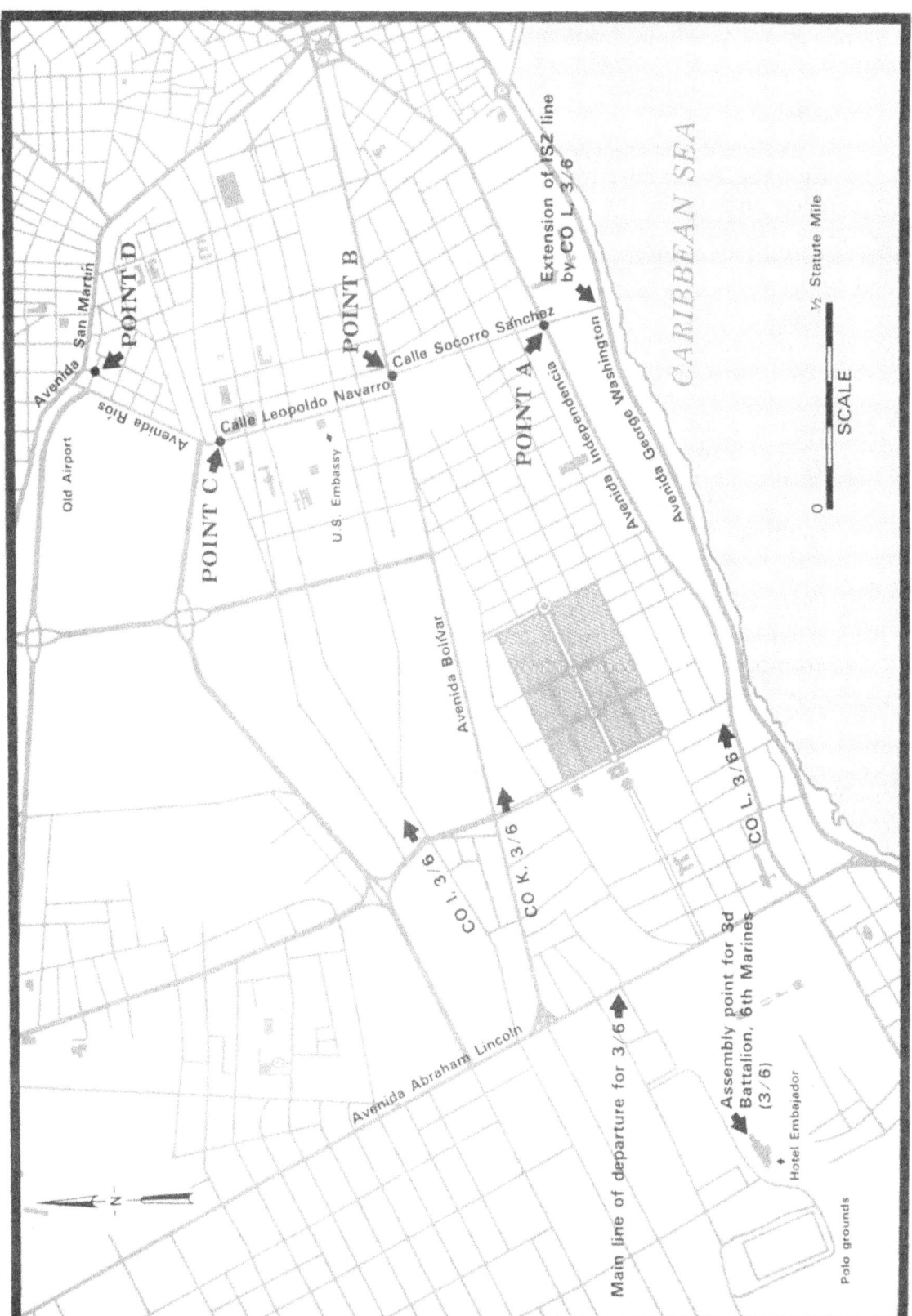

Map 6. U.S. marines establish International Security Zone, 30 April 1965

to reduce the buildings housing the snipers. Although the rockets proved highly effective, a checkpoint established at Point D could not be held. In view of this, Colonel Daughtry ordered the company to consolidate its position at Point C.

By day's end, the Marine position ran in a north-south line from Point C to Avenida George Washington near the sea. The U.S. Embassy occupied a position directly on the line; troops—not land—provided the only buffer between U.S. officials and the rebels, many of whom had yet to be cleared from within the precarious perimeter established by the marines.

While the 82d and the marines were still conducting their respective operations, a meeting convened at San Isidro in midafternoon for the purpose of arranging a cease-fire. Bennett, the papal nuncio, General York (representing Masterson), Wessin, Benoit, and two men representing Caamaño were among those in attendance, as was LBJ's personal emissary, Ambassador Martin, who arrived just as the meeting was getting under way. There followed a long, acrimonious argument between Loyalist officers and Constitutionalist representatives in which each spoke emotionally about atrocities and other crimes allegedly committed by the other side. The fall that morning of Fortress Ozama, from which only four policemen escaped with their lives, added to the intensity of the confrontation. "This was hate, real and naked," Martin later wrote. For a time it appeared as though agreement was beyond reach, but at Martin's urging, Wessin, then Benoit, then the others present,[20] signed a brief document that sought to guarantee the personal safety of all individuals, regardless of political affiliation, and that requested the OAS to send a commission to arbitrate the conflict. The signers wanted Caamaño's personal approval and signature but decided to wait until the next morning before making the hazardous journey to the colonel's headquarters. In the meantime, the nuncio announced the agreement over the radio.[21]

As the cease-fire went into effect, both marines and paratroopers reinforced their positions and waited for nightfall. A platoon from the 82d flew by helicopter to assist marines defending the landing zone near the Embajador. It was a symbolic gesture calculated to demonstrate the 82d's involvement in the effort to protect American lives. Along the eastern edge of the ISZ, the three Marine companies each had a section of 106-mm recoilless rifles to bolster their firepower. Sniper fire continued throughout the night, despite the cease-fire, but once the marines became accustomed to it, their fire discipline improved—that is to say, they stopped returning fire until they had a clear target.[22]

On the west bank of the Ozama, the bridgehead defended by elements of the 82d came under intermittent sniper fire, at times heavy, throughout the night. The division's initial assault force had arrived configured for light operations, but an artillery battalion had brought in 105-mm howitzers, which were set up between San Ididro and the bridgehead. At one point around midnight, when the snipers were particularly active, the 105s fired illumination rounds over the bridgehead. After eight such rounds caused a discernible drop in the rate of sniper fire, a battalion commander, fearing that the burning remains of shells would ignite fires in the shanty town that bordered the bridgehead, ordered the artillery to cease firing. (As it turned out, there would be no more artillery rounds fired in combat by U.S. forces during the intervention.) Well before dawn, sniper fire in the Army sector became sporadic. The cease-fire seemed to be taking effect, but few were optimistic it would last.[23]

The cease-fire agreement certainly caused no celebration among the Loyalists and American officials in Santo Domingo. Believing a cease-fire unwise while rebels still controlled most of the city, Bennett had tried, without success, to convince Washington of his reservations. York regarded the agreement as an obstacle to preventing a Communist takeover, while Masterson informed CINCLANT and the JCS that the agreement was "tenuous" and that he was "not sanguine as to its effectiveness." Rebel elements, Masterson believed, would attempt to probe U.S. positions, and he had accordingly ordered "Army and Marine commanders to hold their positions and defend them as necessary." At San Isidro, Loyalist officers were convinced that the rebels would use a cease-fire to consolidate their positions and to build up their forces. Bennett agreed but reminded the Loyalists that they could also use the respite to regroup for possible action in the event that the cease-fire broke down. Bennett's nudging was hardly needed. Despite having signed the document, the junta talked about future clean-up operations not as a possibility but as an inevitability. Caamaño's thoughts are not known, but many on both sides wondered whether he had enough control to impose the cease-fire on the small armed groups under his command.[24]

The attempt to revise the cease-fire agreement when Martin, Harry Shlaudeman, and the papal nuncio visited Caamaño's headquarters on Saturday led to a complete breakdown in political-military coordination. The colonel, the entourage discovered, had already signed the cease-fire document. When he warned that U.S. troops must not be allowed to cross the cease-fire lines, Martin produced an ESSO oil company map of the city. The map, which Bennett had given him that morning, had the ISZ boundaries sketched in, based on the approximate position of the marines at that time. Martin explained that the marines intended to move the ISZ line two blocks to the east in order to give the U.S. Embassy better protection. Caamaño agreed to the move and accepted the other boundaries. Only later did Martin discover that Masterson and Tompkins also wanted the northern boundary expanded several blocks in order to provide better protection for what were exposed Marine positions in the area. Martin's failure to consult the military before agreeing to changes in the ISZ boundaries prompted Tompkins to object "in the strongest language (politely of course) that to have the military committed unilaterally to new boundaries and rules, and then fail to tell the military, was an unexcusable [sic] piece of madness." Martin offered to reopen negotiations, but both he and Tompkins realized that it was too late for that. For the time being, the agreed upon boundaries would stand.[25]

In one other respect, Martin's political achievement conflicted with what U.S. officers on the scene perceived in terms of military necessity: the ceasefire in place ratified the gap between the marines and the paratroopers. York expressed concern, but he did not have the authority to override President Johnson's personal emissary. As in the case of the ISZ boundaries, it appeared that this aspect of the agreement, unsatisfactory as it was from a military perspective, would not be altered. Lieutenant General Bruce Palmer had other ideas.

*   *   *

Palmer arrived at San Isidro shortly after midnight Saturday. At the White House meeting the previous day, after LBJ had approved activation of the Headquarters, XVIII Airborne Corps, the president reportedly instructed General Wheeler to select the "best general in the Pentagon" to take command of the forces in the Dominican Republic. Wheeler immediately approached Palmer, who was then the Army's deputy chief of staff for operations (DCSOPS) but slated to take over as commanding general of the XVIII Airborne Corps in a few weeks. Palmer, a modest man, attributed his selection in part to Army politics—Wheeler wanted to put in his own man as DCSOPS immediately—and to the desire of LBJ and his advisers to have a general officer from Washington, one presumably attuned to the political-military dimensions of the crisis, placed in the sensitive role as commander of the U.S. forces ashore. Wheeler informed Palmer to leave at once for Fort Bragg, "pick up an austere headquarters with communications support from XVIII Airborne Corps," and fly to Santo Domingo. The chairman of the JCS went on to say that Palmer's "announced mission" was to save American lives but that his "unstated mission" was to prevent a Communist takeover of the Dominican Republic. Palmer was to take all necessary measures to prevent a second Cuba and was promised sufficient forces to "do the job." Wheeler urged Palmer to "get close to Ambassador Bennett and coordinate your actions with him." Finally, the chairman directed that all messages sent by Palmer through the chain of command, that is, through the JTF commander and CINCLANT, should also be sent directly to Wheeler through a back channel. This last directive stemmed from Wheeler's opinion that "communications from the scene of operations coming via the USS *Boxer* and CINCLANT were slow, sketchy, and unreliable."[26]

Breakdowns in communications were not confined exclusively to the Navy. Neither General Bowen, the current commanding general of the XVIII Airborne Corps, nor General York was informed of Palmer's mission. Thus, when Palmer arrived at Bragg on the afternoon of the 30th, a "more than indignant" Bowen asked him, in effect, "What the hell are you doing here?" Palmer told him. During the discussion, the phone rang, and Bowen finally received official notification of what was going on. Palmer got the headquarters segment and communications package he needed but little useful intelligence before setting off in a C-130 for San Isidro. Upon his unexpected arrival, he reluctantly awakened York from a much-needed sleep so that the 82d's commander could brief his replacement as commander of

Lt. Gen. Bruce Palmer, Jr., commander of the U.S. forces in the Dominican Republic

TF 120. "Bob wasn't completely happy about seeing me," Palmer recalled later, "but he recognized the situation and was very good about it." Be that as it may, an underlying tension developed between the two generals that Palmer attributed to York's natural reluctance to relinquish his role as land force commander. But as Palmer was to argue, York had his hands full with the 82d, and a higher echelon commander who could work with the Country Team as a buffer between the combat troops, with their military preoccupations, and the policymakers in Washington, with their political demands, was essential. The strain between York and Palmer would become more severe in the weeks that followed as their perceptions of the intervention diverged.[27]

York's briefing in the division's noisy hangar at San Isidro—megaphones had to be used—convinced Palmer that the situation "was a *very* confused one." What disturbed Palmer most was the cease-fire in place, under which U.S. forces would have to live with the gap between the Army and the Marine positions, with the rebels, "who had initiated a reign of terror and anarchy," operating at will in between. To Palmer, this was militarily unacceptable, and he informed York that he did not recognize the cease-fire for that reason. York agreed, claiming that he had not signed the agreement but had only witnessed it for Masterson. Both generals concluded that a corridor had to be established between the two U.S. positions. As a first step toward that objective, Palmer ordered York to mount a reconnaissance in force that day for the purpose of determining rebel strength within the gap and finding a feasible route for a corridor.[28] Over the next two days, the issue of a corridor became Palmer's primary operational concern, as he tried to undo the consequences of what he considered a failure in political-military coordination.

Around 1000, Palmer flew by helicopter to the U.S. Embassy, landing next door, where Trujillo had maintained his residence. The marines guarding the Embassy were engaged at the time in a firefight with rebel snipers, so Palmer and his pilot hastily scrambled up a fence and dropped onto the Embassy grounds. In the meeting that followed this unceremonious arrival, Bennett expressed his reservations to Palmer regarding the cease-fire agreement and promised to support the general's request for more troops. Whether Palmer, during the course of the conversation, told Bennett about the reconnaissance in force scheduled for later that morning is not clear. At some point, the general did report his plan for an Army-Marine linkup over the telephone to the director of the Joint Staff in Washington, and he had to have informed Masterson in order to get U.S. Marine Corps participation in the operation.[29] But the evidence suggests that Palmer did not inform Bennett, perhaps because he had not had time to form a judgment as to the diplomat's reliability. If this was the case, the cause of political-military cooperation suffered a temporary setback as a result of Palmer's caution.

About the time Martin was meeting with Caamaño on the cease-fire, the reconnaissance in force was getting under way as the marines and 82d sought to make contact near the ISZ (see map 7). Company I of the 3/6 BLT moved northeast without resistance from their position at Point C to the proposed linkup point on Avenida San Martín. At 1025, a reconnaissance platoon and the 1st Platoon, Company C, 1st Battalion, 508th Infantry, set out from the west bank of the Ozama along a route that would take it due west and then southeast to the rendezvous. Unlike the marines, the paratroopers ran into resistance at two points on their march and suffered their first fatality (another man would later die of his wounds). The opposition in both instances was suppressed before movement proceeded, with one platoon getting lost temporarily because of its outdated maps. Nonetheless, the linkup finally occurred in an open field, after which the joint force canvassed the immediate area gathering valuable intelligence until York ordered the patrols to return to their original positions. The 82d's account of the withdrawal order indicates that it was issued because the force was not large enough to "sustain itself in an isolated position." Another account suggests that the order to withdraw came directly from Washington.[30]

Washington became involved after Caamaño complained about the troop movements. In a cable to Santo Domingo, Mann confessed to being puzzled over the colonel's charges, especially after the Defense Department had assured State that the only known troop movements were between the Duarte bridge and San Isidro. Bennett, who was apparently as much in the dark as Mann, waited two hours before replying and then allowed only that the Embassy was receiving rebel protests about some movement by the paratroopers into the city and that the "conflicting reports" were being checked out. In the meantime, Bennett continued, Shlaudeman had told the

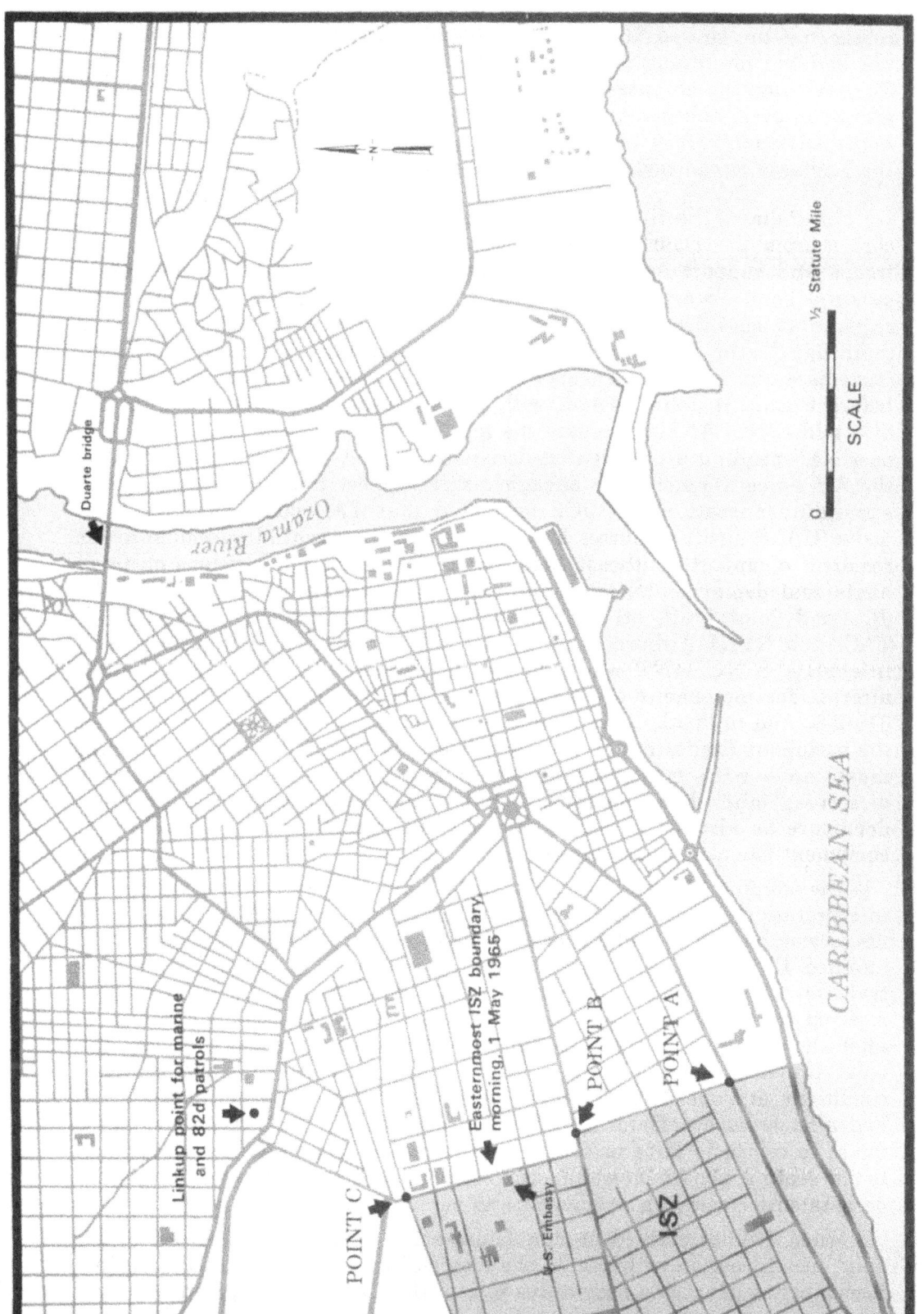

Map 7. Linkup of U.S. Marine and 82d Airborne Division patrols, 1 May 1965

rebels that the United States, while neutral, had "given no commitment as to where our forces might or might not move in execution of their mission." That evening, the ambassador conceded that there was "confusion here this afternoon over movement west of Ozama bridgehead by forces of 82nd Airborne Division." Only at 2040 (in a situation report written at 1830) did the Embassy acknowledge the Army-Marine linkup that afternoon.[31]

* * *

For Palmer, the linkup demonstrated the feasibility of establishing a cordon from the Duarte bridge to the ISZ. The next step was to obtain troops and support for the operation. He would encounter difficulties in securing both. To establish and hold a corridor through rebel territory, he required at least the four additional BCTs York had requested early Friday morning. At the time, York, in making his request, had anticipated an immediate and affirmative response. His optimism seemed warranted. Even before President Johnson met with his advisers later that morning, the JCS told CINCLANT to prepare the four BCTs for deployment "as soon as possible," pending a presidential decision. To quiet expressed concerns that the Air Force did not have enough airlift to meet the requirements of an expanding operation, the JCS indicated that TAC could employ "total active USAF airlift resources less that absolutely essential minimum airlift required to support Southeast Asia." Once LBJ made his decisions on troop alerts and deployments, telephone calls and message traffic between the JCS and Joint Staff, on the one hand, and CINCLANT, CINCSTRIKE, TAC, and XVIII Airborne Corps, on the other, increased in volume and intensity. CINCLANT was to give "maximum priority to positioning aircraft for movement of remaining four BCTs" committed to OPLAN 310/2-65 and to "make maximum preparation for an *immediate* launch" of the battalions (italics mine). The same message "emphasized that this force must move with minimum delay upon receipt of movement execute directive," and that "personnel should be standing by for immediate departure as aircraft are available and all possible advance loading of equipment [should] be accomplished."[32]

The wording of these messages left little doubt that, in the Joint Chiefs' interpretation of LBJ's decisions, the deployment of additional airborne forces was imminent and a matter of great urgency. Two of the four BCTs attained DEFCON 2 status by Friday afternoon, only to wait while their transports sat idle. Hours passed. Finally, that evening, CINCLANT received word that there would be no execute order until the next morning, after the president had met again with his advisers. Sometime later, the Joint Chiefs discovered to their horror that in the crowded and confused conditions at Pope AFB certain elements of the 2d Battalion of the 505th had already taken off for San Isidro. Immediately, the JCS ordered these forces to return to Pope or to divert to Ramey. (Apparently, the troops had found seating aboard Power Pack I's Bravo echelon, which was originally designated for carrying equipment and supplies only.)[33]

When Palmer arrived at San Isidro early Saturday, he learned of the Joint Chiefs' action to withhold the four BCTs, at least for the time being. Remembering Wheeler's assurances to him that he would be given whatever forces necessary to prevent a second Cuba, Palmer immediately requested that troop movements be resumed. But the only additional combat troops he would see that morning were 100 or so "contaminated" paratroopers from the 2d Battalion of the 505th Infantry who, unaware of the recall order, had proceeded to San Isidro. Also landing at the airfield that morning was the lead element of the 15th Field Hospital, a unit the JCS had inserted into the airlift upon receiving Embassy reports of massive casualties in Santo Domingo. York and Palmer were furious. The 82d and the marines already had adequate medical support. From the perspective of the two generals, the purpose of the airlift, once the initial assault forces had landed, was to provide the ground commanders with what they needed, when they needed it. And what they needed Saturday were more combat troops. "A force commander committed to an objective area must be able to request units whose capabilities augment those which are already committed," Palmer later reported, "and he needs to know what sort of units are alerted or en route to join his force." (Palmer was operating under the dubious assumption that higher headquarters had some clue as to the alert or deployment status of the units in question.)[34]

As Palmer and York fumed in the Dominican Republic, President Johnson was reconsidering military movements he had approved only twenty-four hours earlier. The reason for this second White House meeting was simple. The decision to send elements of the 82d to the Dominican Republic had caused a violent reaction throughout Latin America and within the OAS. Riots and mass demonstrations greeted the news, and Latin American leaders—some of whom supported the troop commitment privately—denounced the United States publicly for violating its policy of nonintervention. As criticism mounted, so, too, did the fear on the part of several key presidential advisers that additional military deployments would further alienate friendly governments in the hemisphere, thus jeopardizing the administration's efforts to transform the intervention into a multinational enterprise under OAS auspices. The news that a cease-fire had been arranged Friday afternoon lent weight to this cautious position. LBJ was caught in the middle. He had agreed to emphasize a negotiated settlement. A moratorium on further troop commitments would lend credibility to that position and, perhaps, mollify the Latin Americans long enough for the OAS to send a commission, and possibly troops, to the Dominican Republic. But the cease-fire in place worked out by Martin would, according to Bennett, Palmer, Masterson, and the Pentagon, work to the rebels' advantage, thereby undermining the administration's goal of preventing another Cuba. Stopping the Communists, the military reiterated, required additional troops—the more the better. The wisdom of sending in enough troops to subdue the rebels, either psychologically or militarily, still held. Johnson weighed the advice, then decided on a middle course. He would continue to emphasize the cease-fire and OAS involvement, while honoring Palmer's and Masterson's requests for more troops from the 82d and 4th Marine Expeditionary Brigade (MEB). The 101st would not be deployed at present. As for the U.S. troops gathering in the Dominican Republic, they would not be allowed for the moment to take offensive action to defeat the rebels.[35]

Soon, Palmer, York, and Masterson would have the troops they needed to establish a cordon linking the Army and marines. They still needed authorization to mount the operation. At the Embassy on Saturday afternoon, Palmer contacted Washington—presumably he talked with Wheeler—and presented a strong case for the proposed action in spite of the cease-fire. A cordon, Palmer argued, could follow a route that would bifurcate the southeast part of the city, pushing the rebels into a very small area and giving U.S. troops control over Santo Domingo's telephone exchange, main post office, banks, and other key facilities. The risk entailed in taking this southern route was almost certain confrontation with rebel forces. To reduce the risk, Palmer proposed an alternative: a cordon set up along a line similar to the one used for the Army-Marine linkup that afternoon. Passing north of Ciudad Nueva, such a route would leave key installations in rebel hands but would contain the Constitutionalists.[36]

Before returning to San Isidro Saturday, Palmer also talked with Bennett and Martin and received their support. Martin was prepared to yield to military necessity despite the cease-fire he had negotiated because he realized that the gap left the Constitutionalists in control of the city. But he rejected the introduction of U.S. troops directly into the rebel area for fear that the move would precipitate a bloodbath. He preferred, instead, the alternate route Palmer had broached with Wheeler. After Palmer arrived at San Isidro, he apparently continued his appeal for a cordon when he communicated with LBJ at 0400, 2 May, via an Air Force C-130 "talking bird" located at the airfield.[37]

That Washington was willing to consider such an operation was evident from instructions sent to Palmer, Masterson, Bennett, and Martin on Saturday night and Sunday morning. Each individual was requested to assess the situation and to recommend a course of action to Washington in time for a Sunday morning meeting between the president and his advisers. The directive to Palmer and the one to Masterson came from Wheeler, who expressly raised the issue of establishing a perimeter around the southeast portion of Santo Domingo. From both officers, he wanted to know the most desirable route, the number of U.S. troops to be used, the time it would take to establish and secure the perimeter, and the estimated casualties. Ironically, Palmer, the architect of the idea, never received Wheeler's message. Palmer's copy was sent by mistake to Fort Bragg and not forwarded to him; he therefore did not provide the detailed information Wheeler desired. Instead, he waited for the chairman's response to his proposals of Saturday afternoon, not understanding why Wheeler would hesitate to recommend to the president what was so obviously required on the basis of military necessity. Only later did Palmer learn the reason for Wheeler's recalcitrance. In responding to the JCS inquiry regarding routes and troop requirements, Masterson had indicated that between twelve and eighteen battalions would be needed to carry out the mission. This was two to three times the force of six battalions that Palmer would have recommended. In effect, Masterson's estimate would require the deployment of the 101st Airborne Division. Little wonder for Wheeler's concern.[38]

While Palmer pondered Wheeler's inexplicable silence and waited for instructions, others made his case for him. On 2 May, Bennett, speaking for the Country Team and for Martin (who had by then concluded that the revolt had been taken over by Castroite-Communist elements), strongly urged State to accept Palmer's recommendation to close the gap between the Army and the marines. Masterson, as noted, echoed these sentiments, if not in the exact words that Palmer would have chosen. That afternoon, State instructed Bennett to contact members of the OAS commission (who had just arrived at San Isidro) to determine their opinion as to the establishment of a line of communication (LOC) across the city (the use of the term "cordon" was now forbidden because of its negative connotation). The commission had reservations, but despite its concern that the move might have an adverse effect on the cease-fire, the members approved the plan when they realized that no corridor existed to provide for their safe passage back and forth between San Isidro and the diplomatic heart of the city. Commission members appreciated the deference shown to them, although they might have suspected that it was simply another token gesture to elicit OAS approval for what would be a unilateral U.S. undertaking. Such suspicions would have been well-founded: State had assured Bennett before he made contact with the OAS commission that the LOC would be established regardless of the commission's attitude.[39]

Apparently, several considerations convinced Washington policymakers to accept Palmer's plan: the fragile nature of the cease-fire, a decision to level with the American people regarding the perceived Communist menace, the rationale that a corridor would be used to facilitate the evacuation of American citizens, and the appeal of establishing a perimeter that would isolate the bulk of the rebels. At 2045, President Johnson talked with Bennett and gave him the go ahead to establish the corridor. Later that night, LBJ again went on television to deliver a major address in which he reaffirmed U.S. neutrality in the crisis and announced his decision to send more U.S. troops into the country. To justify additional troop commitments, he revealed publicly for the first time the administration's fears of a Communist takeover in the Dominican Republic and the need for the United States, acting through the OAS, to prevent such a catastrophe. "The American nations cannot, must not, and will not permit the establishment of another Communist government in the Western Hemisphere."[40]

*   *   *

With the president's personal approval and with orders from Wheeler, Palmer was set to "turn loose" the 82d. The operation would occur at night in order to minimize casualties on both sides and among innocent bystanders. At a conference in Bennett's office, Palmer, the ambassador, Tompkins, and Marine Colonel Joe Quilty, the chief of the military group, had already selected the route for establishing the LOC. State had assumed that the operation would follow the same route used for Saturday's linkup, but studying an ESSO map spread before them on the floor, the conferees in Bennett's office considered all possibilities. The southern route of advance was ruled out because it would mean an inevitable clash with the main concentration of rebels, something Washington would not approve. A route that ran north of the ISZ also held out the danger of crossing through rebel hot spots. The route finally chosen "was calculated on the basis of the shortest distance and least rebel resistance." This meant avoiding the dangerous Point D by turning south along Calle San Juan Bosco, which led into Point C, already secured by the marines. In retrospect, all agreed that rejection of the northern-most route was a mistake because it left Radio Santo Domingo in rebel hands. Once the establishment of the LOC rendered a Constitutionalist victory improbable, the propaganda broadcast from the radio station created one of the major obstacles to ending the crisis.[41]

At one minute past midnight on 3 May, the operation began. A Marine platoon moved east along Calle San Juan Bosco to Calle Rosa Duarte.[42] Farther east, three battalions from the 2d Brigade, which had only recently arrived at San Isidro, left the relative security of the 82d's bridgehead and began moving toward the rendezvous.[43] The tactics employed were, in General Palmer's words, "striking":

> Using a leapfrog method, one battalion would move out, secure an area, and hold it. The next battalion on the line would pass through the area held and advance and hold. The third battalion then moved through the two battalion areas and advanced to the Marine position, thus forming a link-up. They encountered only light resistance and contact was made with the marines an hour and 14 minutes later.[44]

Palmer's account fails to mention an incident that took place when the 82d reached the linkup point. Accompanied by General York, the lead elements signaled the marines. At that time, a rebel sniper fired on the 82d's position. The paratroopers killed the sniper, but in the darkness, some marines who heard the fire opened up on the 82d. A second attempt to signal the marines also resulted in a brief firefight. Angry and frustrated, York finally stood up, walked to the middle of the street, and identified himself by yelling. The linkup then took place.[45]

Although declared to be a safe route once several convoys traversed the LOC later on the 3d, the "All American Expressway"—or "Battle Alley," as the LOC came to be called—was widened over the next two days in order to make positions along it more tenable and to "minimize direct fire in the area." The ISZ was again also extended, this time two blocks east to secure the embassies of Ecuador and El Salvador (see map 8).

The LOC, by providing a ground corridor between the Duarte bridge and the ISZ, facilitated communications and the movement of people and supplies. It also served as an alternate evacuation route and allowed paratroopers to begin a series of humanitarian acts that included making food, water, and medicine available to the city's inhabitants—regardless of ideology—who had gone without those necessities for days. Militarily, the LOC split the rebel force and trapped up to 80 percent of Caamaño's troops in Ciudad Nueva. Because U.S. soldiers quickly set up checkpoints along the LOC, the movement of armed rebels into the northern part of Santo Domingo—where they could carry on operations and possibly mount an insurgency in the countryside—was diminished. The LOC, in effect, ended

Map 8. Final disposition of the International Security Zone and line of communication

any possibility that the Constitutionalists could take over the country by military means. They were surrounded and outgunned. Caamaño would have to negotiate or face certain military defeat.

Palmer and York preferred not to allow him the choice. Their primary reason for establishing the corridor had from the beginning been to provide the 82d with an advantageous jumping-off position for an all-out attack on the rebels. As Palmer noted later, "The forces which opened the LOC could have moved southward upon linkup with 4th MEB. Such action would have broken the rebellion early and restored law and order without delay." Palmer planned an attack that combined ground and heliborne operations and would hit Caamaño from all sides at once. The battle, York speculated, "would be over in a matter of hours."[46] All that was needed was authorization to proceed. The word never came. Following the breakdown in political-military coordination that left standing the gap between Marine and airborne units, Palmer had persistently argued that military necessity had to take precedence over political considerations because of the uncertain military situation in the city. The general had been persuasive and had won his case. But the establishment of the LOC opened a new phase in the intervention, a phase in which military considerations would never again override political objectives on an issue the magnitude of the LOC.

With the threat of a Communist takeover removed, the Johnson administration regarded any further U.S. military action as counterproductive to American interests in the Dominican Republic and Latin America. That assessment did not mean, though, that all American troops would be withdrawn. Their presence provided the administration the leverage it needed to forge a political solution to the crisis—a political solution that LBJ prayed the diplomats could achieve quickly before the intervention took on aspects of an occupation. But until negotiations proved fruitful, U.S. soldiers would remain in harm's way, the targets of snipers' bullets, machine-gun fire, and, depending on one's location, popular resentment and mob violence. Just because the intervention had entered a political phase did not eliminate the military dangers. What the transition portended was an increasing number of political restrictions that would interfere with the ability of U.S. troops to counteract these dangers. Frustration would mount in the days and weeks to follow, as American soldiers, having completed the major portion of what combat they would see in the Dominican Republic, experienced the effects of the subordination of military to political considerations. For the soldiers under fire, it was a distasteful lesson and one that no amount of political-military coordination could ever make completely palatable.

Stability Operations II: Adjustments

As U.S. troops occupied the newly established LOC, the military advantage in Santo Domingo shifted irrevocably in their favor. The Constitutionalists could no longer expect to achieve their goals by force of arms. What uncertainty remained concerned the resolution of the crisis. Would there be a diplomatic or military solution? The decision lay with Washington, where President Johnson remained determined to negotiate an end to the civil war. A political settlement involving all Dominican factions, save the extreme left, would presumably be longer lasting and less damaging to America's image in the hemisphere than a settlement imposed by military action. There was, however, one serious drawback to a diplomatic approach: the conditions for its success were not readily at hand. Although surrounded by U.S. marines and paratroopers, the Constitutionalists were in no mood to capitulate. And although the American military presence curtailed much of the wanton killing, the passions and hatred generated during a week of civil war would not be readily allayed. As for the cease-fire arranged on 30 April, both Constitutionalists and Loyalists violated it at will.

As U.S. forces settled in to await resolution of the crisis, several adjustments had to be made. Additional troops and supporting units well beyond those specified in the original contingency plans had to be prepared, deployed, and provided appropriate and adequate supplies. Communications had to be upgraded, and the quality of political and military intelligence improved. A simplified and more efficient command structure was desperately needed. Most of these adjustments would be made before mid-May. Meanwhile, U.S. officials and military officers monitored political developments, which during this two-week period included the formation of two rival Dominican governments, a new cease-fire agreement, a bitter propaganda war, and the arrival of more presidential emissaries from Washington.

Although the crisis had entered a political phase, American troops had to maintain their vigilance against military threats, which up to late May meant the hostile acts of rebel forces to the north and south of the LOC. Also, U.S. commanders had to be prepared to undertake major military initiatives should a breakdown in the diplomatic process occur. Contingency plans had to be ready for a variety of operations, from clearing the remnants of rebel bands from the northern part of Santo Domingo to an all-out attack against the rebel stronghold in Ciudad Nueva.

From the first day of their arrival, U.S. forces in the Dominican Republic began adjusting to the reality they faced and the deficiencies they detected. Inevitably, difficulties arose. Some stemmed from situations over which the United States had little or no control. Others appeared as the intervention, to LBJ's chagrin, began to take on the characteristics of an occupation. Still others reflected shortcomings that had plagued joint operations and political-military coordination in Power Pack from its beginning. When problems developed, flexibility and adaptability became as critical as training and discipline to those trying to devise solutions. Often the determinant of success or failure was simply the knack of knowing when to do something "by the book" and when to throw "the book" away.

* * *

By mid-May, the buildup of U.S. Army, Navy, Air Force, and Marine units in and near the Dominican Republic reached a peak of nearly 24,000 troops. Included in this figure were the 5th Logistics Command, the 15th Field Hospital, the 503d Military Police Battalion, the 50th Signal Battalion, the 218th Military Intelligence (MI) Detachment, the 519th MI Battalion, the 1st Psychological Warfare Battalion, the 42d Civil Affairs Company, and the 7th Special Forces Group. After the White House meeting on 1 May, the Air Force also received orders to move a tactical fighter squadron and a tactical reconnaissance element to Ramey AFB. Prior to the deployment of the 82d, York and Brigadier General Delashaw, the vice commander of the Nineteenth Air Force, had approved plans for the fighters to establish U.S. air superiority over the Dominican Republic and provide escort to the division's initial assault force. When the 3d Brigade departed Pope AFB, however, the tactical fighters were left at Homestead AFB in the United States, a gross violation of doctrine, but one the Joint Chiefs were willing to chance given the political and military urgency of getting the troops to Santo Domingo and the low probability that Cuban aircraft (the Dominican rebels had no air capability) would interfere with the airlift. The squadron of F-100s arrived at Ramey AFB on 2 May. Later, twelve F-104s augmented this group. Until the fighters returned to the United States on 1 June, two planes on a rotational basis were kept on station over the Dominican Republic at all times.[1]

The two principal units composing the intervention continued to be the 82d Airborne Division and the 4th Marine Expeditionary Brigade, the combat elements of which had all deployed to the Dominican Republic by 4 May. Within a week of his arrival at San Isidro, General Palmer had at his disposal nine airborne infantry battalions, an airborne cavalry reconnaissance squadron, and three Marine battalions ashore, with another Marine battalion off shore in reserve. Most of the marines and some other units came to the Dominican Republic in surface transportation; the majority of U.S. troops arrived in aircraft. The airlift, mounted in support of an operation four times larger than that anticipated under outdated Army and Air Force plans, was impressive. TAC managed to assemble 147 C-130s from airfields around the country, the Military Air Transport Service provided up to 57 C-130s and 90 C-124s, and the reserve forces of the Continental Air Command furnished 19 C-119s. By 7 May, these aircraft accounted for 1,600 accident-free sorties, in which the crews flew to San Isidro and recycled back to Pope to pick up further loads before returning to San Isidro. It was a grueling schedule aggravated by frequent bad weather, few navigational aids, and inadequate briefings on required formations. Adverse conditions notwithstanding, the crews unloaded 16,500 troops and 16,000 tons of equipment and supplies in the Dominican Republic before operations began to wind down after the 7th.[2]

In assessing the airlift as a whole, Army commanders offered praise no less ebullient than that of their Air Force counterparts. Yet when these same Army commanders examined specific aspects of the airlift, praise occasionally yielded to irritation. Hasty planning and haphazard loading procedures resulted in some aircraft arriving at San Isidro without their full loads of equipment and supplies or with trucks, jeeps, and other vehicles not crammed, as they should have been, with rations, water, and ammunition. More critical, the JCS, Palmer, and York all stressed that combat troops should be deployed with "minimum essential equipment." Yet despite these explicit instructions, they could not at first convince those responsible for loading the aircraft that much of the heavy equipment preplanned to accompany each Power Pack element was not needed. Although York understood that readjusting force packages was a "herculean task," he had no sympathy for anyone who refused to make adjustments simply because they were not "according to plan." The general had, for example, all the 2½-ton trucks he needed yet continued to get more. "It appears," he later observed, "that in some respects the Army is still fighting World War II. The back-up required to fight an *SS* division in Europe is not a good guide to use when determining the support required to fight irregular forces in stability operations." The 82d did not need every item on its TOE. "We must," he concluded, "in conjunction with the Air Force, develop procedures permitting great flexibility and quick response to changing tactical and support requirements."[3]

During the first phase of the Power Pack airlift, Palmer echoed York in complaining about the Air Force's slavish devotion to preplanned "packaging" procedures. Not only did Palmer experience delays in getting the combat units he needed, but he also found it difficult to obtain priority seating for intelligence analysts, military police, and civil affairs and signal personnel and other specialists needed in larger numbers than estimated in the original plans. Palmer's irritation over inflexible procedures was not assuaged when chaos engulfed the airlift after the deployment of Power Pack's first echelon. As the general noted later, only Power Pack I moved to San Isidro as a clearly defined package, after which the requirement to identify units in subsequent packages was "either forgotten or ignored." The schedule according to which later echelons deployed further aroused Palmer's ire. He and York argued that aircraft in the initial assault package returning to Pope should be permitted to depart again for San

Isidro as soon as they were loaded with men and supplies. What both generals wanted was for the JCS to authorize a continuous, around-the-clock "airstream" of recycling transports. The appeal made little headway at first. Reluctant to depart from established procedures, the JCS would authorize departures from Pope only after all the planes in a given package had been loaded. This serial approach, in York's opinion, was a mistake in that it caused fatigue among troops who, once aboard the C-130s, were required to wait an inordinate time until other planes were loaded and the JCS issued an execute order. For his part, Palmer cited the enormous problems the serial approach created at San Isidro when aircraft in a given package, arriving within minutes of each other, overtaxed the limited landing and unloading facilities at the airfield. The absence of standard procedures for handling incoming aircraft at San Isidro during the first several days further aggravated the situation. The JCS finally authorized an airstream operation but only after representatives of the 82d made numerous and vigorous remonstrations.[4]

In suggesting ways to overcome the problems experienced with the airlift during the Dominican crisis, Palmer recommended that the troop list in an OPLAN be "treated as a shopping list from which the commander

C-130 transports lined up at San Isidro

charged with execution of the plan can request units according to the actual situation in the objective area." York seconded this suggestion by urging those responsible for preparing the troop, equipment, and supply lists to heed the requirements of the ground commander in distinguishing what was "really necessary" from what was "nice to have." In perhaps the most telling comment of all, York intimated that had the situation in the Dominican Republic been "more volatile," the inflexibility of a packaging system that denied the necessary priority to troops and additional ammunition could have left the 82d highly vulnerable during the first days of the intervention.[5]

For the marines and paratroopers entering the Dominican Republic, whatever confusion or delays they might have experienced getting there were quickly forgotten once they began acclimating themselves to an unfamiliar country and carrying out their specific missions. For elements of the 4th MEB, that meant securing the ISZ until units of an inter-American peace force then being assembled could assume the responsibility.[6] As for the cavalry squadron and nine airborne infantry battalions of the 82d, their assignments encompassed three locations. In the area around San Isidro, a brigade took part in training exercises while providing security for the airfield, the division reserve, and the 82d's command post (which had been moved after only a few days from the noisy hangar at San Isidro to rooms in a military academy nearby). Another brigade of two battalions was deployed to secure positions along the Ozama River and the eastern approaches to the Duarte bridge. Of "primary interest" was the area west of the Ozama, including the LOC, "which was used as the focal point for mission assignment and unit rotation." Because of the intense activity along the LOC, the brigade task force of three battalions that initially occupied the area was reinforced by a fourth battalion on 8 May. According to a plan devised by York, all "infantry battalions were rotated within the area of operations so that each battalion would become familiar with each specific mission and get combat initiated," receiving "practical experience in conducting relief-in-place, in defense of a river line and in operations in built up areas." Other units organic to the division, together with nondivisional elements, set up operations in the most available places they could find that would enable them to perform their tasks efficiently and in safety.[7]

*   *   *

As the troops arrived in the Dominican Republic, their impressions of the country varied. Some were struck most by the "searing sun" and the way it was blotted out virtually every afternoon by torrential rains; others by the "just plain squalor" of the city and the sight of naked children playing in mud puddles; others by the condition of the wartime capital, in which garbage littered the streets, electrical power and telephone service worked sporadically, and food and water were scarce commodities; and still others by the range of emotions with which the noncombatant population greeted a foreign army—emotions ranging from friendly welcomes to vulgar hostility. Whatever their initial impressions, all soldiers from Palmer and

A paratrooper manning his position at the Duarte bridge

York down to the enlisted men manning their posts shared one basic need: a desire for information on the situation they faced.

For the commanders, the list of intelligence requirements was interminable, encompassing both political and military, strategic and tactical, geographical and psychological, logistical and legal information. For the combat soldier, the list was shorter: he wished only to know about the men trying to kill him. Few American troops, particularly those in the first waves, had been adequately briefed, yet almost to a man, they assumed that the rebels were the enemy. The fighting required to establish U.S. positions in the ISZ, along the Ozama, and within the LOC, together with the constant sniping and firefights that followed, transformed assumption into conviction. So, too, did the contrast between the treatment accorded those soldiers who came into contact with Loyalist troops and those who, because of inaccurate maps or unfamiliarity with the city, strayed into rebel territory: from the Loyalists, one could expect friendly conversation and a cold beer, from the rebels, a bullet or a harsh interrogation and public denunciation for propaganda purposes (after which those who survived their errant wanderings in Ciudad Nueva were usually returned to American lines promptly). Military briefers quickly adopted the practice of referring to the Loyalists as "friendlies," the Constitutionalists as "unfriendlies." Talk among American soldiers about "killing commies" or going downtown to "finish them off" also betrayed more than a hint of partisanship. As one "exasperated" colonel put it, "What the hell, those who shoot at us are the enemy and those who don't are friends." The logic seemed irrefutable, but when the media reported the discrepancy between these statements and the formal proclamations of U.S. neutrality emanating from Washington and the U.S. Embassy, the credibility of the administration and the military was again called into question.[8]

Official proclamations notwithstanding, for soldiers under fire it was an easy task to identify the enemy. It was quite another to acquire current, accurate intelligence as to his numbers, leaders, armaments, deployment, and organization. When York and Palmer arrived at San Isidro, that kind of reliable information was simply not available to them or their subordinates. "Information concerning the enemy was practically non-existent," complained one unit afterward. Nor did higher headquarters and other U.S.-based sources provide much enlightenment. The first CINCLANT intelligence summary arrived midmorning on 1 May but did little to clarify the situation. As for information provided by the Continental Army Tactical Intelligence Center, Palmer's assessment was blunt: following the deployment of troops, it was of no value, the organization not having the assets to support a corps in the field. For the general, "The immediate G2 task consisted of discharging current Order of Battle data on rebel forces to meet urgent tactical needs." Because that intelligence would have to be derived on the scene, the first thing to do was to contact individuals in the Dominican Republic who had already collected information pertinent to the Army's needs. Divisional intelligence assets, augmented by elements of the 519th MI Battalion sent from Bragg, established liaison with CIA, Embassy, MAAG, JTF 122, Marine Corps, and Dominican intelligence personnel during the first days of the intervention.[9] Approaches to Peace Corps workers also yielded some valuable information, even though many of the young volunteers, sympathetic to the Constitutionalist cause, resented their government's attempts to suppress the revolt.

An overlay from the 4th MEB helped update U.S. maps, while information from most of the other sources proved useful. If the military had any problem in the exchange of data, it was with the CIA. The record here seems mixed. Some U.S. military intelligence officers benefited from their contacts with their CIA counterparts; others complained that agency men were inept amateurs who refused to share information, possibly because they did not possess any worth sharing. When LBJ sent twenty-four Spanish-speaking agents from the Federal Bureau of Investigation into Santo Domingo, the move was widely interpreted as the president's attempt to establish a reliable intelligence operation in the wake of what he considered to be the unsatisfactory performance of the CIA, especially in the area of compiling a credible list of Communist agents taking part in the revolt. Military intelligence officers found the FBI competent, professional, and willing to share what information it accumulated on Dominican Communists and their links with American academicians and other groups in the States. The CIA held a lower opinion of FBI competency, although the agency's new chief of station managed to establish a cordial working relationship with the head of the FBI team, a personal friend.[10]

Palmer's headquarters and the 82d both suffered from shortages of intelligence personnel, including those Spanish-speaking MI officers who had been sent to Vietnam. Furthermore, the equipment designed to intercept enemy communications was built for use against the Soviet Union; it proved incapable of picking up rebel transmissions from cheap Japanese walkie-talkies. Despite these drawbacks, the Army managed within the first week of the intervention to mount a comprehensive and highly informative intelligence operation. The first real breakthrough came at the tactical level, when the 3d Brigade patrols made their initial linkup with the marines on 1 May. In their trek across the city, the patrols reported rebel roadblock, sniper, and machine-gun positions; the kinds of small arms the rebels were using; the intensity of the opposition; and the fact that the Constitutionalists possessed at least some tanks captured from *CEFA* forces. With the establishment of the LOC, information from frontline troops inundated the corps and divisional G2 and threatened to swamp the meager staffs. In the meantime, U.S. counterintelligence specialists began compiling personality files and lists that categorized rebel activists according to their political affiliation, ideological commitments, and degrees of involvement in the revolt. The files and lists had to be built from raw information because the CIA and Embassy staffs had burned many of their records during the early days of the revolt out of fear the Embassy might be overrun.[11]

Of enormous value to the Army's intelligence-counterintelligence effort was the human intelligence (HUMINT) contained in "Detainee Interrogation Reports." On the morning of 1 May, the 3d Brigade requested transportation for prisoners of war, who were "coming in bunches." At first, the XVIII and 82d were not sure what to do with the prisoners, who, to avoid legal complications, would thereafter be referred to as "detainees." Without adequate facilities or military police to handle rebels who surrendered or were captured, U.S. troops turned the first group of detainees over to the junta, which apparently executed them soon afterwards. Appalled, U.S. Army commanders accelerated efforts to acquire more military police, to turn the division's Detainee Collection Point into a detainee center, and to set up a corps detainee center in the Sans Souci peninsula at the southernmost point of the Ozama's east bank. Once these facilities became operational, detainees would receive their initial interrogations at makeshift brigade holding areas and then be sent to Sans Souci. There, MI teams, counterintelligence officers, and others in need of information attended the interrogation sessions.[12]

The sessions at Sans Souci did not go smoothly at first. Although official files indicated that nearly all U.S. interrogators spoke fluent Spanish, in reality, many did not. To address this problem, MI officers requested that Hispanic-American paratroopers be assigned to the corps' detainee center, but brigade and battalion commanders were reluctant to deplete the 82d's Spanish-speaking assets in the LOC. Consequently, Puerto Rican soldiers were sent directly from their country to Sans Souci. There, they were to serve as interpreters until those interrogators with only a rudimentary knowledge of Spanish could, through on-the-job training, attain the proficiency necessary for conducting interviews on their own. This stopgap measure solved one problem but created another. The fact that most rebels were not Communists but men fighting for a return to constitutional government convinced several of the newly arrived Puerto Ricans that the United States was backing the wrong side in the civil war. (Many

Paratroopers cover group of suspected rebels

non-Puerto Ricans among the U.S. troops in Santo Domingo, it should be noted, shared this view.) Sympathy for rebel ideals led some Puerto Ricans to misinterpret questions and answers in deliberate attempts to keep individual detainees out of trouble. When caught, the offending interpreters were transferred out of the area. These isolated incidents did not appreciably affect the quality of intelligence coming out of Sans Souci. They did demonstrate that the U.S. military was not impervious to the controversy surrounding the Dominican intervention.[13]

The operation at San Souci provided interested U.S. parties not only with tactical intelligence of a strictly military value but with political information concerning the motives, background, organization, and personalities of the rebels. At corps level, political intelligence was essential, given the political-military nature of the intervention; it was also in short supply. Initially, corps intelligence did not have attached to it a political officer versed in Dominican history and politics. It therefore depended on other in-country U.S. resources for a panoramic view of what was transpiring. The Sans Souci interrogations helped to reduce this dependency. So, too, did disenchanted Constitutionalists, who were recruited by MI personnel, debriefed at safe houses, and sent back to their rebel bands to gather additional information. Handling these informants without compromising them was a delicate task. So, too, was crossing into the rebel zone to get a firsthand look at conditions there. For that mission, MI and Special Forces personnel needed civilian clothing, forged documents, proficiency in Spanish, and luck. During the early days of the intervention, all but the last commodity were in short supply. Even when an operative completed a successful reconnaissance, he still had to reenter the LOC. Dressed in mufti and without official identification, he had to convince a checkpoint guard with no knowledge of the operation that they both worked for the U.S. military. One way around this difficulty was to take Green Berets who knew about the covert activities and station them at various checkpoints to identify the returning infiltrators.[14]

Another military source of intelligence was aerial reconnaissance and photography. The 82d had its own aviation battalion, which after 4 May met some of the division's need for aerial reconnaissance, although other duties prevented Army aircraft from being used solely for that purpose. More suited to the task was the Air Force's 363d Composite Reconnaissance Squadron, which arrived at Ramey AFB on 2 May. Composed of six RF-101s, three RB-66s, and an augmented photo-processing cell, the squadron provided aerial photographs on request. During political negotiations, the photos provided a means of verifying whether either side had violated agreed-upon troop dispositions. For tactical purposes, aerial shots revealed not only the location of troops but also key urban terrain features that did not appear on military maps, including the detailed city maps that were available to U.S. troops after 7 May.

Air Force reconnaissance flights began on 3 May but immediately encountered difficulties. Inclement weather and restrictions that prohibited flights below 1,500 feet over Santo Domingo impeded performance. More important, units in need of up-to-date information complained about the lag time between the request for aerial photos and their delivery. Army units wanted no more than a five- to six-hour turnaround but often experienced delays of up to twelve hours between submitting a request and receiving the desired photos. That each request had to pass through TF 120 for approval before being forwarded to the Joint Air Force/Army, Direct Air Support Center for implementation accounted for part of the problem. Excessive demands for prints and duplications compounded the delays by overwhelming the capabilities of the photo processing unit. A 50 percent reduction in the print distribution list and the dispatch of an MI warrant officer to familiarize the photo processing unit with Army requirements helped to reduce the delivery time. Even so, Palmer, while benefiting from the political intelligence provided in aerial photos, reported that Air Force reconnaissance was never fully exploited for tactical purposes.[15]

Despite the variety of problems encountered in gathering information about the rebels, by mid-May, U.S. troops had a fairly accurate order of battle and other essential information about opposing forces in Santo Domingo.[16] The new estimates reduced the number of rebels to between 2,000 and 4,000, operating in 15- to 20-man commando units, each responsible for a certain portion of the city. The commandos ostensibly fought for Caamaño, but most analysts and several rebels, including Caamaño in a few candid moments, doubted that he exerted firm control over all the small bands. Many of the commando groups operated behind the façade of a labor union, student body, political party, or some other organization. Military intelligence had identified the commanders of most units and their headquarters. The U.S. soldiers who manned checkpoints possessed updated wanted lists of individuals who should be detained on sight.[17] The current intelligence about the Constitutionalist forces in Santo Domingo did not end the sniping incidents and firefights, but it gave soldiers on the front line a much better idea of what they were up against.

Military commanders plagued during the early days of the intervention by a dearth of information concerning the status of rebels in Santo Domingo knew even less about conditions throughout the Dominican Republic. Was the rebellion spreading beyond the capital? Would Washington soon face a Communist insurgency in the countryside? Lyndon Johnson wanted to know. More to the point, he became obsessed with finding out. The new director of central intelligence, Admiral Raborn, was the first to feel the pressure from the White House. Raborn, in turn, asked David Phillips, designated to take over as chief of station in the Dominican Republic in early June, how many men the agency had reporting from the countryside. Phillips replied that there was an agent in Santiago. More to the point, he reported that liaison contacts and agents monitoring the Dominican government's communications reported that, in general, the countryside was quiet. The civil war was having little serious impact outside the capital. This news satisfied neither the president nor Raborn, the latter of whom issued what to Phillips was a "ridiculous order" to send CIA officers into the interior. Phillips complied and sent nine men into the countryside on 2 May. The most urgent message he received once his teams fanned out was from a chief of outpost complaining, "The mosquitoes are killing us."[18]

Like their CIA counterparts, the U.S. military commanders in the Dominican Republic also learned that one could not ignore the curiosity of their demanding commander in chief. Following LBJ's meeting with his advisers on 1 May, General Wheeler dispatched a message that began, "At highest level meeting this morning it was recognized that intelligence and activities of dissident groups outside the Santo Domingo area is sparse." To correct the deficiency, Ambassador Bennett, the U.S. military, and the CIA were to mount "a coordinated effort to obtain [the] needed information." The military was to provide ground vehicles and helicopters for the undertaking, "to include using medical evacuation helicopters marked with the Red Cross." The next day, Bennett reported that he and Palmer concurred in the importance of the mission and hoped to launch it the next morning. The code name of the operation would be Green Chopper.[19]

The XVIII Airborne Corps, the Embassy, the CIA, and AID coordinated and executed the first Green Chopper missions. Assessment teams visited seven towns between 3 and 5 May in order "to determine popular feelings and to assess political, military, and economic conditions." While this was taking place, the 7th Special Forces Group(-) arrived from Fort Bragg. The group's arrival was not atypical of units entering the country in the later echelons of Power Pack. At Pope AFB, the Green Berets had received a "space available" priority; that is, they experienced the chaos of scrambling for whatever seats they could find aboard available aircraft. They arrived at San Isidro with little information or essential equipment, "completely inadequate" communications for field work, and too many operational and too few support personnel (cooks, mechanics, communicators, etc.). Despite these problems, once enough men and equipment had been assembled on 4 May, the unit became operational under Palmer's command. The next day, the Green Berets took over the Green Chopper missions, driving or flying in civilian clothes to towns throughout the countryside, often accompanied by Embassy or AID personnel to lend credibility to cover stories about conducting economic, agricultural, or medical surveys. Working undercover, the men established residency in their assigned towns and began collecting information. (Over time, the cover stories broke down because the Special Forces teams "were using U.S. Army equipment and were resupplied by U.S. Army personnel using military aircraft.") Between thirty-four and fifty towns were visited, several of which were short on critical supplies. There was also an occasional anti-American agitator to be found. But on the whole, the Special Forces reports for Green Chopper confirmed what Phillips had told Raborn: the countryside was quiet. Lyndon Johnson could rest easy. There was no incipient insurgency in the interior. The fate of the Dominican Republic would be determined in Santo Domingo, where the presence of U.S. troops precluded the possibility of a rebel victory by military means.[20]

*   *   *

While MI officers, Special Forces, and various staffs worked to improve the quality of intelligence available to U.S. forces in the Dominican Republic, an effort was under way to streamline the chain of command from Washington to Santo Domingo and to upgrade the communications available to military commanders in the field, particularly Palmer.[21] The two efforts were interrelated. Upon his arrival, Palmer had become the de facto land force commander (see figures 2 and 3), but his formal elevation to Commander, United States Forces, Dominican Republic (USCOMDOMREP) did not occur until one week later. The delay in upgrading his status from a task force commander in charge of all U.S. Army and Marine elements ashore to that of the commander of a Joint Headquarters, U.S. Forces, Dominican Republic (USFORDOMREP), stemmed from an unanticipated shortcoming: for nearly a week, Palmer lacked an independent network that would allow him to communicate with the numerous people both in the Dominican Republic and abroad whom his new responsibilities would require him to consult on a daily basis.

When Palmer entered the country on 1 May, he brought with him only the small portion of the XVIII Airborne Corps' signal elements authorized by Wheeler. The 82d's communications equipment at San Isidro enhanced his meager capabilities, but not by much. Both corps and division communications were geared to tactical operations involving relatively short

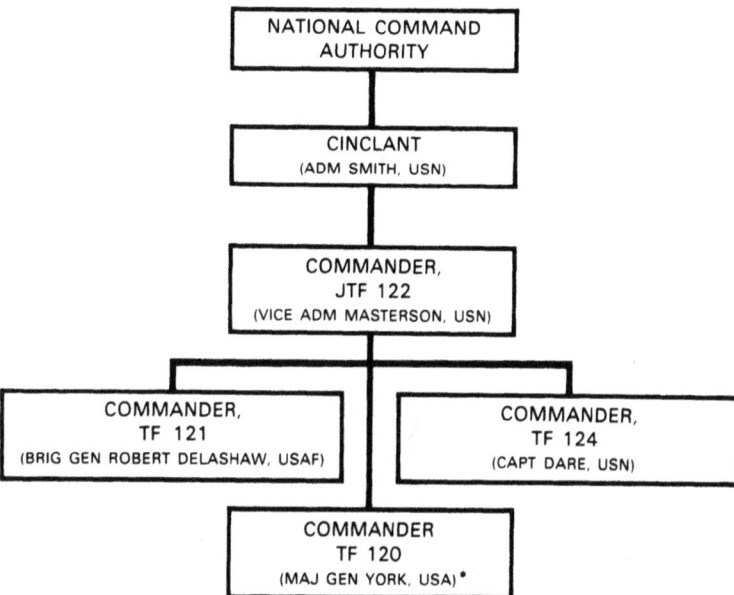

*For a short period, Maj. Gen. York commanded all land forces ashore.

Figure 2. U.S. command relationships, 30 April 1965

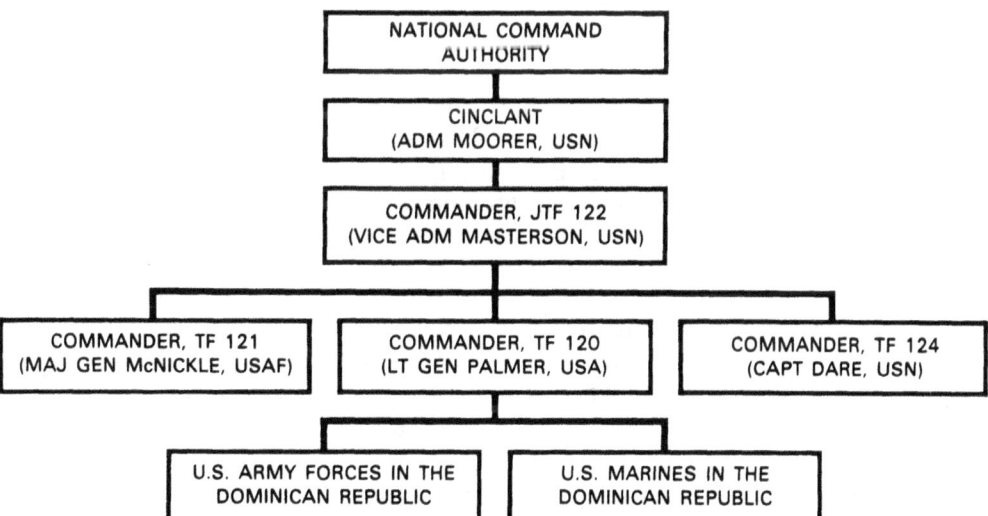

Figure 3. U.S. command relationships, 1 May 1965

distances. But by direction of the JCS, Palmer was to assume the role of a theater commander, which meant he needed a *strategic* communications capability that would enable him to contact policymakers far from Dominican shores. Until he acquired this capability, he made do with what he had. By midmorning on the 1st, his small Special Security Office—a special

U.S. Air Force C-130 "talking bird" at San Isidro

communications detachment with its own codes—had established secure communications with Fort Bragg and DA, enabling Palmer to send his first back-channel message to General Wheeler. By afternoon, Palmer could talk from San Isidro directly with Masterson on the *Boxer*, even though the admiral's flag ship could only operate on one of several radio nets and had to lower its antenna—and thus cease communications—during flight operations off its deck. (On 3 May, Masterson transferred his flag to the *Newport News*, which had excellent communication facilities for joint operations.) Also, once Palmer discovered that the Air Force's "talking bird" had landed at San Isidro (a fact unknown to the corps' signal officer), the general used the plane's sophisticated communications gear to talk with the president and other Washington officials.

But these communications capabilities were still woefully inadequate and, more important, inconvenient, being located at San Isidro. Palmer, realizing the soundness of Wheeler's advice to work as closely as possible with Ambassador Bennett, wanted to move his headquarters next door to the U.S. Embassy as soon as possible. On 2 May, he transferred his command post by helicopter (no overland route being available yet) to the Embassy grounds; the remainder of his headquarters at San Isidro was instructed to follow as soon as it acquired the means to do so. Bennett readily shared the Embassy's communications facilities with the general, but these, too, left much to be desired. The only reliable communication between the Embassy and Masterson was by helicopter and ham radio. Cable traffic with Washington was secure, but telephone contact was being monitored by the rebels who controlled the telephone exchange. Palmer tried to solve his problem by requesting CINCSTRIKE, General Adams, to loan him one of STRICOM's two Joint Communications Support Elements, which were tailor-made for the sort of independent and secure strategic capability Palmer so desperately needed. But CINCSTRIKE refused without comment, although Palmer later concluded that Adams, who had collided with CINCLANT during the early phases of the crisis, had adopted a "dog-in-the-manger" attitude, withholding from Palmer (and, indirectly, from CINCLANT) a communications element Adams could easily have parted with on a temporary basis.

The Defense Communication Agency rescued Palmer from the dismal situation he confronted. It provided long-range communications that enabled him on 3 May to move his headquarters into the former Trujillo residence next to the Embassy and, on 4 May, to communicate with CINCLANT without having to use Masterson, the JTF commander, as a go-between. On the 4th, Palmer became Commander, U.S. Land Forces, Dominican Republic (LAND FORCES ASHORE) (see figure 4), with Masterson still controlling the forces assigned to the intervention with the exception of the Army and Marine units under Palmer's command. A debate ensued as to whether Palmer or Masterson would control the Air Force Task Force 121. Palmer prevailed. On 7 May, the day he formally became the commander of what was in essence a subunified command under LANTCOM (see figure 5), Palmer exercised operational control over all Army forces, the 4th MEB, and all Air Force and Navy elements in-country. The Navy Task Force 124 and the Air Force Task Force 121 retained a separate identity under CINCLANT but were placed in support of Palmer's joint headquarters, USFORDOMREP. Under these arrangements, JTF 122 became a redundant command and, according to doctrine, was disestablished.

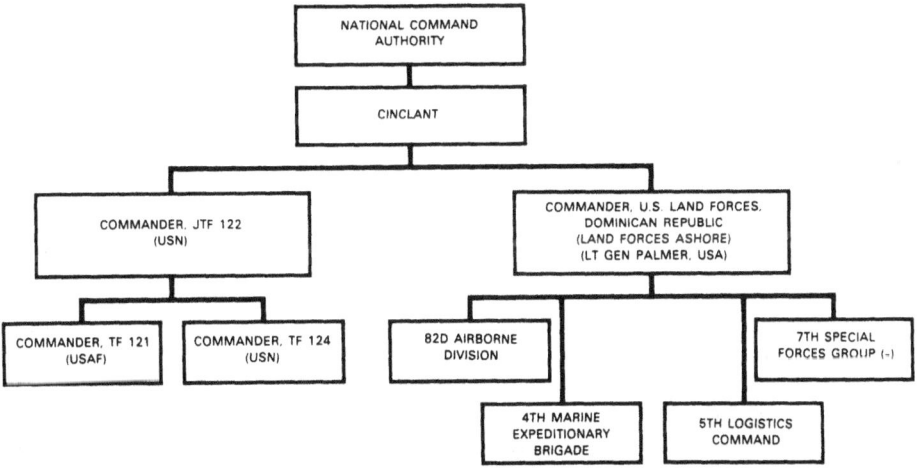

Figure 4. U.S. command relationships, 4—6 May 1965

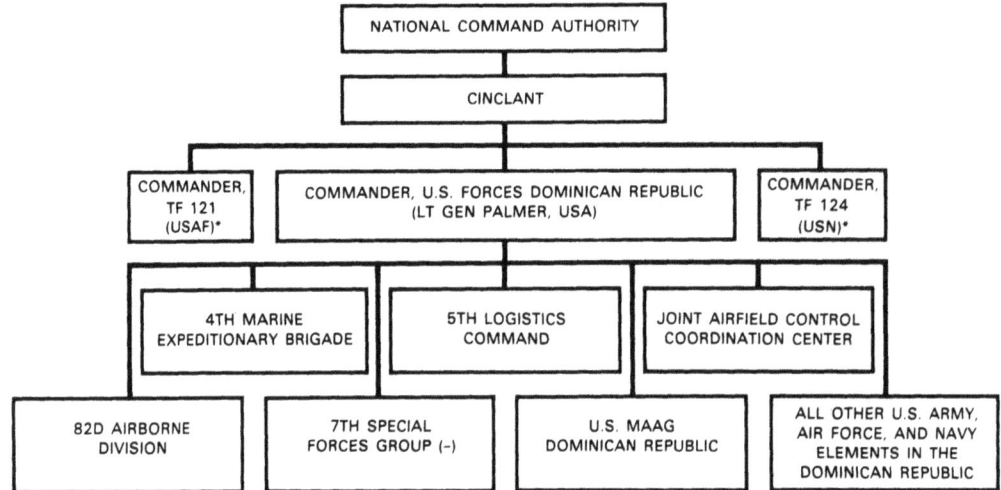

*TF 121 and TF 124 assumed supporting roles to the ground forces, with General Palmer authorized direct liaison with the commanders of each TF in order to levy support requirements. In December 1965, the JCS dissolved TF 121 and TF 124 and established a permanent headquarters command for all U.S. forces in the Dominican Republic.

Figure 5. U.S. command relationships, 7 May 1965

Palmer's new title did not appreciably alter his relationship with the Embassy's Country Team. As ambassador, Bennett would exercise responsibility for policy execution but not operational control over U.S. troops, although prior to Palmer's appointment, Washington had given Bennett a good deal of latitude in directing the movement of those forces. With Palmer on the scene, that would change, but not dramatically unless the ambassador and the general disagreed over the deployment and activities of the troops. In that case, Palmer, now Bennett's senior military adviser, would argue his position not only with the ambassador but up the military chain of command, from CINCLANT to the JCS (the latter of whom would present his position to the secretary of defense and the president). But such divisive disagreement rarely occurred. Palmer felt that Bennett on occasion excluded him from critical information, and this led to some stormy sessions. But on the whole, the two men established a close and cordial working relationship and personal friendship as they coordinated efforts to use the U.S. military presence to the best advantage in seeking a political settlement.

* * *

Political maneuvering among all parties to the conflict began the day after the establishment of the LOC demonstrated U.S. power and ended any possibility of an all-out rebel attack on the San Isidro junta. Denied a military victory, the rebels quickly shifted tactics and launched a vigorous political-propaganda offensive, the first shot of which came on 4 May, when a Constitutionalist "congress" elected Caamaño "president" of the country. While these ceremonies were taking place, U.S. officials were pursuing their own campaign to form a more suitable government. Essentially this meant easing out Colonel Benoit's San Isidro junta—identified by too many Dominicans with reaction and repression—and finding an alternative government that would enjoy popular support. Here LBJ's emissary, John Bartlow Martin, with Ambassador Bennett's support, took the lead by championing General Imbert, a man still regarded by many Dominicans (although fewer than Martin realized) as a national hero for his role in assassinating Trujillo. Imbert had a private army of 2,000 men, but what made him an attractive candidate in Martin's eyes was the estrangement between the general and the San Isidro officers, including Wessin. Caamaño, Martin knew, would never deal with Wessin, the man most rebels blamed for starting the civil war. But, Martin believed, "a rapprochement between Caamaño and Imbert was not impossible."

Prompted by U.S. officials, Imbert would head a slate of five candidates who would constitute a Government of National Reconstruction (GNR). Imbert picked Benoit immediately as the second candidate so as not to alienate completely the existing junta. The other three candidates were to be civilians, but delays arose in trying to recruit them. As Bennett reported to State, few persons were qualified for the positions, and most who were expressed their reluctance to serve. After a rigorous search, the candidates materialized, and on 7 May, Imbert was sworn in as president of the GNR. Bennett recommended immediate U.S. recognition of the new government, but State demurred: such a move could adversely affect the next step in the stabilization process as envisaged by Washington and the OAS—namely, arranging an agreement between "President" Caamaño and "President" Imbert to form a provisional government committed to early elections. Even though both "governments" encouraged this expectation when they signed the Act of Santo Domingo, an OAS-drafted document that spelled out in greater detail the cease-fire accord, the rapprochement Martin predicted proved elusive.[22]

At first, the main stumbling block to an accord between the GNR and the Constitutionalists seemed to be Caamaño's insistence that he would not meet with Imbert until certain officers linked to the San Isidro group left the country. U.S. officials persuaded Imbert to accept the condition, but the key to progress was Wessin, an "honorable man," according to Bennett, but the "bete-noir of the revolution." When Wessin promised Palmer and Bennett that he would resign for the sake of the country and accept a position abroad, prospects for peace improved.

In an all too familiar pattern, they just as quickly declined. Against the background of cease-fire violations on both sides, efforts to get Caamaño and Imbert together proved futile. Bennett, Palmer, and Martin doubted that Caamaño was a "free agent"; Martin suspected that radical elements within the colonel's entourage were deliberately trying to sabotage a political compromise. Caamaño, for his part, expressed similar sentiments about Imbert, whom he saw as the puppet of the Trujillist generals, particularly Wessin, who had immediately "welched" on his pledge to leave the country. Bennett also reported that the GNR, after an encouraging beginning, was encountering difficulties in trying to run the country. He attributed this, in part, to the fact that the GNR controlled neither the critical Dominican financial institutions located in Ciudad Nueva nor the industrial plants north of the LOC. Most of all, Bennett believed, the government suffered from the constant barrage of vituperative anti-American, anti-GNR propaganda spewing forth from Radio Santo Domingo. He denounced the propaganda offensive as the "main thorn in GNR's (and our) side." But if the Constitutionalists were proving intransigent, so was Imbert. U.S. officials began to doubt whether the general would accept Caamaño or any of his followers into a new government. Imbert talked increasingly about taking military action against the rebels, a course from which Martin tried to dissuade him by arguing that GNR forces could not defeat Caamaño's, even if the United States would allow them to try, which, Martin declared, it would not.[23]

Martin should not have been so categorical. As the chances for an early political settlement slipped away, the possibility of some form of military action increased dramatically. An incident on 13 May illustrated the danger. Without consulting U.S. officials, Imbert sent five F-51s to knock out Radio Santo Domingo. The planes hit the target, taking it off the air for the remainder of the day, but one pilot fired erratically into U.S., rebel, *and Loyalist* positions near the radio station, wounding one U.S. marine. In perhaps the only display of true unity during the intervention, Americans, Loyalists, and Constitutionalists all returned fire and succeeded in downing the errant flyer, who was then rescued by a U.S. helicopter. Bennett lodged a protest with the OAS Commission over this flagrant violation of the cease-fire, but in his report to Washington, he admitted that it was "hard to rap GNR for having taken an action to remove installation which was poisoning whole body politic." In another indication of his private sentiments, Bennett had already voiced his concern that U.S. neutrality during the political negotiations was working against the GNR and assisting the rebels in consolidating what positions they held in the key northern industrial area of the city. The military situation, in his view, was unclear but not good, and while the United States would continue to work for a political solution, it could not discount the possibility of being "compelled to assist GNR militarily if present situation deteriorates to point of becoming untenable."[24]

For Bennett and Palmer, the immediate source of military concern was the situation north of the LOC. Since 10 May, rebel forces had been attacking GNR troops stationed in the strategically located Transportation Headquarters. In response to the fighting, Imbert was infiltrating reinforcements into the area. Meanwhile, economic life in the north had come to a standstill as factories closed. Food riots soon broke out. It was an intolerable situation that had to be dealt with swiftly if the city hoped to avoid even greater economic chaos. Based on their own observations and a gloomy report from the OAS Commission, Bennett and Palmer held little hope for a political solution to the problem. As Palmer wrote, echoing Bennett's previous warning, "military actions may be soon required to break the present stalemate and make any progress towards stability and establish law and order." The question was, who would take the required action?[25]

On 13 May, Palmer and Bennett recommended unilateral U.S. military action to restore order north of the LOC. The operation would take place in three phases. Phase I would involve extending the LOC in a search and clear operation that would seize Radio Santo Domingo. Phase II would involve extending the ISZ northward to Avenida San Martín, which would serve as the line of departure for Phase III, a sweep of the north to the Isabela River. During the last phase, rebel forces would be captured or destroyed, and industrial complexes would be seized and secured. Bennett and Palmer predicted that Dominicans in northern Santo Domingo would welcome the restoration of order and economic activity. While this plan was working its way through channels to Washington, Imbert informed Martin that his forces in the north, some 600 to 900 men, were under orders to extend their control gradually throughout the industrial area.[26] A major military confrontation with the rebels, initiated by U.S. forces or GNR troops or the two working together, seemed but hours away.

This was not welcome news to President Johnson, who, unlike U.S. officials on the scene, tended to blame Imbert for the drift toward military action. "I'm not going down in history as the man responsible for putting another Trujillo in power," he is reported to have said in referring to the

President Johnson with his national security adviser, McGeorge Bundy

general. Hoping to be able to restore order through diplomatic means, LBJ decided to send Bundy, Vance, Mann, and Vaughn to Santo Domingo. The thrust of Bundy's instructions was to sacrifice the GNR, if necessary, in favor of a more moderate government that would guarantee the safety of the Dominican military and the removal or detention of Communists and Castroites. Palmer, upon hearing that the mission was en route, was not pleased. To him, it was but another example of interference from higher political authorities who lacked an in-depth appreciation of the complexity of the "local picture." Bundy's team, he later commented sarcastically, expected to achieve a "quick and dirty" settlement within forty-eight hours. To Palmer, this constituted pure fantasy.[27]

Bundy and the others arrived in Santo Domingo on 15 May, the very day Imbert mounted a massive offensive, *operación limpieza* (Operation Cleanup), to clear all rebels out of the north. Most U.S. officials and military officers in Santo Domingo knew of the impending attack and gave it their tacit blessing. Charges that American troops actually assisted in the operation, either actively or by allowing GNR troops to cross the LOC into the north, have never been substantiated. As a rule, Imbert circumvented the LOC in transporting his forces north. If some trucks did pass through the LOC, it was an exception to the rule and done without Palmer's approval. Palmer did authorize two-man U.S. liaison teams to meet with GNR soldiers in the field so that as Imbert's sweep approached the LOC, the risk of firing into U.S. positions would be minimized.[28]

Contrary to the expectations of American officers, Imbert's offensive appeared as though it would succeed, albeit at a very bloody cost in rebel and innocent civilian lives. At the Embassy, Bundy and others consulted with Washington about sending U.S. troops north to establish a new, north-south LOC that would, as with the current east-west one, separate the two sides. Although Palmer indicated that this could be done, he was skeptical about sending American troops into the middle of a situation in which they might be fired on from both sides. As it turned out, planning for the new corridor could not keep pace with GNR advances; while Washington was still considering the proposal, Imbert completed his sweep of the north, clearing out the rebels and capturing Radio Santo Domingo.[29]

The success of *operación limpieza* had several consequences, some anticipated, some not. The rebels were now truly isolated in Ciudad Nueva, and Imbert began putting pressure on the United States to let his troops cross the LOC, the only barrier to total victory. York sympathized with the request. (On 19 May, the 82d had published its own contingency plan for reducing the rebel stronghold.) But Washington emphatically disagreed. There would be no further major military engagements by either side; the United States would see to it. On 16 May, while Imbert's offensive was still in progress, Palmer received an indication of what was to come when LBJ instructed him to use U.S. forces to prevent GNR naval and air force units from taking part in the fighting. At San Isidro, the U.S. battalion charged with airfield security immediately moved obstacles onto the runway even as GNR pilots were starting the engines of their F-51s. By 21 May,

U.S. paratroopers as they prevent F-51s from taking off at San Isidro airfield

when a Red Cross-negotiated truce became a new cease-fire at OAS urging, U.S. behavior was truly neutral for the first time since the beginning of the crisis.[30]

Neutrality did not hasten a political solution. Having suffered the reversal in the north, Caamaño was more amenable to talking, but Imbert, "flushed with success," was not. Bundy's efforts to organize a provisional government around Silvestre Antonio Guzmán, a moderate *PRD* member, broke down because Imbert would not accept the arrangement and because, at the last minute, Guzmán reneged on his promise to exile various Communist leaders. Palmer endured no distress over the failure of the Guzmán formula. Although as a military man he did not say so for the record, the general believed, as did Imbert, that a Guzmán government would be dominated or taken over by the Communists.[31] When Bundy realized the futility of his efforts, he packed his bags and turned further peace negotiations over to the OAS.

With the failure of the Bundy mission at the end of May, a political solution to the Dominican crisis seemed a distant hope at best. American troops would remain in the country for an indefinite time, not so much to fight as to serve as peacekeepers. The work entailed would be at times challenging and dangerous, at other times frustrating and tedious. To the individual soldier, the nightly firefights and his noncombat duties would become a matter of routine to which he would adjust. But few really comprehended why the United States, with the military power it had assembled in Santo Domingo, simply could not take military action to secure a political settlement. Not to let soldiers do what they were trained to do seemed confusing, even senseless.

Stability Operations III: Peacekeeping

Once Washington ruled out a military solution to the Dominican crisis, much of the ambiguity surrounding the objectives of U.S. forces in Santo Domingo dissipated. American soldiers would assume a peacekeeping role, the purpose of which was to create and maintain the stability needed by political negotiators—many of whom wore military uniforms—to forge a lasting peace. Peacekeeping did not prohibit the use of force to achieve stability; it did, however, restrict the ways in which force could be applied. To a degree unparalleled in U.S. military history, paratroopers and marines in Santo Domingo found their actions governed by a plethora of politically and militarily motivated directives, guidelines, and rules of engagement. In general, these proclamations dictated that combat operations would be defensive in nature and that soldiers would engage in a variety of activities normally performed by civilian agencies and officials.

U.S. authorities did not issue the rules of engagement and other guidelines in a single package, but piecemeal in response to specific situations. Nevertheless, American forces began to get a clearer idea of what was expected of them immediately after the LOC came into existence. Troops received copies of both LBJ's 2 May speech, in which the president justified U.S. intervention, and a fact sheet that called for the military to protect or evacuate foreign nationals, initiate humanitarian programs, help restore order, and prevent a Communist victory.[1] Although these general missions applied to the Dominican Republic as a whole, most of the activity aimed at accomplishing them would take place in Santo Domingo with its complex of streets, built-up areas, industrial and financial districts, service facilities, and dense population. Militarily, this meant that American forces would engage in city fighting to a degree not experienced since Korea.[2]

The marines and the 82d both had been trained in urban combat, but they were hardly experts in it. The 82d, for example, conducted an annual urban terrain course, last offered in mid-1964. Since then, new men without this training had joined the division, while paratroopers who had taken the course had become rusty in these skills. World War II and Korean War veterans among U.S. units in Santo Domingo added the insight of personal experience to what training the troops had received.[3] For whatever else needed to be learned—and it was considerable—combat would be the in-

U.S. observation post

structor. Invariably, the first lesson brought home to inexperienced soldiers was that at times a strict adherence to doctrine made good sense; at other times, it did not. In those cases where anomalous situations rendered doctrine inadequate or irrelevant, common sense, flexibility, improvisation, and a generous portion of luck often spelled the difference between success and disaster.

Soldiers manning the ISZ, LOC, and east bank of the Ozama combined traditional tactics and innovative measures to secure and defend their positions opposite the armed rebels. In accordance with long-standing practice, they arranged observation posts (OPs) and individual rifle positions to enhance the firepower of automatic weapons. The resulting network of fortified positions commanded excellent fields of fire and observation. In an urban environment, as a member of the 82d later wrote, one had to make "a rapid mental adjustment from 'high ground and critical terrain' to key buildings and objectives." As a result, command posts were placed in the center of buildings, as much out of harm's way as possible, while observation posts were located predominantly on towers and on the rooftops or upper floors of tall buildings. Paratroopers on top of an eight-story flour mill on the east bank of the Ozama enjoyed a panoramic view of Ciudad Nueva—a bit of military voyeurism the rebels found most disconcerting as evidenced by the amount of fire they directed at the OP, especially after a helicopter deposited a 106-mm recoilless rifle on the mill's roof. While the application of military principles concerning high ground and clear and interlocking fields of fire proved useful in securing positions in and around Santo Domingo, other less conventional approaches proved equally rewarding. Within the city, vehicles abandoned during the early days of the civil war served as excellent OPs when manned by one or two soldiers with makeshift periscopes.[4]

The occupation of key facilities received careful attention, as demonstrated by the decision on 30 April to include the power plant on the west bank of the Ozama within the 82d's bridgehead and by the marines' incorporation within the ISZ of the Hotel Embajador, a university, and various residences and official buildings. Unfortunately for the Americans, these master strokes were all too few in number. On the debit side, Radio Santo Domingo had deliberately or inadvertently been left outside the LOC, while many industrial, financial, and civic buildings were also located in rebel-held areas. In fact, most key facilities lay under Constitutionist control until late May, when the GNR captured some during its sweep of the north. Still, U.S. occupation of the power plant made it possible for those running the installation to provide some critical services and, on occasion, to indulge in some mischievous fun: aside from being able to bring electricity to Santo Domingo on a sporadic basis, the troops could shut down Caamaño's air conditioners at will.[5]

Whether manning an observation post, going on patrol, or simply crossing an exposed area to get to the power plant or some other facility, Americans located within sight of Constitutionalist territory quickly learned that

Dominicans and U.S. troops take cover from sniper fire

the greatest threat to their personal safety was not an all-out Constitutionalist attack on U.S. positions (an unlikely prospect) or a projectile launched by an angry Dominican demonstrator; rather, it was the ubiquitous rebel sniper whose harassment of the foreign invaders became a routine but dangerous fact of daily life.

Sniper fire accounted for the majority of American casualties during the intervention. While trees and other natural objects provided some protection from fire, man-made structures afforded little in the way of a shield. The bullet from a sniper's high-powered rifle passed easily through lumber and concrete blocks, the most common building materials in the Dominican Republic. Solid concrete offered some protection but tended to fragment and cause ricochets. For maximum security, soldiers relied on sandbags piled three high in relatively unexposed areas and up to fifteen high on flat rooftops and the like.

The troops at first returned the sniper fire, but the rules of engagement restricted their choice of weapons. The 106-mm recoilless rifle was the largest weapon that could be employed. The advantage of the 106-mm was that it not only killed the sniper but usually destroyed his cover as well. The disadvantage was that sometimes an entire building would be leveled to kill one man. Furthermore, a 106-mm round would sometimes pass through three or four shanties grouped together, thereby increasing the risk of killing or wounding innocent civilians. The back blast of a recoilless rifle fired in one of Santo Domingo's narrow streets or alleys could also destroy poorly built houses in a friendly area. All told, the 106s were best reserved for knocking holes in substantial structures or in the walls of buildings soldiers wished to pass through during the course of a patrol or attack. The recoilless rifle was also ideal for use against the rebels' antiquated armor and against large groups of isolated rebels. And, in at least one case, a recoilless rifle crew on the east bank of the Ozama River sank a boat that had just delivered what was presumed to be ammunition to the Constitutionalists on the west bank. (The rule against firing unless fired on prevented the crew from destroying the ship and its cargo, but as the boat departed the dock area, presumably heading back to Cuba to take on more ammunition or up-country to unload more weapons, rebels on board fired at American positions. With the approval of higher headquarters, the recoilless rifle crew put one round into the superstructure and ended the firefight. The next morning, a second round at the waterline sank the boat off Sans Souci. A Special Forces team brought in to examine the boat's contents found a few small arms, three or four bodies, and five cases of Black Label beer.)[6]

The M79 grenade launcher and the .50-caliber machine gun and spotting rifle served much better as antisniper weapons. The grenade could easily destroy a room in which a sniper was operating and do it without the collateral damage of the recoilless rifle. The .50-caliber machine gun had much the same effect, as its bullets could penetrate the most common construction materials in the Dominican Republic. When U.S. troops could actually see a sniper, the .50-caliber spotting rifle on a 106 presented a "surgical" way to eliminate the problem, either by targeting the sniper him-

This rebel tank was destroyed by one round from a 106-mm recoilless rifle

self or by placing a round where he was likely to be standing, usually to the immediate right of a window. The M16 rifle was less reliable against snipers given its small caliber and the fact that troops did not have telescopic sights. (Some enterprising men, however, ordered rifle scopes from sporting goods stores back in the United States and converted the scopes to fit their M16s; others brought in M1s with scopes.) A shortage of parts, frequent jamming, and the rebels' possession of 7-mm Mausers (which had greater range than the M16s) resulted in the M16 receiving less than enthusiastic reviews from many of its users.[7]

Marines and paratroopers also took preemptive measures to diminish the volume of sniper fire into their positions. These included widening the LOC, conducting house-to-house searches, and clearing buildings likely to serve as sniper haunts or ammunition caches. Each of these measures necessitated going out on patrol, a dreadful prospect in a built-up, urban area. One company commander in the 82d who later served two tours in Vietnam and took part in the Grenada operation reminisced that patrolling in Santo Domingo was "very, very frightening." Curious Dominicans who talked, laughed, and waved as the soldiers passed by caused only minor distractions. The real terror stemmed from knowing that even when patrolling procedures were executed flawlessly, soldiers still stood exposed to enemy counter-

U.S. troops firing a .50-caliber machine gun

measures. True cover was a luxury. Streets and intersections offered clear fields of fire for rebel gunners. Moreover, few walls or houses could stop even small-arms rounds, and ricochets off pavement or within doorways could often do more damage than a direct hit. Troops also worried about being lured into rebel cross fire. Platoon and squad leaders shared the additional burden of having to be concerned with the adverse effects that casualties might have on unit morale and discipline.

Dangers did not diminish when a patrol reached its objective, especially if the objective were a several-story building that had to be cleared. Doctrine dictated that buildings be cleared from the top down. But in a built-up area, rooftops often became death traps because of their exposure to nearby buildings that were taller and to which the enemy had access. One platoon in the 82d paid dearly to learn this lesson. Assembled on a roof prior to entering a building, it was decimated by a concealed sniper standing in a bathtub and firing a Thompson submachine gun from a building only twenty-five feet away. In light of these dangers, doctrine yielded to common sense. When necessary, buildings would be cleared from the bottom up, with adequate covering fire to discourage anxious snipers.[8]

Within the LOC, expansion of the corridor by patrolling alleviated some of the sniper fire directed at the main east-west avenue, but it increased the instances of friendly fire. Commanders discarded the practice of defending the widened corridor in depth after sniper fire one night resulted in elements of a second-echelon battalion firing into American troops on the front line instead of over their heads. This incident led to the establishment of quick-reaction forces that could plug any break in the line in the

Marine sniper sighting his target

U.S. troops on patrol in Santo Domingo

event of an attack. Defense of the LOC would thereafter be "keyed to a line of rooftop and street positions on the perimeters with no depth."⁹

A second cause of friendly fire had to do with the configuration of the LOC near the ISZ and with lapses of fire discipline. It was not uncommon, according to one source, for rebel snipers to fire over the heads of Army defenders into the security zone, thus prompting the Leathernecks to return fire that often fell short into the 82d's positions. Such episodes did little to diminish interservice rivalry.¹⁰

In addition to the dangers posed by snipers, friendly fire, and constant patrolling, soldiers stationed in the LOC confronted problems arising from the corridor's unique traffic-control function. Dominicans wishing to pass from northern Santo Domingo into Ciudad Nueva, or vice versa, invariably had to traverse the LOC, where makeshift barricades of concertina wire, sandbags, and oil drums shut off side streets and alleys, channeling pedestrian and vehicular traffic into a series of checkpoints and roadblocks erected at five or so strategic locations. Nearly 50,000 people a day traversed the corridor making congestion a chronic problem that was compounded by the "undisciplined driving habits" of Dominican cabbies and by an insufficient number of Spanish-speaking troops at the critical bottlenecks. Military police, supported by Army troops and Dominican policemen, manned the checkpoints, where they looked for "subversive" agents and, more important, weapons. The intention was to prevent the flow of arms in either direction across the line. No Dominicans (with the exception of national policemen) could enter the corridor with a weapon, a rule that disrupted the Constitutionalists' efforts during the first half of May to send arms north for the purpose of using them against pockets of Loyalist troops or simply of caching them for retrieval at a later date should the Americans take over Ciudad Nueva.

The rebels refused to be deterred by U.S. surveillance measures and adopted several ruses to achieve their objective. Guns were placed in automobile gas tanks. Hearses and ambulances loaded with concealed weapons instead of bodies cleared checkpoints without being searched, often as American soldiers removed their helmets out of respect. After the subterfuge was discovered, the treatment accorded such vehicles at roadblocks became anything but respectful: MPs undertook vigorous searches, even opening coffins that did not appear completely sealed. Another rebel tactic was to create a diversion or mount a full-scale sniper attack during which a vehicle containing weapons would attempt to run a roadblock during the confusion. Again, frustrated American traffic controllers devised countermeasures. The rapid emplacement of emergency barricades during such disruptions discouraged speeding cars and trucks, as did the occasional lobbing of a grenade from an M79 launcher into their paths.[11]

One rebel deception for smuggling arms across the LOC lent itself to no immediate counteraction. While all Dominican males entering and exiting the corridor were frisked, females were spared the procedure lest the indignity

Pedestrians and vehicles creating congestion at an LOC checkpoint

Vehicles lined up at a U.S. checkpoint

of it incite a riot. Thus, women and young girls wearing loose-fitting dresses or maternity clothes could easily slip grenades, pistols, and ammunition through the checkpoints. Efforts by U.S. authorities to obtain female inspectors failed, while less delicate suggestions for eliminating the practice were dismissed out of hand. Reports written during the last part of May claimed that the problem still lacked a solution, although photographs of checkpoint activity indicate otherwise. One photo in particular shows an American soldier with a mine detector and a determined look dutifully passing the device in the vicinity of a young woman's skirt.[12]

Having difficulties crossing over the LOC, the rebels decided to go under it via the city's sewer system. A highly successful ploy at first, the Americans eventually realized what was happening and once again devised countermeasures. A Special Forces team acquired a plan of the sewer system and passed it to corps and division. The Green Berets also assisted the 82d in reconnaissance missions in the sewers, while Army engineers emplaced a series of booby traps that included mines, grenades, barbed wire, trip flares, and, according to some sources, chemical agents. During these preparations, the two sides would often meet, and an underground firefight would ensue. After the engineers installed the obstacles to underground traffic, soldiers above ground removed the manhole covers, lowered lights on wires, and began maintaining a 24-hour watch (in twenty-minute shifts) over the open holes. Underground infiltration fell off markedly after that.[13]

A paratrooper uses a mine detector to determine if these Dominican women are concealing weapons

The neutralization of the sewer network was but one example of an operation involving clandestine activities during the Dominican intervention. Some of the missions carried out by Green Berets and the 82d, either separately or in tandem, are still classified; certain others are not. Mention has already been made of Green Chopper, the search of the sunken boat, and obtaining the sewer plans and reconnoitering the underground labyrinth. In another clandestine operation, a team from the 82d, after managing to get the blueprints of the telephone cables running from Ciudad Nueva to the north, again went underground, this time to sever the cables and impair

Manholes had to be watched to prevent rebels from using the sewer system to pass under the LOC

Caamaño's ability to coordinate rebel activities north of the LOC. In another operation, Army Special Forces teamed up with a Navy sea-air-land (SEALS) team to investigate reports of a cache of Cuban arms located near Samana

Bay. The "reconnaissance indicated no arms caches or 3d country involvement in this area."[14]

Some of the most important clandestine operations during the intervention attempted to silence Radio Santo Domingo (RSD). Although a poor people by U.S. standards, virtually every Dominican family owned a radio and, because of the country's high illiteracy rate, relied on it heavily for information. RSD, with "numerous outlets, studios, and transmitter sites," was the country's national station, capable of being heard throughout the island. In the hands of the rebels, the station became a powerful propaganda weapon—in fact, the "biggest thorn" in the side of the Americans. While David Phillips was still at Langley, he received a telephone call from a CIA agent with a blunt message. "The difference in Santo Domingo," the agent shouted, "lies in that radio station. If the rebels continue their propaganda they will take over the entire country. The radio must be silenced!"[15]

U.S. officials in the Dominican Republic received a similar message from State advising, "Availability of this station to rebel forces highly undesirable and prejudicial to our interest." As though it needed to be said, State indicated its "wish to deny this facility to rebels." Efforts to accommodate this

Radio Santo Domingo

wish met with little success. The problem was that nothing seemed to work. Naval vessels offshore and the Army Security Agency both tried to jam RSD broadcasts, but neither had powerful enough equipment to interfere more than temporarily with the broadcasting range of a commercial station. On 8 and 10 May, Special Forces teams mounted successful air assault operations against RSD transmitter sites at Alto Bandero and La Vega, respectively, thereby reducing the effectiveness of RSD broadcasts in those and surrounding areas. The day after the Special Forces seized the La Vega transmitter, a team of paratroopers and Green Berets slipped into the north and severed telecommunication lines. The operation failed to shut down the radio station, but it did disrupt the telephone system used by the rebels for tactical purposes. By 13 May, Palmer had had enough and requested permission from Washington to mount an overt military operation against RSD. Before he received an answer, the GNR's F-51s attacked the station and knocked it off the air. The following day, Imbert's own special forces destroyed an alternate transmitter and studio north of the Duarte bridge. Finally, during *operación limpieza*, the GNR captured Radio Santo Domingo.[16] The Americans were delighted, at least until they discovered that Imbert had no intention of relinquishing the station to the OAS.

*   *   *

The removal of bodies, many of which had been left in the streets for days, was a top priority

In mid-May, U.S. Special Forces personnel in Santo Domingo received new orders. Described in an after-action report, the mission was "... to assist the 82d Airborne Division civic action program. This overt civic action mission was a cover for many covert Special Forces activities, and was designed to create an impression that Special Forces was primarily engaged in a civic action mission in the Dominican Republic."[17]

What constituted the "many covert" activities is not clear from the available evidence. Sources concerning the civic action program, on the other hand, are readily available, thanks to the efforts of civil affairs officers to preserve them.[18] A civic action-civil affairs program began as soon as marines and paratroopers established positions in and around Santo Domingo. Something had to be done to alleviate the deplorable conditions in the city and suburbs. Garbage and bodies littered the streets, electrical power outages were frequent, potable water was in short supply, and a starving and war-weary population required food and medical attention. Hospitals were crowded, with physicians practicing by candlelight. At first, the U.S. military's response to the shortages and human suffering consisted of little more than the voluntary sharing of C rations with hungry Dominicans or the providing of impromptu medical treatment. On 3 May, a bonafide civic action program supplanted voluntarism, as marines and the 82d distributed rice, powdered milk, cornmeal, beans, cooking oil, water, and clothing to the population. At the Embassy's request, Washington authorized the distribution of food to people on "both sides" in the civil war,[19] so long as they were unarmed. In all, over 15,000 tons of food and 15,000 pounds of clothing would exchange hands, not only in Santo Domingo but in the countryside as well.

At first, troops unfamiliar with civic action procedures exercised little effective control. As mobs of hungry Dominicans stormed distribution points, several members from a single family could each make off with a full family allotment. Some Dominicans, after having received their initial handout, simply hid it close by and returned for more. As soldiers distributing food and clothing gained experience, they enacted measures such as ration cards to curb such abuses. Free medical clinics also enjoyed a high volume of business, although the crowds requiring the doctors' attention were much better behaved. The medical supplies needed to run the clinics came from the United States, the first batch arriving on 1 May as the result of an Embassy request, with succeeding shipments beginning on 5 May.

While Marine and Army troops dispensed food and medicine, military engineers worked to restore power and water to Santo Domingo and to repair the city's incinerator so that garbage collection could resume. For the most part, the division's engineers lacked the equipment and the skills to repair and operate large facilities such as waterworks, incinerators, and power plants, but with the assistance of civilian and military experts, they managed to put the plants in operation. What the engineers resented, though, were orders that they personally take charge of ridding Santo Domingo's streets of garbage. "Clean up the streets, hell—we came here to fight!"

U.S. soldiers distributing food to Dominicans in war-torn Santo Domingo

summarized their feelings, if somewhat inelegantly. The engineers followed orders, although as time passed, they delegated more and more of the actual collection work to the Dominicans, who, the soldiers argued, had much to relearn in the way of proper sanitation procedures.

There was also an unofficial side to the civic action program, seen primarily in the eagerness with which several U.S. units "adopted" orphanages in the Santo Domingo area. Out of their own pockets and occasionally (in completely unauthorized actions) from military stockpiles, soldiers provided the children with food, clothing, and supplies. They also played with them when time permitted and thrilled many with short helicopter rides. The soldiers' wives at Fort Bragg and elsewhere also contributed food and clothing to the orphans (as well as to other needy Dominicans). Moreover, before redeploying to the United States, units passed the hat and cleaned out their inventories to see that the orphanages would remain provisioned, at least for the near future.

The civic action program was but part of a larger civil affairs operation that focused on Santo Domingo but also included the countryside. The undertaking was massive and, in the opinion of an 82d company commander, "one of the most important missions during these early days." The indispensable military unit in the planning, administration, coordination, and implementation of this extensive civilian-military enterprise was the

42d Civil Affairs (CA) Company (augmented with personnel possessing civil affairs experience) out of Fort Gordon, Georgia. Elements of the 42d began arriving at San Isidro on 2 May; by the 6th, the company had begun normal operations under the command of XVIII Airborne Corps, but providing assistance to the 4th MEB, the 5th Logistics Command, and each of the 82d's three brigades. Initial operations aimed at performing humanitarian missions and restoring public utilities and services. To accomplish this, the company organized along the lines of functional teams.

Some of the teams accomplished their missions; others did not, often through no fault of their own. For example, although normal civilian legal processes had become a casualty of the Dominican civil war, the U.S. command did not assume the powers of local government, nor did it advise the 42d's Legal Team as to the status of U.S. forces in the Dominican Republic vis-à-vis international law, treaties, and other agreements. Consequently, the Legal Team had little to do but advise other functional teams on the legal ramifications of their activities. In another case, the Dominican minister of health, perhaps fearing the consequences of cooperating with the American military, refused to provide assistance to the Public Health Team in such critical areas as insect control and refuse disposal. The Public Education Team, in conjunction with AID and CARE representatives and local school officials, did help to reopen elementary schools for a short time until faculty shortages forced the schools to close once again. As for the high schools, there was no attempt to reopen them because of the Communist elements they supposedly harbored. The Economics Team met with bankers in an attempt to restore financial operations to the country, but after two weeks, U.S. Embassy and AID officials pushed the military out of these negotiations.

More successful were the efforts of the Public Facilities Team and the Public Welfare Team. The Public Facilities Team's assistance was instrumental in restoring garbage collection, electricity, and water to the city. The Public Welfare Team focused on many areas of the Dominican economy, but "by far the biggest responsibility of the team was that of food distribution to the people." With the goal of returning food control to the proper welfare agencies as soon as possible, the Public Welfare Team, working with AID officials and private agencies, initiated "a massive civil relief food distribution program." The first step involved AID procuring rice from local sources and having it transported to the Hotel Embajador, there to be hauled in military trucks to distribution points within the corridor. More food became available when the military situation permitted civilian transports to unload their cargo. On 5 May, relief supplies from the United States began arriving at Haina. The 82d dispatched trucks to the port to lessen the time between unloading and distribution.

While the operation at Haina was still under way, responsibility for food relief and economic aid programs was transferred to Assistant Secretary of State (designate) for Economic Affairs Anthony Solomon, who returned to the Dominican Republic in mid-May with a team of specialists. The food program suffered some disruption while Solomon assessed the situation, then agreed to plans AID had made some ten days earlier. In the meantime, the Public Welfare Team continued to monitor the five battalion distribution points in Santo Domingo. (Civilian agencies also assumed responsibility for food and medical assistance in the villages and countryside, although civilian officials were often accompanied by 82d medical personnel.) In critiquing the program it had helped to establish, the Public Welfare Team recommended that in future food distribution operations, companies, not battalions, should run distribution points; only adult women should receive food; and normal welfare agencies should take over food distribution as soon as possible.

One general problem that plagued the civil affairs effort occurred in the realm of civilian-military cooperation and coordination. With many of their key facilities located in rebel territory, State and AID officials had allowed the 42d Civil Affairs Company to assume many of their respective functions. When the civilian officials found it possible to operate again, they often began to do so without informing the 42d, thus causing duplication of efforts. There was also a tendency on each side to be ignorant of the functions and capabilities of the other. Still, despite these and the other problems mentioned above, the civil affairs effort, on the whole, was highly successful.

The civic action and civil affairs programs sought to provide humanitarian aid, assist in stabilizing the country, and win the "hearts and minds" of the Dominican people. The last two goals coincided with efforts undertaken by Army psychological warfare specialists.[20] When U.S. troops entered the country, an urgent need arose to explain to the population the goals of American policy, the positive side of the intervention, and the need to restore order and democracy. Latin American specialists working for the United States Information Service (USIS) in Santo Domingo could have performed these tasks except that their printing and broadcast equipment were located in buildings controlled by the rebels. The 1st Psychological Warfare (PSYWAR) Battalion at Fort Bragg and the 1st PSYWAR Company (Field Army) had the necessary equipment to support USIS, but because the OPLAN called for the deployment of only a small, light mobile detachment, the company and the entire battalion did not reach the Dominican Republic until 7 May, and then largely at the insistence of Mr. Hewson Ryan, associate director of the United States Information Agency (USIA), who would direct all psychological operations in the Dominican Republic.

Ryan arrived at San Isidro from Washington on 2 May accompanied by one of the PSYWAR groups that entered the country piecemeal. When Ryan found out that one of his missions would be to deny the rebels the ability to broadcast their views freely—a mission "contrary to previous US policy and [his] own personal philosophy"—he voiced his objections, but "nevertheless carried on with vigor and skill."[21] He demonstrated that "vigor" by sending Carl Rowan, the director of USIA, a curtly worded request to help expedite the arrival of military printing equipment, the shortage of which, according to Ryan, was "seriously handicapping leaflet and poster output." Despite this handicap, USIS managed to have the military launch its first pamphlet drop over Santo Domingo using two Air Force C-47s.[22]

When the 1st Psychological Warfare Battalion arrived in the Dominican Republic, it brought with it mobile printing presses, mobile broadcasting facilities, a loudspeaker capability to broadcast from trucks and from the two C-47s, and ultimately, heavy, mobile printing equipment. The loudspeaker trucks proved more effective than the aircraft in imparting information. Wherever the trucks would stop, hundreds of Dominicans would gather round to hear the latest news and receive leaflets and pamphlets, which by the end of May were being printed at a rate of 70,000 per day. On 5 May, the battalion's mobile broadcast, "The Voice of the Security Zone," hit the airwaves and was powerful enough to be picked up deep in the interior. In addition to these highly visible activities, battalion propaganda analysts helped interrogate rebel detainees to gain feedback on the PSYWAR effort and to uncover areas in which rebels and civilians alike were vulnerable to propaganda. Military specialists helped write scripts and other forms of propaganda, but USIS determined the themes of the material and retained tight control over all information disseminated by the battalion. Leaflets bearing pictures of Presidents Kennedy and LBJ and pamphlets extolling

PSYWAR team with speaker mounted on jeep

the virtues of the OAS and the evils of communism became standard, if innocuous, fare. Some propaganda, however, was blatantly false, as USIS officials tried to convince the population that the intervention was a benevolent undertaking. One of the battalion's after-action reports listed among the USIS-imposed propaganda themes such fictions as the "landing was made only for peaceful and humanitarian ends," and the "US government supports neither side nor has it given military or material aid to either faction."

On the whole, civilian-military cooperation in the psychological warfare effort was "remarkably successful." It was not, however, entirely devoid of friction. Besides feeling constrained by USIS control, 1st PSYWAR Battalion

Examples of PSYWAR material distributed to Dominicans during the intervention

personnel believed that civilian agencies had little understanding of the military's capabilities. Conversely, civilian participants often complained about delays in the delivery of Army equipment and then about the outdated material and the poor quality of products they received. At the time, General Palmer praised the PSYWAR effort but complained about "antiquated and unsuitable equipment." Upon reflection, however, he conceded that in psychological operations, Americans are "amateurs" because "we operate in an open society with a free press, and the thought of propaganda is kind of foreign . . . revolting to us," as opposed to the Communists who "can beautifully integrate the psychological aspects into all their operations." Referring specifically to PSYWAR operations in the Dominican Republic, Palmer maintained that the Americans were "good at it technically," but that "we didn't really know how . . . to communicate with people in that way, because we're just not used to the idea of using [propaganda] as a weapon."[23]

Just how effective were the civic action-civil affairs programs and the psychological operations in winning the hearts and minds of the Dominican population? The question is impossible to answer. Surveys by military personnel were conducted to learn the feelings of the Dominican people toward Americans, rebels, the OAS, etc., but the results were highly unreliable. For instance, persons conducting a survey on occasion would deliberately word questions in such a way as to obtain answers they thought would work to the military's advantage, while respondents would often tell an interviewer what they thought he wanted to hear.[24]

Undoubtedly, the food, clothing, and medical programs won friends among locals who had initially opposed the intervention. According to one 82d report, "Civil assistance has been the single most important factor in building a favorable image of the airborne soldier." Personal contact was indispensable to this goal, and fact sheets issued to the soldiers instructed them on proper conduct.[25] But despite this and other efforts to promote good relations, some friction between Dominicans and U.S. troops was inevitable. To begin with, the marines and the 82d were resented as an occupation army. The use of U.S. troops to break up demonstrations, despite the restraint exercised in doing so, also created hostility, as did "the immorality of some American soldiers who did not distinguish between professional prostitutes and ordinary Dominican girls." (The incidence of venereal disease in the Dominican Republic was high enough to make a lasting impression on several officers who tried various measures to curtail their troops' sexual liaisons with women other than the ubiquitous and "clean" camp followers.) In day-to-day dealings with Dominican citizens, a racial slur or an ugly incident could also undo a great deal of good will in seconds. In one particularly tragic occurrence, a soldier requesting an Alka Seltzer of a teenager who worked in a drug store thought that the boy had poisoned him. He shot and killed the teenager on the spot. A visit by General York to the neighborhood to offer his personal condolences could not assuage the bitterness caused by the tragedy.[26]

In a more positive vein, many Dominicans simply appreciated the fact that, with few exceptions, the intervention reduced the previously uncontrollable bloodletting of the civil war. While in a crowd, locals would often hurl abuse or more tangible objects at soldiers manning the front lines. Alone, a Dominican would often offer the Americans beer and whisper words of appreciation for the job they were doing. Perhaps indifference—or more aptly ambivalence—best describes the feelings of most Dominicans once Americans became a familiar presence among them. Few U.S. troops who served in the country fail to recall the words of a piece of graffiti that became more and more common as the intervention continued: *Fuera Yanqui—y lléveme contigo* (Yankee go home—and take me with you).[27]

* * *

"Discipline" is the word used most frequently, then and now, by soldiers describing the critical element in the performance of U.S. troops in the Dominican intervention. When manning a frontline position, discipline enabled a soldier to endure sniper fire every night without firing back at shadows or overreacting in an angry outburst causing unnecessary death and destruction. During riot-control operations, it took discipline to hold one's fire and stand firmly in the face of a hostile, often violent, mob. Discipline also enabled a soldier to cope with the tedium of day-to-day routine despite numerous recreational, educational, and training programs established to keep him occupied when not on duty.[28] But most of all, soldiers had to be disciplined to observe the numerous and increasingly complex rules of engagement imposed on them by higher authorities.

The initial rules of engagement made sense in both humanitarian and political terms. Prohibitions on the use of artillery (the 82d redeployed all but one battery by the end of May), tanks (the marines did not use theirs in action and the 82d left theirs at Bragg), and mortars prevented a conflagration in the congested tinderbox of Santo Domingo. Thus, few disputed the necessity of this restriction. The order not to fire unless fired on, while not so readily embraced, still fell within the realm of the necessary, especially during the early period of the intervention when an aggressive spirit, imperfect fire discipline, a belief in a military solution, and an instinctive fear of unknown dangers could have led to needless killing and, consequently, diplomatic complications. The policy of providing food, clothes, and medicine to all needy Dominicans regardless of political allegiance struck some soldiers as being unnecessarily magnanimous considering that a person picking up food in the afternoon might be shooting at you that night; yet from a humanitarian and public relations perspective, the policy was essential lest the United States be accused of partisan behavior and, worse, of allowing women and children to suffer needlessly.

Once the ISZ and LOC were established, the political concerns that dictated every phase of the intervention became even more pronounced. That meant a simultaneous rise in Washington's fears that some unforeseen incident would disrupt movement toward a political solution. Beginning on 3 May, to lessen the chance of such an incident, restrictions on the use of military power in the Dominican Republic became even more numerous and complex.[29] (Veterans of the intervention have chosen less charitable words

Celebrities entertained U.S. troops in the Dominican Republic. Here, Joey Heatherton dances as part of the Bob Hope Show.

to describe the rules of engagement: "dumb," "crazy," "mind-boggling," "demoralizing," "convoluted," and "confusing" are but a sample of the printable ones.)[30] That there would be no military solution to the crisis—as had been expected—was frustrating to Masterson, Palmer, York, and the other soldiers down through the ranks, even though the emphasis on diplomacy ultimately proved the wiser course for achieving long-term Dominican stability. Where frustration gave way to anger was in those cases in which civilian and military leaders in Washington appeared to ignore military considerations completely as they seemingly sacrificed the safety and morale of American soldiers in Santo Domingo on the altar of political considerations. The general rule not to fire unless fired on soon gave way to a succession of other rules, ending with a prohibition against firing unless one's position was in imminent danger of being overrun. Once the rebels realized this new situation, they took full advantage of it. A sniper with rifle in hand would often swagger down the middle of the street toward an American position, casually walk into a nearby building, choose his firing position, expend his ammunition, leave the building, and offer an obscene gesture as he departed the area. In response to this, U.S. troops could only hope to have time to take cover and escape the deadly ricochets—all the while wondering how the death of one sniper could undermine efforts to achieve a political settlement.

The procession of restrictions that emanated from higher authorities in May was not confined to general guidelines. Many pertained to specific tactical details. For example, riot control agents and CS (tear gas) grenades could not be used without permission of higher authorities, units west of the Ozama could not patrol, flamethrowers would not be used, and so on. When some Army units along the LOC set up a string of lights on their perimeter to deter sniper attacks at night, Constitutionalist protests to a United Nations team (viewed by all U.S. officials as prorebel) resulted in instructions from Washington to remove the lights. As Chief of Staff of the Army General Harold K. Johnson wrote a subordinate, "One thing that must be remembered... is that the command of squads has now been transferred to Washington and is not necessarily limited to the Pentagon either!"[31]

For commanders of combat units concerned with the safety and morale of their men, the rules of engagement created a dilemma. To obey the rules might further political objectives, but at the cost of American lives and of conceding certain advantages to the enemy. To disobey the rules would violate one of the most sacred tenets of command and risk court-martial. The enterprising commander thus looked for loopholes or ways to bend the rules without technically breaking them. One illustrative case involved an airborne company in the southwest portion of the LOC. The position overlooked the National Palace, which was located in the rebel zone but occupied by Loyalist troops. The company established liaison with the Loyalists, whom they regarded as friends if not allies. As the contacts increased, so, too, did the Americans' conviction that the Palace must not fall to the rebels. Since the building was surrounded on three sides by open areas, there existed little danger that a firefight would set that portion of the city ablaze. In view of

The Presidential or National Palace

this, the company commander in question made preparations for an "artillery" barrage by stringing together several 3.5-mm rocket launchers and by mounting several M79s on wheels that adjusted fire when moved. When the Constitutionalists attacked the Palace, the airborne company waited for the inevitable round that would overshoot its mark and land in or near the American position. Having been "fired upon," the company launched its rockets and grenades in a devastating fusillade. A sympathetic battalion commander kept his subordinate out of trouble, but eventually a new rule of engagement plugged the loophole by forbidding any kind of firing in the vicinity of the National Palace.

Some of the rules of engagement were essential; others were inexcusably at odds with rational military practice. At times, officials in Washington, in their zeal to manipulate the military for political objectives, evinced little understanding of basic military requirements. Conversely, U.S. soldiers in the Dominican Republic, by their own admission, were not well versed in the nature of political-military operations. "Most of us were now beginning to experience a new phenomena [sic] of modern war—the political control of military operations," wrote one airborne soldier. "Here again was a condition for which we had not properly trained."[32] The training would come with the job, as after 3 June, a second round of political negotiations would dominate the crisis and the military's role in it.

The IAPF and the Peace Settlement 8

Although firefights and sniping incidents continued throughout the intervention, significant combat operations in Santo Domingo, with one exception, ceased after the GNR sweep of the northern part of the city during the third week in May. After *operación limpieza*, the cordon of U.S. troops facing Constitutionalist forces in Ciudad Nueva acquired a dual function: it continued to keep the bulk of Caamaño's forces bottled up, but it now protected them as well from any effort by the Government of National Reconstruction to impose a military solution to the crisis. That the United States would pay more than lip service to its proclaimed "neutrality" came as an unpleasant surprise to President Imbert. When the incredulous general declared that U.S. troops would not stop him should there be "no other way out" than to break the cease-fire and attack Caamaño, Embassy officials took swift "action to set him straight on this." As he quickly learned, the U.S. military presence was now "directed toward maintaining the cease-fire and developing a negotiated settlement that would provide a broad based U.S. oriented government." On 2 June, Imbert appeared to accept this reality, albeit reluctantly, when he "announced full support of the OAS and proposed OAS-sponsored elections as a way out of the deadlocked political issues."[1]

The general's reference to the OAS is significant. The failure of the Bundy mission in late May to arrange a political settlement signaled an end to unilateral U.S. initiatives to open negotiations between the two sides. The OAS moved with uncharacteristic alacrity into the void created by Bundy's departure. Dr. José A. Mora, the OAS secretary general who had been in Santo Domingo since 1 May, attempted to keep the possibility of negotiations alive until he could transfer peacemaking functions to a new three-man OAS Committee. Palmer hailed the arrival of the committee on 4 June as the beginning of "a new era." "The arena is now almost purely political and psychological," he reported, "with the military furnishing the power back-up as the necessary muscle to enforce a solution." As another indication that the crisis was entering a new phase, the military muscle to which Palmer referred would, in the form of the Inter-American Peace Force (IAPF), come under the jurisdiction of the OAS. With these political and military initiatives, the OAS, according to one U.S. source, "assumed the responsibility for the stability operation."[2]

Ellsworth Bunker, the U.S. ambassador to the OAS

In the political realm, OAS leadership was more nominal than real. Ambassador Ellsworth Bunker of the United States headed the three-man commission as its principal negotiator—the man who called the shots—and he took his guidance more often from the White House than from the OAS. Despite the multilateral façade, the United States would retain tight control over the political process.

A strong case cannot be so readily made for U.S. domination of the IAPF. The idea for a multilateral military force within the hemisphere did not originate with the Dominican crisis. As early as 1961, the United States had broached the idea of a permanent inter-American military organization. Among the unstated reasons for doing so was a belief that such an organization would deter intrahemispheric conflicts, discourage pro-Communist tendencies, promote security within Latin American countries, and, in the event of a hemispheric crisis, obviate unilateral U.S. intervention. The OAS made little progress toward enacting the proposal, in part because the Pentagon wanted U.S. operational control over the regional force, in part because Latin Americans feared that an IAPF would serve as a thinly disguised cover for a return to Big Stick diplomacy.[3] Both these concerns would affect efforts to establish a multilateral force during the Dominican revolt.

From the early days of the crisis, the Johnson administration sought to wrap U.S. activities in the mantle of hemispheric support. Appreciative of OAS support for the deployment of marines, LBJ, ever sensitive to criticism, recoiled when several members of the organization reacted bitterly to his sending in the 82d Division without consulting them. It fell to Bunker, as U.S. ambassador to the OAS, to explain Washington's unilateral intervention to his colleagues in an effort to repair the damage. The main thrust of his argument was that, having no hemispheric military force to which it could turn, the United States had to go it alone to protect its citizens and interests. To counter charges that the United States was returning to a policy of intervening at will in the internal affairs of other nations in the hemisphere, Bunker proposed on 1 May an OAS resolution calling on member states to provide military contingents for duty in the Dominican Republic. To improve the chances for prompt passage of the resolution, U.S. officials promised to provide airlift for any Latin American troops sent into the troubled country. They also mounted a massive lobbying campaign in Washington, in Santo Domingo, and throughout the hemisphere to promote the measure. On 6 May, after what seemed an interminable debate, the foreign ministers of the OAS, meeting in Washington, passed the resolution by a vote of fourteen to five (Chile, Ecuador, Mexico, Peru, and Uruguay voting in the negative), with Venezuela abstaining.[4]

The decision to establish what was initially called the Inter-American Armed Force (IAAF) gave President Johnson, in the words of a recent study, "a legitimate umbrella under which to operate" until details concerning the composition, organization, command, and support of the unit could be worked out. Even during the debate, U.S. diplomats and military officers, through a series of discussions with their Latin American counterparts, had tried to determine what countries would or could furnish troops for the multilateral force. As early as 5 May, CINCSOUTH had compiled a list of units that certain Latin American countries might agree to contribute to the IAAF. Encompassing a wide range of forces from a Uruguayan platoon to two battalions each from Argentina and Brazil, the list had to be pared after 6 May because it included some of the countries that had voted against the resolution. After the vote, U.S. diplomats intensified their drive to encourage Latin American governments to contribute forces. For its part, the JCS made known its preference for Latin American infantry units trained in counterguerrilla and riot-control tactics. As late as 9 May, the administration still hoped for the participation of Argentina, Brazil, Venezuela, Colombia, and the five Central American nations. Most of these expectations fell victim to domestic politics in several key countries, to public demonstrations against the U.S. intervention, or, in the case of Argentina, to concern over the role Brazil would play in the IAAF. When the final troop list appeared, it included (in addition to the United States) only six Latin American countries: Brazil (1,130 men), Honduras (250), Paraguay (184), Nicaragua (160), Costa Rica (21 military policemen), and El Salvador (3 staff officers).[5]

CINCSOUTH and CINCAFLANT worked out arrangements for Operation Press Ahead, the airlifting of the Latin American contingents to the Dominican Republic. The first units to arrive, with only two hours' notice to U.S. officials in Santo Domingo, composed a reinforced rifle company

Honduran troops arriving in the Dominican Republic

from Honduras. Despite the high morale of the men, the condition of the company left those officers who met it dejected. "The unit's total organizational equipment," USFORDOMREP reported, "consisted of a still crated kitchen it had never seen before." As for the men, each had only a mess kit, poncho, M1 rifle, and twenty rounds of ammunition. The Pentagon had anticipated and State had promised U.S. supplies and training by Special Forces "A" Teams for Latin American units. But neither agency had foreseen the extent to which it would be called upon to fulfill this commitment. The Honduran unit presented the worst case. In addition to the Class I, II, and V supplies and tentage that the United States furnished all the Latin contingents, the Hondurans also required fatigues, socks, and underwear.

To U.S. commanders on the scene, the Military Assistance Program for Latin America seemed seriously flawed. The Hondurans so depleted existing supplies in the Dominican Republic that Palmer, through Admiral Moorer, urged CINCSOUTH not to deploy further OAS contingents to the Dominican Republic "until they are equipped to exist and function in the field." Once referred to Washington, the request died from lack of presidential support. LBJ wanted an operative multinational peace force, and he wanted it immediately. The best Palmer was able to extract from Washington was a directive from Secretary of Defense McNamara to the effect that "additional food, clothing, tentage, and non-U.S. standard ammunition be sent directly to the Dominican Republic from storage depots in the continental United States."[6]

If establishing the IAAF proved a logistical headache, it was nothing compared to the nightmare Palmer endured in trying to place the command under U.S. control. On the day the OAS approved the combined force, the State and Defense Departments named Bennett the U.S. coordinator for working out, in the words of the resolution, the "technical measures necessary to establish a Unified Command of the OAS." Palmer was to work with Bennett, and both were to "prepare recommendations as to [the] structure and functioning of [the] Unified Command and submit these to Washington for approval before commencing discussions with [Latin American] Force Commanders or OAS Committee."[7]

Three days later, Bennett and Palmer submitted their recommendations for the IAAF command structure. A combined staff, they suggested, should follow the U.S. example because "most Latin American officers who would be nominated for these assignments would probably have been exposed to U.S. staff procedures and structure in CONUS schools." Within the staff, U.S. officers should fill the posts of secretary, C4 (logistics), and C6 (communications), "as a minimum." (On 11 May, Palmer established a separate staff section, J7, within his command. Called the Director of Military Affairs for Inter-American Armed Forces, it would provide the nucleus of the U.S. contribution to the combined staff, once the latter became operational.) In connection with another matter, Palmer and Bennett had the opportunity to convey their conviction that the commander of the IAAF "should be a US General Officer, probably of three star rank."[8]

On one point, Palmer was insistent: nothing should be allowed to interfere with the freedom of action of U.S. forces. That the IAAF could pose such a threat came across in his and Bennett's warning—which could hardly have come as a revelation to their superiors—that "should OAS Commission refuse to authorize IAAF to take action, high level Washington decision would be required with respect to possible unilateral US action by other units." The "other units" would be U.S. forces not committed to the IAAF, for in Palmer's view, it would be folly to place more than a token brigade under OAS jurisdiction. But regardless of the number of U.S. troops attached to the force, their freedom of action and, consequently, the furtherance of U.S. interests could only be ensured by the appointment of a U.S. commander.[9]

From a purely military standpoint, the position taken by Palmer and Bennett made good sense. Diplomatically, however, it was untenable. The OAS would accept nothing less than the subordination of all U.S. troops to the operational control of a Latin American IAAF commander. In the words of one study, "An intra-regional military peace-keeping force under OAS control was far more palatable in Latin America than was one under U.S. control; at the same time, the regional force would tend to seek the same goals as the United States—ending the strife and preventing a Communist takeover." Recognizing these realities and unwilling to risk a return to unilateralism with all of its adverse consequences, the State Department, with the support of Secretary of Defense McNamara, overrode the strenuous and frequently voiced objections of Palmer, Bennett, Moorer, and the JCS and acceded to the Latin American demands. As General Wheeler explained to Palmer and Moorer, "We devised the IAF concept for the purpose of giving an international cover to American military involvement in the Dominican Republic and to legitimize our activities in world opinion by identifying them with the OAS." All U.S. troops in the Dominican Republic would serve in the IAAF under a Latin American general. On 22 May, the 13th Plenary Session of the OAS requested that Brazil designate the IAAF commander and the United States the deputy commander. General Hugo Panasco Alvim and General Palmer were so named. Because Alvim would not arrive in the Dominican Republic for a week, Palmer became acting commander until 29 May, when the Brazilian general assumed command.[10]

A formal ceremony to sign the Act Establishing the Inter-American Force (the word "Armed" being dropped from the title) took place on 23 May at the Hotel Embajador. The document stated, in part, that while assigned to the force, members would remain in their national services but "serve under the authority of the Organization of American States and subject to the instructions of the Commander through the chain of command. Command of national contingents, less operational control, shall remain vested in the commanders of the respective national contingents." The IAF would consist of "the Unified Command and the national contingencies of Member States assigned to it," while the Unified Command would "consist of the Commander of the Inter-American Force, the Deputy Commander, and the Staff." The "sole purpose" of the force would be "that of cooperating in the restoration of normal conditions in the Dominican Republic, in maintaining the security of its inhabitants and the inviolability of human rights, and in the establishment of an atmosphere of peace and conciliation that will permit the functioning of democratic institutions." The headquarters of the IAF would be located in the Hotel Jaragua. On 2 June, in another change in title, the IAF became the Inter-American Peace Force (IAPF) (see figure 6).[11]

Once Alvim arrived, he "exercised command in the fullest sense," reserving for himself the final word on major decisions. Despite that, he and Palmer worked well together on the whole, with the American deputy managing to acquire, through a variety of ways, as much flexibility and freedom of action as he could hope for under the circumstances. Alvim began by

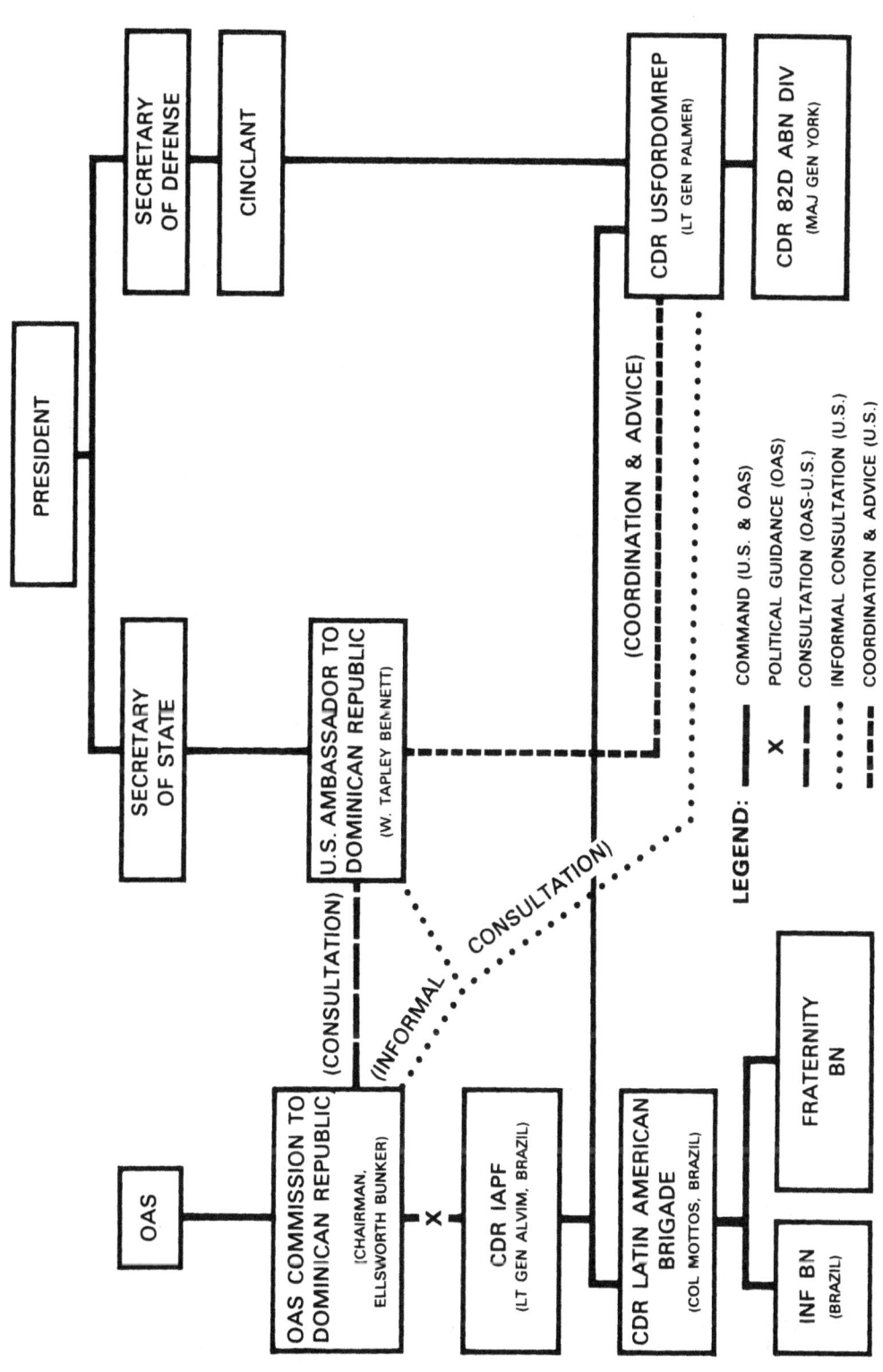

Figure 6. U.S. and OAS relationships, Dominican Republic, May–June 1965

General Palmer presents OAS flag to General Alvim at command ceremony

accepting all of Palmer's recommendations on key staff positions, save one: the chief of staff would be a Latin American officer, his deputy a U.S. officer—not vice versa. The Brazilian general appointed U.S. officers to the C4 and C6 positions and as deputies to Latin American officers assigned to the remaining slots (see figure 7). An equal number of U.S. and Latin American officers headed the 156-man headquarters staff, the vast majority of which was composed of American enlisted men. Palmer had ensured the imbalance when he set up J7, which now expanded and formed the cadre for the IAPF staff. The shrewdness of the move provided the deputy commander with one technique of influencing IAPF activities: an officer on Palmer's USFORDOMREP staff would prepare a paper prescribing what the U.S. general wanted and then pass the paper to a U.S. officer on the combined staff to "develop and promulgate as an IAPF action." Also placing Latin American commanders and staff officers at a disadvantage was the leverage the United States accrued within the IAPF simply by providing it with over half its troop strength and almost all its logistical support.[12]

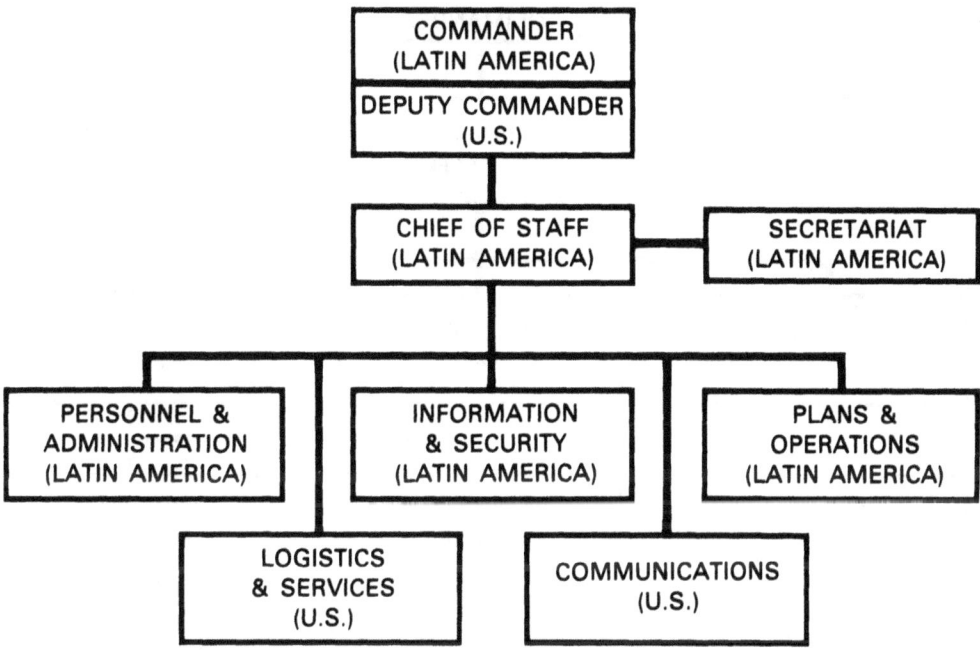

Figure 7. Headquarters, IAPF

Published on 29 June, IAPF Force Regulations gave Palmer a good deal of latitude to act in the name of the commander.[13] The organization of IAPF combat elements into two separate forces, one U.S., the other Latin American, further strengthened Palmer's hand. A Latin American brigade (later subdivided into a Brazilian Battalion and a Fraternity Battalion, the latter comprising a Brazilian marine company and the remaining Latin units) operated under a Brazilian colonel, while USFORDOMREP retained its identity as the U.S. contingent (see figure 8). Alvim tried to assume direct command of the 82d, but Palmer deflected the move, thus ensuring that orders to American forces would have to be channeled through him.[14] According to Lawrence Greenberg's analysis of the IAPF,

> this procedure satisfied Palmer, Moorer, and the joint chiefs' concerns about placing U.S. troops under the direct control of a foreign commander. In theory, U.S. forces would be under the operational control of the Inter-American Peace Force and, through it, the Organization of American States. In reality, they remained under the direct control of General Palmer, whom before he had

left for the island, General Wheeler had told that the president expected [Palmer] to follow directives from his national chain of command should differences between U.S. and OAS objectives arise.[15]

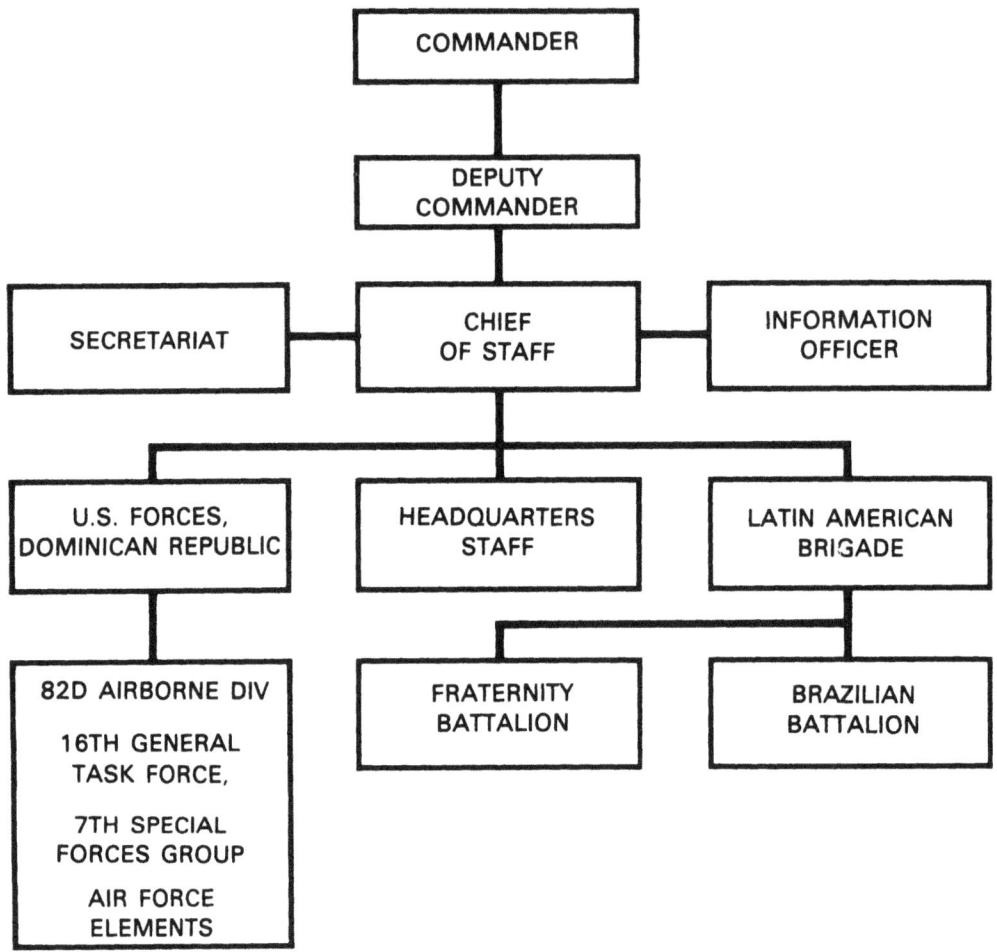

Figure 8. Organization, IAPF

Once the IAPF began to function, certain difficulties emerged. One had to do with finding suitable and language-qualified U.S. and Latin American staff personnel. Another concerned the uncoordinated and inappropriate tasks assigned the force by anyone associated with the OAS in the Dominican Republic. Most important, from the U.S. standpoint, was getting Alvim to approve a series of troop withdrawals that U.S. military leaders considered prudent. One reason Washington had pushed so hard for a Latin American military contingent to the Dominican Republic was to enable the president to reduce the Yankee presence in that country by at least 10,000 men. The withdrawal would signify a good-faith gesture in the spirit of multilateralism and provide soldiers needed to protect American interests elsewhere in the world. Once the Latin American contingents began to arrive at San Isidro, the JCS solicited recommendations for U.S. troop withdrawals. CINCLANT's argument that the marines should be pulled out first in order to restore the U.S. capability to undertake military action in the Caribbean prevailed. By the time Alvim assumed command of the IAPF, the first Marine units had already pulled out. He readily approved redeployment of the others, and by 6 June, they, too, had left. Alvim also authorized redeployment of a number of units from the 82d before he became cautious during the summer and began to insist that further U.S. troop withdrawals await progress toward a negotiated settlement. Palmer chipped away at Alvim's position with mixed results. At one point in mid-June, he requested that Washington approve the deployment of an Army tank unit to bolster IAPF firepower, to intimidate opponents, and to use as an inducement for Alvim to release another infantry battalion. (By the time State endorsed the deployment of a tank company, a political settlement in the Dominican Republic was being implemented, and U.S. troop withdrawals had resumed.) In late June, Palmer did manage to obtain Alvim's blessing for a plan that entailed leaving behind, in the wake of peace negotiations, one three-battalion brigade of the 82d plus some miscellaneous units as the U.S. contribution to the IAPF until OAS-sponsored elections could be held.[16]

Upon reflection, Palmer came to agree that the creation of the IAPF was "a profound historical event with far-reaching implications." Yet he could not bring himself to endorse a permanent inter-American military force,

First contingent of U.S. marines leaving the Dominican Republic

at least not without stringent reservations, the foremost being that the United States make no commitment that would impair its freedom of action and ability to respond rapidly in a crisis. Above all, he felt that the commander of such a force should be a U.S. general officer. In the Dominican Republic, the United States for the "first time in its history," Palmer contended, had turned over field command of its combat forces to a foreign officer. That "serious error" should never be repeated.[17]

* * *

As the Latin American Brigade became operational, its contingents performed a variety of duties. On 29 May, Brazilian troops relieved U.S. forces in the ISZ and western edge of the LOC. The Brazilians engaged in civic action projects, while three-man observer teams, composed of a Honduran, a Costa Rican, and an American team, patrolled all areas in Santo Domingo except Ciudad Nueva. Other IAPF teams investigated cease-fire violations, including several charges from the Constitutionalists that GNR troops were lobbing mortar shells into the rebel stronghold. At first, the IAPF was inclined to dismiss the allegations as propaganda, but newly acquired counter-mortar radar pinpointed the alleged firing location in northern Santo Domingo. Concrete evidence that Wessin's forces had violated the cease-fire brought an end to the attacks. The most grisly assignment for the investigation teams was looking into such atrocities as the mass execution of prisoners committed by both sides at the height of the brutal civil war.[18]

The presence of Latin American troops within the IAPF did not lead to good relations between the Constitutionalists and the multinational force. Quite the contrary. As IAPF units took up positions in the ISZ and LOC, the rebels launched a propaganda campaign intended to foment dissension within the ranks of the Latin American Brigade. The United States, the rebels charged, had given the Brazilians the most rigorous and dangerous assignments in the IAPF. Palmer responded to the allegations by arranging with Alvim to give the Latin Americans only the Palace area and a small portion of the ISZ to hold. The rebels then dropped their "soft-line" approach in favor of hurling rocks and verbal insults at the Latin Americans. On 6 July, the rebels even mounted a military probe of positions manned by the Latin American IAPF contingents. Showing contempt for the rules of engagement, the Latin Americans responded to the probe by starting a prolonged firefight. Soon thereafter, Constitutionalists began hoisting the first "Brazilian, Go Home" signs. Palmer applauded the failure of the propaganda offensive but regretted the "trigger-happiness on the part of [Latin American IAPF] troops which was later to be almost disastrous from the point of view of the negotiations."[19]

Palmer's concerns on this point were not immediately voiced. In fact, within days after becoming operational, the IAPF headquarters scored a negotiating coup that boosted morale among the staff and helped legitimize the new peacekeeping organization. The breakthrough involved the festering situation at the National Palace, an isolated bastion of several hundred Loyalist troops within the rebel sector. The rebels, beginning in early May,

Latin American members of the IAPF man a position on the LOC

had tried without success and, in one case, with the loss of several prominent leaders, to dislodge their opponents by force. Given the symbolic importance of controlling the building, State had authorized Bennett and Palmer to take military action if in their judgment it was the only way to save the lives of the soldiers from an all-out rebel attack. The Constitutionalists, having engaged in several firefights with U.S. units manning that portion of the LOC, had no desire to precipitate such a confrontation or to see the national monument destroyed. To defuse the situation, they entered into unsuccessful negotiations with the OAS and the GNR. In late May, the IAPF joined the talks and secured an agreement, reached on 1 June. Under the accord, GNR forces would be withdrawn, except for a token platoon of twenty-five men, and Brazilian troops would secure the building and the newly created demilitarized zone surrounding it. The next day, the agreement went into effect without incident.[20]

With the Palace neutralized, Palmer turned his attention to providing better security for the vital power plant, that, although controlled by the 82d, was vulnerable to rebel fire from an old hospital nearby. At one point in mid-May, the general had considered using military force "to push our lines further out in order to provide better security to both US troops and the facility, as [the] power plant is now practically on the front line." He decided, instead, to negotiate with the Constitutionalists in an attempt to accomplish the same goal. On 10 June, however, negotiations collapsed when the rebels rejected IAPF proposals to extend the security line.[21] It was a tragic decision on the part of the Constitutionalists. Within days, Palmer would obtain his new security line and more in the bloodiest battle of the intervention pitting U.S. troops against Caamaño's forces.

IAPF officers and U.S. officials in Santo Domingo had anticipated some rebel military activity on 14 June, a national holiday, but the rally held that day in Ciudad Nueva was small and controlled. That night, a brief firefight broke out after a group of rebels fired into a Brazilian position, but it was a negligible engagement, apparently unauthorized by Caamaño. A rebel colonel later apologized to the Brazilians and promised courts-martial for the instigators, thus prompting IAPF speculation about rebel morale, unity, and frustrations.[22]

Discord within the Constitutionalist camp and Caamaño's inability to control his decentralized forces were what probably led some rebel groups to shoot into U.S. and Brazilian positions the next morning. The IAPF units under attack, particularly the 1st Battalions of the 505th and 508th Infantries, returned the small-arms fire in what began as just another "routine" firefight. But when the 505th suffered a casualty, the paratroopers "retaliated for their loss by generosity in terms of ammo expenditures."[23] The rebels, too, escalated from small arms to tear gas grenades, .50-caliber machine guns, 20-mm guns, mortars, rocket launchers, and tank fire. The 82d responded with every weapon allowed under the rules of engagement. Within two hours, a pitched battle was under way. The 82d hastily devised a plan to clear the area of rebels, and late that morning, York received permission from Alvim and Palmer to take the offensive. The 1st Battalion of the 508th launched the attack, supported from the LOC by the 2d Battalion of the 505th. Moving southward into rebel territory, the 1st Battalion met heavy resistance but managed within two hours to advance several blocks. The rapidity of the advance and the apparent disintegration of rebel forces to the front soon had Alvim and York thinking about pushing all the way to the Ozama.

The timely arrival of Palmer, apparently on orders from Washington, prevented such a move. In what several sources have described as an emotional exchange between Palmer and York, the deputy IAPF commander ordered the attack halted, even though everyone present realized that a military solution to the crisis would require only a few more hours. "I felt terrible about it," Palmer would recall years later, and "Alvim didn't like it worth a damn." York, although "sore," gained at least one concession. A company of the 1st Battalion of the 508th had moved west to capture the hospital near the power plant, something Palmer had failed to obtain through negotiations. Although committed to a political solution, even Palmer could not envision returning this key facility. He therefore ordered York to hold and secure the 82d's gains that morning. For his part, Palmer would return to headquarters and attempt to get permission for the 82d to incorporate those gains into the LOC. Traveling in a jeep without a radio, Palmer could not be contacted en route to headquarters, and York used the interval to have the 1st Battalion, 505th Infantry, seize two additional blocks to the west. Moving out about 1600 local time, the paratroopers accomplished their mission by maneuvering through backyards and buildings to avoid open streets. By the time Palmer contacted York with approval to hold his ground, the LOC had been extended even farther into rebel territory. No American officer, including Palmer, seemed to mind. If there were regrets, they were over the decision not to deliver a knockout blow to the rebels as they cast off their uniforms and headed for the Ozama River. Even Bennett told Palmer, "It's too bad you didn't let the 82d go." An incredulous Palmer could only reply, "Are you joking?"

The fighting continued one more day, but there were no further advances by the IAPF. The 82d sustained thirty-one casualties, three of whom later died. The Brazilians, who had orders to remain on the defensive, suffered five wounded. U.S. sources estimated rebel casualties at 99 killed and more than 100 wounded. (Some sources place the rebel casualties, including civilians, at 300.) As a result of the fighting, U.S. troops extended the area of the LOC about thirty square blocks. When the United Nations Observer Team in the Dominican Republic demanded a return to the status quo ante, Alvim refused. Retention of the new positions shrank the rebel stronghold, provided the IAPF with better fields of fire and more security for the power plant, and served notice that the OAS, not the UN, was going to call the shots in the Dominican crisis. As for the rebels, after the fighting on 15—16 June, they became reluctant to attack U.S. positions. One rebel spokesman, in describing the action on the 15th, explained how, after a modest exchange of gunfire, "the Americans opened up and started shooting like crazy—like they were attacking Russia." After the 16th, deliberate harassment was directed primarily at Latin American troops, who engaged in "vigorous return fire," much to Palmer's chagrin. The Hondurans particularly, Palmer became fond of saying, "loved to throw hand grenades like popcorn."[24]

*   *   *

The mauling the Constitutionalists received on the 15th made them more amenable, but not yet committed, to a negotiated settlement, while rebel misfortunes only stiffened the resolve of Imbert's GNR to gain recognition as the provisional government of the country. Palmer had little sympathy for either side at this point: "Although Imbert is *not* a winner and shouldn't be considered so," he wrote, "Caamaño and his communist associates are definitely losers." Given the passions and political differences separating the two contenders, diplomacy promised little more than prolonged negotiations to end the civil war. Yet no matter how ponderous, negotiations also held out the best hope for restoring and, more important, maintaining stability without recourse to military dictatorship. The ad hoc OAS committee, in Palmer's opinion, had to find and "impose" a political solution occupying the "practical middle ground" between extreme Left and Right.[25]

Palmer's sentiments coincided with Bunker's instructions to establish a "middle road" government not necessarily associated with the belligerents.

A Constitutionalist rally in Santo Domingo

On 18 June, the OAS committee presented both sides a set of general propositions that could serve as the basis for a negotiated settlement. The key passages called for the establishment of a provisional government representing "all sectors" within the country, to be followed by OAS-sponsored elections. Neither the Constitutionalists nor the GNR rushed to embrace the OAS formula. In the rebel camp, Communist elements proclaimed their intention to continue fighting even if Caamaño agreed to a provisional government, while from Puerto Rico, Juan Bosch complicated matters by urging his followers to reject a provisional government headed by Héctor García-Godoy, a Dominican businessman and diplomat and the OAS's hand-picked moderate candidate for interim president. Meanwhile, the GNR alternated between endorsing OAS attempts to create a provisional government and proclaiming that the GNR itself legally constituted such a government. Each side, Constitutionalist and Loyalist, sought to improve its respective bargaining position by mounting a war of nerves against the other that included demonstrations, propaganda, and military incidents.[26]

In early August, the ad hoc OAS Committee published an Act of Reconciliation, again a series of general propositions to be used as the basis for a negotiated settlement. As part of the package, the Constitutionalists and GNR were to accept the OAS-sponsored Provisional Government of García-Godoy as the "sole and sovereign government of the Dominican Republic," agree to the dismantlement of rebel defenses and the incorporation of Ciudad Nueva into the ISZ on a temporary basis, be the recipients of a general amnesty, turn arms carried by civilians over to the government, and, without punitive measures, reintegrate into the regular armed forces members of the military who had defected to the rebel side. Furthermore, upon installment of a provisional government, the military would "return to their barracks and place themselves under the orders of their Commander in Chief, the Provisional President."[27]

Three weeks of intense negotiations followed, during which the Act of Reconciliation was revised several times. In Palmer's opinion, alterations designed to placate Caamaño so "watered down" the military and security aspects of the plan that he and Alvim "finally stated on 22 August that we could not accept any further changes." Imbert went further by rejecting the proposed agreement and reneging on his promise to resign in favor of García-Godoy. But Imbert's position by this time was weak. Revelations of GNR atrocities had undermined his public image,[28] and his political authority suffered from a U.S. decision to stop financing the GNR until an agreement was reached. When Imbert refused to discuss the matter of his resignation with the OAS or García-Godoy, Bunker turned to the CIA chief of station, who in a meeting at Imbert's home assured the GNR leader that the United States would not allow the disintegration of the Dominican military or the fall of the country to the Communists. With these reassurances, Imbert resigned on 30 August, citing U.S. pressure as one reason for his decision.

Extremists on both sides tried to sabotage the agreement—the rebels by attacking IAPF lines, Wessin's forces by firing mortars into the rebel area. But U.S. troops showed their usual restraint, and countermortar radar again provided evidence that only a small group was involved. On 31 August, Caamaño signed the Act of Reconciliation for the rebels. After receiving written clarification from García-Godoy on certain ambiguous parts of the agreement pertaining to demilitarization, disarmament, and the reintegration of rebel soldiers, the military chiefs who had served Imbert signed the act on behalf of the GNR. On 3 September, García-Godoy took the oath of office as president of the Provisional Government.[29]

If any person deserved credit for the settlement, it was Ellsworth Bunker. The dominant figure in the negotiations, "he was very much his own man," whose interpretation of trends in Latin America dictated his "basic negotiating posture." Latin America, he believed, was moving inexorably to the Left. The United States could not stop this movement but with insight and patience might moderate it before it reached the Communist extreme. Thus, Bunker was more willing than Imbert, Bennett, Alvim, and Palmer to make concessions to Caamaño's Constitutionalists. Not that Palmer was completely unsympathetic to Bunker's views. In some respects, Bunker served as Palmer's tutor in Latin American realities. Added to this tutelage were the insights the general gained from his close working relationship with Bennett. Daily communications with diplomatic, political, and military officials in the United States revealed to Palmer the complex considerations affecting U.S. policy in the Dominican Republic. That the general came to advocate a political solution to the country's crisis says much about the education he received during this assignment. When the new CIA chief of station first met the general that summer, he judged Palmer to be "possessed of a political sensitivity unusual in field officers."[30]

On the subject of the peace settlement, Palmer admired Bunker's negotiating method, which was to "allow pressures to build up just short of an explosion and, if by that time an agreement had not been reached between the two sides, to present a final OAS proposal and drive hard for what amounted to an imposed solution." The general also liked the way Bunker used the implied threat of force to move negotiations along, even though the OAS ambassador was adamantly opposed to a military solution. Palmer was less laudatory about Bunker's failure to seek IAPF advice about certain military provisions of the settlement, provisions that Palmer believed would "weaken or destroy the effectiveness of the Dominican Armed Forces," the "only effective, indigenous force capable of preventing a return to the chaos and mob rule of April 1965 or of countering a seizure of power by Leftist extremists following the withdrawal of the IAPF."[31] That Palmer's concerns along these lines were well founded became apparent as the IAPF shed its neutrality and became the protector of the new Provisional Government.

*   *   *

The inauguration of Garcia-Godoy did not bring an immediate stop to violence and political passions, but for the most part, these remained at a manageable level. With the installation of the new government, formal U.S. troop withdrawals resumed after a two-month hiatus. During the interval, however, individuals had been reassigned and not replaced (because of the buildup and combat losses in Vietnam), dropping the strength of USFORDOMREP to under 10,000 men—at least 3,000 below authorized strength. Some battalions were operating at only 50 percent of full strength. Not until October did USFORDOMREP receive a priority on individual replacements. By then, redeployment of units was reducing the U.S. contribution to the IAPF to the three-battalion brigade (plus miscellaneous units) that Palmer had proposed in June. When completed, troop withdrawals would leave 6,000 U.S. soldiers in the country as part of an IAPF totaling 8,800. Palmer and Alvim agreed that unless the civil war resumed, this force would be capable of restoring order and protecting the Provisional Government.[32]

Between the establishment of the Provisional Government and the elections held in June the following year, the IAPF had to intervene only a handful of times to save Garcia-Godoy's somewhat shaky administration or to quell disorders that threatened the country's stability. The first test of the IAPF's new role of protector came within a week after Garcia-Godoy assumed office; it involved the difficult task of getting General Wessin y Wessin to leave the country. Always resented because of his elite position, the general had become the object of even more controversy because of his decision to bombard and strafe the city on 25 April, thus triggering the civil war. Even before the formation of the Provisional Government, it was generally assumed that Garcia-Godoy would have to accede to Constitutionalist demands for Wessin's ouster in order to achieve rebel adherence to the Act of Reconciliation. Wessin's belief that the presidency of Garcia-Godoy was the first step toward a Communist takeover of the country further weakened the general's standing. When the Provisional Government became a reality, the IAPF made access into the LOC and ISZ easier but continued to block the eastern end of the Duarte bridge to prevent *CEFA* troops from entering Santo Domingo in an attempt to overthrow the government and resume the civil war.[33]

On 5 September, the new president abolished *CEFA* as a separate force (a directive that was ignored) and called for its integration into the Dominican Army. The next day, after Wessin held a press conference to declare his willingness to lead the country in a crusade against communism, García-Godoy could no longer avoid the inevitable. On the 8th, with his military chiefs and Bennett present, the president told Wessin face-to-face that the general would have to leave the country. Wessin agreed but early the next morning began to mobilize his unit for a march on the city. The IAPF reacted immediately. When *CEFA* forces began to move, they were quickly intercepted and escorted to their Armor Center, where the commanding officer agreed to confine them to the compound. On Palmer's orders, IAPF troops blockaded the Armor Center, surrounded Wessin's headquarters, and, with the aid of helicopters, moved into the landing zone near the general's house. With the troops in place, Alvim, Palmer, and the Dominican military chiefs proceeded to Wessin's home, where Alvim "called upon the Saints in the Catholic Church" in an emotional appeal for Wessin to leave the country. When Wessin temporized, Palmer bluntly instructed the interpreter, "You tell him he has no choice; he is going!" Palmer also conveyed to Wessin that force would be used if necessary. Wessin relented. The matter was settled, although some anxious moments occurred when the emissaries escorted Wessin through an angry group of guards who feared that their boss was being taken away to be shot.

Before going to the airport, Wessin asked to be allowed to say good-bye to his troops at an academy near San Isidro. Palmer agreed but lost Wessin's car in the dark. At that point, according to Palmer, "we tore off to San Isidro. Everybody in a different car chasing each other." When Wessin did not show up at the airfield, Palmer ordered the 82d's assistant commander, Jack Deane, to fetch the general. In an extraordinary act of courage, Deane bluffed his way into the *CEFA* fortress and returned to San Isidro with the wayward Dominican. It was, in Palmer's words, a "delicate mission." Wessin "had a whole compound armed to the teeth. It was really fortunate that something didn't happen there. A spark could have ignited that thing and I don't know what the hell would have happened." That night, after a tearful farewell at San Isidro, Wessin boarded a plane for Panama, an interim stop before proceeding to Miami, where he became the Dominican consul general. The general's departure, Palmer noted, "was a great blow to conservatives and rightist extremists."[34]

Because the rebels refused to surrender their weapons until they felt secure from attack by the Dominican military, Wessin's departure constituted a first step toward the demilitarization of Ciudad Nueva. It would also be the last for over a month. In the interval, the rebel area experienced a breakdown in law and order, as gangsters and right-wing and left-wing hit squads roamed the streets and Communist-inspired propaganda and bombings intensified. There were also indications that the Communists were planning a terrorist campaign against IAPF and government personnel. In an attempt to force García-Godoy to take action to remedy the situation, Palmer devised a plan to dismantle the LOC and ISZ surrounding the rebel area, thus creating a vacuum that the president would have to fill. To lessen the chances for conflict and to protect the Constitutionalists from reprisals, the plan called for the removal of rebel military forces under IAPF escort to the 27th of July barracks. Caamaño agreed to the plan, and on 13 and 14 October, military police and troops from the 82d evacuated the rebel military. Checkpoints around the camp ensured that only Caamaño and a handful of select officers and their bodyguards carried arms outside the area. Concurrently, the IAPF dismantled the checkpoints and barriers that had separated Loyalists from Constitutionalists.[35]

The next phase of the plan called for García-Godoy to demilitarize what had been the rebel zone by sending in his own military, which he distrusted, or the IAPF. He did neither. Instead, he stalled and then accepted an alternate plan put forward by the UN observers and Caamaño to have Ciudad Nueva searched by four-man teams over a period of several days. Palmer was livid. He dismissed the new plan as "patently absurd," and as he predicted, its results were "completely ineffectual." The enactment of the farce confirmed for him what he had suspected for some time: García-Godoy was a "spineless" man who kowtowed to Leftist elements while gratuitously alienating his own military chiefs. With five U.S. airborne battalions and a tank company still in the country, together with the Latin American Brigade, Palmer postponed further troop redeployments and sought authorization for the IAPF to clear the city—whether García-Godoy approved or not. Knowing that several hundred hard-core rebels had reentered Ciudad Nueva from the 27th of July camp, he urged immediate action before rebel forces increased to such proportions as to threaten a renewal of hostilities.[36]

Bunker, Alvim, and State liked Palmer's plan. Even García-Godoy approved it after having first received a nod from Caamaño, who hoped "to persuade the hard-core rebels remaining in the city to allow a bloodless entry." At the last minute, a nervous Dominican president tried to cancel the operation, only to learn that the IAPF was already committed. The IAPF troops—three airborne infantry battalions, the tank company, and the Latin American Brigade—crossed into Ciudad Nueva from all directions at dawn, 25 October. Meeting only scattered resistance and neither suffering nor inflicting casualties, the IAPF secured the area in an hour. The operation uncovered few arms caches but did yield an unexpected prize—"a fine haul of incriminating Communist documents." When informed that the area had been pacified without bloodshed, a "hoarse and nervous" García-Godoy "finally calmed down."[37]

The Wessin affair and the demilitarization of Ciudad Nueva brought home to García-Godoy in different ways "the fact that the IAPF was the

A sample of rebel arms seized by U.S. troops

key to his survival." It was also the protective shield for former rebels—so long as they stayed within Santo Domingo. What could happen when they did not was vividly illustrated by an episode on a Sunday in mid-December, when Caamaño insisted, against all advice, on attending a memorial mass for a slain rebel buried outside Santiago, a Loyalist bastion to the north of the capital.[38] Sunday was traditionally a day for church, drink, and recreation. When the arrival of Caamaño and his armed entourage became known to the "rummed up" populace, the situation in Santiago became extremely volatile. As could have been predicted, shooting broke out at the cemetery, and Caamaño and over 100 of his followers fled to refuge nearby in the Hotel Matum. Three hundred former Loyalist troops stationed in Santiago surrounded the hotel and opened fire. Caamaño returned the fire, and a battle lasting several hours commenced. Guests of the hotel, including a Puerto Rican circus troop, became virtual hostages of the former rebels. A State Department counsel stationed in Santiago went into the Matum in an effort to mediate a cease-fire but succeeded only in adding his name to the hostage list. A U.S. military intelligence officer who had observed these developments telephoned the grim news to Santo Domingo. His report that Loyalist forces were using tanks (without high-explosive rounds, however, that could have destroyed the hotel) and that Americans numbered among the hostages moved the IAPF to action.

In hopes of avoiding a bloodbath at the hotel, García-Godoy authorized the IAPF command to dispatch troops to Santiago. A company of the 2d Battalion, 508th Infantry, departed within an hour of being alerted. The battalion commander, Lieutenant Colonel John Costa, followed a short time later. After receiving a briefing at the Santiago airfield, he went with a small party by jeep to the hotel. The IAPF company followed on foot. When Costa reached the hotel, he passed through the line of angry Dominican soldiers surrounding the building and went inside to talk to Caamaño. The former rebel leader was visibly nervous and looking for an honorable way out of his predicament. Against the advice of his suspicious and more militant advisers, he accepted Costa's word that the IAPF would protect him and his men. Soon thereafter, the hostages were released.

By then, the IAPF company had arrived, and Costa had placed it between the opposing forces. He also declared himself to be in charge of the situation, much to the chagrin of the Dominican commander who wanted to storm the hotel. Several tense hours passed with the disposition of forces resembling a small-scale model of Santo Domingo during the height of the U.S. intervention. Bad weather delayed the dispatch of more helicopters from the capital, but once they arrived on Monday, the evacuation of Caamaño's group proceeded peacefully. An incident that could have plunged the country back into civil war had been narrowly averted, despite the casualties suffered by both sides (four Constitutionalists and eleven Loyalists killed and eighteen others wounded).

The Hotel Matum affair was followed by yet another crisis, this one bringing to a head the tension that had been building since September between García-Godoy and his military chiefs. As all parties to the peace settlement clearly understood, the Act of Reconciliation did not resolve the issues that had led to civil war, it only provided the mechanism for doing so. The Provisional Government needed as wide a base of support as possible, which meant that García-Godoy, aside from having to prove that he was not a U.S. puppet, had to give moderate Leftists some hope that the government could implement some reforms lest the moderates move farther to the Left. Hence, the president's deference to Caamaño and the appointment of former rebels to cabinet positions that angered and alarmed most American officials.[39] Caamaño and others from the rebel side, as one of the conditions for their cooperation, demanded the removal of prominent Loyalist officers—beginning with Wessin and moving on to other military chiefs, including the newly appointed secretary for the armed forces, Rivera Caminero. Because García-Godoy was not certain he could trust his military chiefs to support him and his overtures to the Left, he was inclined to accept Caamaño's demands.

Before that could happen, Palmer was telling the OAS Committee in forceful terms that he would only support the dismissal of the military chiefs if ordered to do so by the highest authorities in Washington. Even then,

Helicopter at Santiago airfield awaiting evacuation of Caamaño's entourage

Palmer warned, Alvim and the Latin American IAPF officers would probably refuse to support the government thereafter, in which case the IAPF would dissolve. These were strong words coming from a military officer on what could be construed as a political issue. But Palmer and Alvim fervently believed that the current secretary and service chiefs of the Dominican armed forces were best qualified to control the military situation in the country. The replacement of these men by incompetents would pave the way for a left-wing takeover of the government, conservative countermeasures, and the renewal of civil war. Bunker accepted Palmer's assessment and worked to prevent—or at least forestall—dismissal of the chiefs. (Palmer, it should be noted, also used his powers of persuasion with the chiefs to keep them working with García-Godoy and, in one instance, from mounting a coup against him.) In November, after the demilitarization of Ciudad Nueva, relations between the Dominican president and his military officers improved, but not to the extent of removing fundamental differences over what paths the government should take in ruling the country.[40]

The Hotel Matum affair in December convinced many Caamaño supporters that the military chiefs still sought to defeat the Constitutionalist movement. Several segments of the population, including the sugar workers—"the mainstay of the slowly reviving economy"—threatened to go on strike unless the president fired Rivera Caminero and the three military chiefs. Bunker argued with García-Godoy against bowing precipitately to these demands but to no avail. The president was determined to act. Accepting that, Bunker then proposed a solution whereby military leaders from each side would leave the country. García-Godoy agreed. But on 6 January 1966, when he issued a decree announcing the overseas posting of his military chiefs and certain Constitutionalist officers—including Caamaño—Rivera Caminero and other officers who had reluctantly supported García-Godoy up to that point broke with the government and seized the main radio station. García-Godoy, through the OAS Committee, instructed the IAPF to suppress the attempted coup. Alvim refused, saying that "he did not take orders from the Dominican government." Under OAS pressure, he reluctantly changed his mind and committed the IAPF. Backed by troops, he and Palmer then met the leaders of the uprising and worked out an end to the crisis. In the aftermath, Caamaño agreed to an overseas assignment and departed the country later in the month. In February, García-Godoy maneuvered Rivera Caminero and the service chiefs into resigning. He replaced them with officers he considered more sympathetic to civilian democracy.[41]

The attempted military coup in January had at least two serious consequences for the U.S. involvement in the post-civil war phase of the Dominican crisis. The first effect was to undermine U.S. plans to reorganize and reform the Dominican armed forces, the goal being to make them more professional, less corrupt, and enthusiastic supporters of civilian democracy—in short, an apolitical force that would stand as a bulwark against right-wing and, more important, left-wing extremism. After the events of January and February, the United States feared that an intensive reform and rebuilding program would only increase demoralization within military ranks,

Caamaño Deño (right) talks with Ambassador Ellsworth Bunker (back to camera) prior to the colonel's departure from the Dominican Republic

thus further weakening the institution and its ability to maintain security and order. In effect, the well-intentioned—if slightly unrealistic—U.S. program became a casualty of political necessity. The withdrawal of 82d units, which Palmer had resumed in November, would soon leave the United States with little leverage to initiate an overhaul of the Dominican forces.[42]

A second consequence of the January uprising was to call into question the reliability of Alvim as the IAPF commander. The success of the political settlement depended on placing the IAPF at the disposal of the Provisional Government when need be, but Alvim—in temporarily putting his conservative principles and sympathy for the military chiefs above his assigned duties—had hesitated. For all anyone knew, if the general found subsequent orders to be equally odious, he might refuse altogether to commit his forces. To preclude that possibility, Bunker, during a visit to Brazil in mid-January, arranged for the general's removal. Alvim would be recalled, ostensibly as a part of a routine rotation and a decision to downgrade the rank of the commanding officers in the IAPF. That meant that Palmer would leave the country as well, another measure to save Alvim's face. The changes in command proceeded as planned. Palmer returned to the United States on 17 January 1966, leaving Brigadier General Robert Linvill in charge of the three-battalion brigade that now formed the core of USFORDOMREP. Alvim returned to Brazil in February.[43]

On 1 March, a three-month campaign for elections scheduled for 1 June began. The two leading candidates were Balaguer and Bosch, both of whom had returned to the country, the former in June 1965, the latter, that September. Most American officials predicted a Bosch victory, but since his return, the rebels' ostensible leader had confined himself to his home, where he spent most of the campaign (earning himself the epithet, *"Juan de la cueva"* [Juan of the cave]). Balaguer, on the other hand, campaigned vigorously and won by 57 percent of the vote. Remaining IAPF forces began redeploying even before Balaguer took office on 1 July. On 21 September, the last units left the country as U.S. intervention in the Dominican Republic came to an end.

As the 82d and other American units returned home or to other duty stations, they left behind a more stable situation in which democracy, however fragile, had been restored, and a Communist takeover, however remote, had been averted. In accomplishing this, 27 U.S. soldiers had been killed in action and 172 wounded. For the Dominicans, the civil war and the return to a kind of stability acceptable to the United States had taken a much higher toll, estimated at at least 3,000 killed. Even critics of the intervention agree that had the United States not stepped in to end the hostilities, the figure would have been much higher.

Conclusions 9

In the Dominican crisis of 1965—66, President Johnson wanted to prevent the establishment of a "second Cuba" in the hemisphere but in such a way as not to open the administration to charges of "another Hungary." He succeeded on both counts. Whatever possibility existed that Communist groups would seize power vanished with the introduction of U.S. troops, whereas a subsequent political agreement between the two warring Dominican factions obviated the use of all-out U.S. force to suppress a popular revolt, as the Soviets had done in Budapest.[1]

From the perspective of U.S. security interests in Latin America, the intervention was a *qualified* success. With the election of Balaguer, a stability acceptable to the United States returned to the republic. To be sure, the methods used to maintain this stability, while by no means comparable to the excesses of the Trujillo regime, have at times seemed harsh by U.S. standards. Hundreds of politically motivated killings "continued into the early 1970s," and other drastic measures were used to repress radical opposition to the Balaguer government.[2] Furthermore, the 1965 settlement failed to eliminate the country's deep-rooted economic and social weaknesses. Still, while repression continued and discontent exists, the magnitude of the problems, when compared to the upheaval of 1965, have given American citizens and policymakers little cause for alarm. For the U.S. government, an occasional riot in Santo Domingo pales in comparison to the ongoing guerrilla war in El Salvador or the U.S.-backed insurgency against the Sandinistas. Relatively speaking, the Dominican Republic appears to be one of the more stable countries in the Caribbean area.

There are other reasons for considering the Dominican intervention only a qualified success. Through their actions, the Johnson administration and the U.S. military establishment raised doubts and evoked criticism in several quarters. Among various groups in Latin America and the United States, LBJ's decision to deploy the 82d Airborne Division without consulting Latin American allies provoked anger and heightened fears of a resurgence of U.S. imperialism in the hemisphere. Resolutions establishing an OAS negotiating commission and multinational peace force were supposed to deflect criticism of U.S. unilateralism, but opponents of the intervention dismissed these measures as little more than a pretext for the assertion of U.S. power and influence. Political divisions in Latin America over the intervention sapped the OAS of its effectiveness, while the pressures Washington brought to bear on the organization and the domination U.S. Ambassador Ellsworth Bunker asserted over the second OAS Committee caused the image of the OAS to suffer. Many Latin Americans had always regarded the OAS as a tool of U.S. imperialism. During the Dominican crisis, critics joked that the Spanish acronym for the organization, *OEA (Organización de Estados Americanos)*, really stood for *"Otro Engaño Americano"* (another American trick).[3]

Not only did the United States provide the vast majority of soldiers and supplies to the Inter-American Peace Force, U.S. officers also tried to block the appointment of a Latin American general as the IAPF commander. Of the military considerations behind this effort, the desire to retain America's freedom of action was paramount. When this rationale became public knowledge, however, it seemed to contradict the spirit of multilateralism the White House was espousing. Even though some Latin leaders applauded U.S. policy, either publicly or privately, the number of Latin American states who declined to send soldiers to the Dominican Republic in most cases illustrated the depth of anti-American feelings generated by the intervention. As Abraham Lowenthal observed in 1969, "The idea of an Inter-American Force composed of units from democratic countries in the hemisphere... seems to have died as a result of its premature birth in the Dominican context."[4]

Above all else, the crisis demonstrated to Latin Americans that when the rhetoric of the Good Neighbor conflicted with vital U.S. interests, the latter, usually explained in terms of anticommunism and the preservation of hemispheric solidarity, would hold sway over the former. The United States, as a great power, would do what it considered in its best interests. Although it would prefer to act in association with allies and friends, it would go it alone if need be. This position is axiomatic for all great powers. Still, when the unilateral approach is followed in this hemisphere, Latin American countries, ever sensitive to infringements on their sovereignty and to the historical record of U.S. interventions and gunboat diplomacy, will become understandably agitated and resentful.

Many countries outside the hemisphere condemned the intervention. Predictably, the Soviet Union was one of its severest critics. The intervention gave the Kremlin a long-lasting supply of ammunition for public denunciations of U.S. imperialism. In private conversations with American officials, however, Russian references to the intervention have assumed a more expedient cast, as U.S. incursions in the Caribbean area are equated with Soviet intervention in Hungary, Czechoslovakia, and Afghanistan—countries that Russia considers to be within *its* sphere of influence.

President Johnson anticipated the criticism he received from abroad, though he underestimated its range and intensity. He was not prepared for the criticism he received at home, especially from fellow liberal politicians and statesmen and from academicians. The criticism developed around three overlapping themes. One asserted simply that the United States had displayed bad judgment and an "arrogance of power" (to use Senator William

Fulbright's phrase) in intervening in the internal affairs of a sovereign country. A second theme charged the administration with grossly exaggerating Communist involvement and the threat of a Communist victory in the Dominican revolt. A list of supposed Communist agents actively participating in the revolt was compiled by the CIA on short notice to silence critics on this point, but the list contained so many errors—duplicate names, the names of dead people, people out of the country or in jail—that it only fueled the controversy and brought down LBJ's wrath on the agency. A third theme held that the administration had misinformed the American people and the world about its reasons for intervening in the Dominican Republic and about its "neutrality" in the civil war. Taken together, these charges against the administration created the first crack in the bipartisan cold war consensus that had provided the underpinning of U.S. foreign policy for twenty years. With Vietnam, this weakened foundation and the edifice it supported collapsed. But it was the Dominican intervention, not the Vietnam War, that opened the "credibility gap" that would simultaneously undermine presidential prerogatives in international affairs and bring about a long overdue reassessment of the basic tenets of U.S. foreign policy.

LBJ was hardly the first president to suffer criticism for his handling of an international crisis involving U.S. forces. (The Truman-MacArthur controversy during the Korean War comes readily to mind.) But the Dominican intervention represented the first time in historical memory (meaning, for most Americans, World War II and after) where U.S. troops in the field became the subject of adverse commentary. Field commanders who had fought against Hitler, Tojo, or Kim Il-sung, had generally regarded media correspondents as allies in the war effort. Eisenhower's deal with Darlan in World War II or MacArthur's call for total victory in the Far East during the Korean War may have stirred controversy, but units engaged in combat were generally immune from such critical analyses.

That immunity expired with the Dominican crisis. There were several basic reasons for this. One was that the administration's insistence on maintaining the fiction of U.S. neutrality during the first month of the crisis forced military public affairs personnel to echo the official line in press briefings in Santo Domingo, even though correspondents covering the city could readily see and hear evidence to the contrary. Of the correspondents who inundated the Dominican Republic beginning in late April, only the most dimwitted—or those old-timers who believed that patriotism dictated an uncritical acceptance of the official line—could overlook U.S. assistance to the Loyalists in the form of advice, equipment, intelligence, and moral support. The Loyalists themselves sought to identify their cause with U.S. goals, which did not help U.S. credibility. Realizing this, the State Department, at one point, informed Bennett that it "would be particularly helpful if [Wessin] could be persuaded to stop playing the 'Star Spangled Banner' over [the] San Isidro radio station."[5]

Responsibility for the deteriorating relationship between the media and the military in Santo Domingo rested in part on those correspondents who, through bias, chose to discount official accounts that *were* correct or who distorted news for the sake of a good story (as in the case of the CBS report of Loyalist troops entering the LOC).[6] Other newsmen simply misinterpreted events they witnessed in the city. For its part, the military also contributed to the strains that developed. As General Palmer conceded at the time, the military "simply did not have a first-class press and public affairs set-up in the DOMREP," and thus, "our handling of the press was not well done." When correspondents confronted briefers with discrepancies between America's proclaimed neutrality and the military's close ties to the Loyalists, the briefers often refused comment or misrepresented the facts, thereby reinforcing the media's skepticism. Some correspondents stopped attending the daily military briefings; some offered to hold press briefings for the military.[7]

The military's ongoing conflict with certain correspondents in the Dominican Republic became a matter of public record. Other problems, namely those that afflicted the military in planning and executing the intervention, either were not publicized or were not considered newsworthy. The military itself would have to remedy these problems, which, in the tradition of the services, were addressed in an avalanche of after-action reports, debriefings, roundtable discussions, and interminable official studies. To begin at the top and work down, the JCS, the president's principal military advisers, found themselves locked out of several critical meetings where military operations were discussed by LBJ and his civilian advisers. To be sure, Secretary of Defense McNamara served as a conduit between the White House and the JCS, but this did not compensate for the inability of the Joint Chiefs to perform their advisory function under optimum conditions. On those occasions when General Wheeler, the chairman of the JCS, was called on for advice, he often presented the views of the JCS eloquently. There were critical times, however, when the JCS was simply ignorant of what was happening further down the chain of command. During the deployment phase, for example, units were often in the objective area before the JCS had issued the necessary execution orders. One can only speculate on the reaction of a task force commander on receiving a message to prepare for an operation that had already been completed. And one can only imagine LBJ's state of mind when, in attempting to control operations from the top, he received inaccurate or outdated information.

The problem of military communications permeated the chain of command. Wheeler bristled when he could not obtain timely information from LANTCOM or the commander of JTF 122, a shortcoming attributable in part to the inadequate U.S. communications equipment located at the scene of the action. The difficulties Masterson encountered in trying to talk directly to Embassy officials during the first week of the intervention brought into question the relevance of a naval officer having operational control over a land operation that he could not be present to direct. That the Navy did not seem to comprehend the procedures and requirements of a large airborne force further called into question naval direction of Power Pack. Little wonder that Wheeler insisted on the appointment of a land force commander and then instructed him to report directly to the JCS as well as through the chain of command. Once Palmer received adequate communications facilities to comply with this instruction, JTF 122 became irrelevant to the operation and, according to existing doctrine,[8] was disestablished. At the same time, CINCLANT found that his operational command over the land forces involved in the intervention had become more nominal than real.

Poor coordination, communications, and command and control had a disruptive effect on virtually every requirement for sending an Army division, Marine MEB, and other forces to the Dominican Republic. With respect to coordination, the CINCLANT OPLAN listed the forces that could be called on for the purpose of intervening in a Dominican crisis, but it provided little useful information concerning the target area itself. In addition, the OPLANs of the Army and Air Force components were woefully outdated. While no OPLAN can anticipate all contingencies and requirements, the above deficiencies complicated the hectic planning efforts on the part of hastily convened, inadequately informed, geographically separated, and insufficiently manned joint staffs. Considering these handicaps, it is notable that the staffs accomplished what they did during the first few days of the alert. Indeed, their work might have suffered had it not been for competing demands, such as the Blue Chip exercise, and the unanticipated and rapid escalation of troop requirements. Last-minute priorities set by higher authorities further complicated matters, hindered better coordination, encouraged the tendency toward inflexibility, and added to the general confusion.

The number of commands and headquarters taking part in the deployment phase of the operation hindered orderly communications and aggravated the problem of effective coordination and control. At one extreme, CINCLANT often bypassed CINCSTRIKE in an attempt to facilitate deployment. At the other extreme, planners would be contacted by too many "higher authorities" hoping to play some part in the operation. The XVIII Airborne Corps or 82d at Bragg, for example, would often receive verbal messages from one source, only to have them contradicted by follow-up messages from another source. York's admonition that "Headquarters at all levels must phase out of operational channels as quickly as possible..." and that "If the shots are to be controlled at DOD/DA or higher level, intervening headquarters should provide support but not attempt to interpret guidance," constituted sound advice under the circumstances.[9]

Once in the Dominican Republic, York and Palmer sent urgent requests for more combat troops and then waited, partly because political decisions had to be made, partly because of problems in planning and deployment procedures. Delays in sending the kinds of troops and equipment requested by the field commander occurred when key personnel refused to deviate from load and deployment plans or, conversely, when chaos resulted from the failure to observe any plan. Higher headquarters added to the confusion when they rearranged transport priorities without consulting with the commanders in Santo Domingo.

Once the troops did arrive in the Dominican Republic, they knew little about the situation. In part, their ignorance resulted from a dearth of accurate information. Assessments contained in State and CIA cables were often unsubstantiated, biased, or irrelevant. When accurate political and mission-oriented information did exist prior to the commitment of troops, it was withheld from some key officers because of an obsession with operational security. Most of the intelligence essential to the operation was acquired by U.S. troops *after* they had entered the country and made direct contact with Dominicans on both sides. Military intelligence officers bemoaned the low priority given HUMINT (intelligence acquired from people instead of from technical devices) prior to the intervention, and valuable time was later spent in setting up the networks and facilities for acquiring such information (one of the most productive sources of intelligence in military operations short of all-out war).

The intelligence failure, together with the delays in sending combat troops and supplies, could have had fatal consequences had the United States confronted a formidable conventional force or well-trained urban guerrillas. Had that occurred, the marines and paratroopers would have ultimately prevailed, but the U.S. casualty figures would have been much higher than 47 dead (27 in combat) and 172 wounded. Fortune was kind. The Constitutionalist forces the Americans faced lacked discipline, training, cohesion, and sophisticated weapons. Because the U.S. Navy and Air Force could interdict any supplies, troops, or aircraft entering the country from external sources, the rebels could expect little more than moral support from sympathetic countries. Also, by intervening during the early days of the civil war, the United States did not allow either side to develop a conventional or unconventional threat that could inflict heavy casualties on U.S. forces. Noting these advantages, Palmer, in his first commander's summary, emphasized that the Dominican intervention should be regarded as "a special case," not necessarily applicable in larger countries where an insurgency had had a chance to plant firm roots. "If the situation has been allowed to deteriorate," Palmer wrote, "we had better think twice before we commit our force to a large country—it may be a bottomless pit."[10] Palmer's ability to grasp the larger ramifications of a specific operation had been one of the reasons for his selection as the commmander of U.S. forces in the Dominican intervention.

Palmer was also one of a small group of U.S. officers who truly grasped the "political-military" nature of the undertaking. In all cases in which the United States employs military force, political authorities define the strategic objectives of an operation. This function has traditionally been within the purview of America's foreign policy establishment. Indeed, the military expect policymakers to define these objectives, but in clear terms so that military personnel know what is expected of them and can plan accordingly. In the Dominican crisis, the goal of preventing a Communist victory was made clear from the start. But whether the military would help achieve that goal through intimidation or force could not be determined until several weeks after the initial U.S. forces landed. At the time, and in retrospect, critics have faulted U.S. political authorities for not understanding or not paying attention to the military's requirement for a clear mission statement. But this criticism, while it has some merit, fails to comprehend the perspective of the president and his advisers. For a variety of reasons, they wanted to avoid ordering the military to mount a major offensive. But until they were certain that the rebels could not overthrow the Loyalist junta or Imbert's GNR, an unequivocal decision as to the precise employment of U.S. troops could not be made. Uncertainty, with its consequences for political-military coordination, was inherent in the rapidly changing situation in the Dominican Republic.

Just as the determination of strategic objectives by political authorities was in keeping with tradition, so, too, was the president's choice of what military units would be committed to the intervention. All parties privy to the deliberations culminating in the president's decision to send in an overwhelming force in hopes of intimidating or, failing that, defeating the rebels were in agreement. The consensus broke down, however, over the control Washington wished to exert over military activity and operations. That political authorities would assume direct control of military operations had immediate repercussions. As noted, CINCLANT's operational command over U.S. forces committed within his area of operations was at times nominal. Just as CINCLANT often excluded CINCSTRIKE from the chain of command, so Washington often bypassed CINCLANT or only perfunctorily involved him in the making of critical military decisions. Unified commanders had been taught to play a more important role during a crisis.

As the two principal land force commanders in the Dominican Republic, York and Palmer realized upon their arrival that they and their subordinates would not have the free hand in operational and tactical matters that military tradition revered and officers expected. Washington's delay in sending both men the combat troops they requested and Palmer's ordeal in getting Washington to approve the LOC brought home the lesson that political considerations would govern the scope of military operations. Neither general liked the constraints placed on him, but whereas York, a commander who was very close to the troops of his division, refused to accept the validity of the restraints, Palmer, as the "theater commander," adjusted to them. While Palmer never ceased to be an on-the-scene spokesman for military necessity, he gradually came to comprehend the complexity of the Dominican situation and to accept the wisdom of a political settlement. It went against his professional experience and training to enforce the more odious rules of engagement, but he carried out his orders knowing that a political solution would, in the long run, be best for U.S. interests and for the Dominican Republic. Had a general officer not possessed of Palmer's "political sensitivity" been in charge of the U.S. forces, the outcome of the crisis might have been decidedly different.

For the marines and paratroopers who faced rebel bullets, the stringent rules of engagement imposed by Washington and USFORDOMREP made little sense. The troops had been trained to fight upon deployment. Yet with few exceptions, the combat they experienced in the Dominican Republic was against snipers, not formal military units. Soldiers cursed the restrictions and wondered why the military had not better trained them for political-military operations. Such training no doubt would have been valuable, although the lesson of restraint can be quickly forgotten when a soldier comes under fire and is told he cannot defend himself unless he is about to be overrun. Some rules of engagement, such as the restriction against return fire unless one's position were being threatened, were ludicrous. Most rules, however, were essential for improving the prospects for a negotiated settlement. While officers in charge of combat units cannot be expected to appreciate rules of engagement that place the safety of their men in jeopardy and should challenge those that do so gratuitously, they should also be prepared in contingency operations to confront such restraints. Officers who expect a free hand in such situations are bound to become frustrated and disillusioned, perhaps to the point where their performance as leaders would be affected.

If restraint provided the key to a political solution to the crisis, discipline provided the key to restraint. By all accounts, the U.S. troops involved in the Dominican intervention demonstrated remarkable discipline in performing the full range of duties assigned to them and in resisting temptations to retaliate when provoked. The mere presence of the troops ended the worst of the bloodshed that characterized the first phase of the civil war. The discipline of U.S. troops ensured that thousands more would not join the almost 3,000 Dominicans killed prior to the intervention. For this, most of the population of Santo Domingo were grateful, although they did not always express their gratitude publicly.

In the context of a political-military operation, the Dominican crisis, at the time, seemed the apotheosis of limited war theories of civilian management applied to the real world. For civilian policymakers, the ultimate success of the Dominican enterprise encouraged the further application of the theories in Vietnam. The military came out of the Dominican Republic divided in its views. A few officers begrudgingly came to accept political management as inevitable and at times necessary in situations in which the primary purpose of military operations was to support efforts to arrange political solutions. Most officers, however, criticized "overcontrol and overmanagement" by civilians, unwarranted intrusions for which Johnson and especially McNamara were held in contempt. In late 1965, General Wheeler spoke for these critics when he asked "discretion for field commanders to 'exercise command . . . on the spot,' free of having their hands tied by . . . theorists at higher headquarters."[11] Between the poles of acceptance and criticism, several officers and enlisted men who served in the Dominican Republic recognized that neither the professional military nor the civilian policymakers and their representatives understood the needs, requirements, and problems with which the other had to grapple. From among the military personnel who lamented this ignorance, appeals emanated for greater training in political-military operations at all levels throughout the civilian and military chains of command. The appeals went unheeded. It was easier to use the management of the Dominican crisis as an argument for or against limited war theories than to derive from the experience insights that might promote better understanding and more efficient interaction between civilian policymakers and military officers during times of crisis. (As a cautionary note, one should avoid overstating the benefits of better political-military understanding in a constantly changing situation. Understanding cannot always cut through the confusion and ambiguity inherent in an international crisis.)

Power Pack, in the final analysis, should be approached cautiously when used as a model for contingency and peacekeeping operations. Individual operations should be evaluated on their own merits and with an open mind as to the degree of political control and military restrictions necessary to achieve U.S. objectives. Nonetheless, the Dominican crisis provides us with useful insights and reveals recurrent patterns that arise in such contingency operations. Problems that developed in Power Pack have occurred all too frequently in other joint and combined operations. The experiences of Power Pack also indicate that the Vietnam War was not an aberration in terms of political-military interaction. In a world of nuclear weapons, the idea that a field commander and his troops will automatically be given complete freedom to perform their mission is outdated and inherently dangerous. This observation, however, does not make operating under politically imposed restraints any easier for men under fire, and in this sense, the Dominican intervention stands as a tribute to the discipline and training of American soldiers. Equally important, it demonstrated the ability of soldiers to adapt quickly when reality has failed to conform to their expectations and when changing circumstances involved new roles, force structures, and command relationships. Flexibility and adaptability were critical to the successful execution of missions to which the marines and paratroopers probably gave little or no thought prior to deployment.

Despite the frustrations and problems that surfaced during the Dominican intervention, Power Pack, when judged by the criteria Generals Johnson and Palmer established, fulfilled the requirements of a successful stability operation. The Marines and Army performed a variety of functions that included combat, civic action, civil affairs, psychological warfare, and special operations. The ramifications of these activities carried well beyond the strictly military sphere into areas affecting politics, economics, society, and public opinion. As a result of the stability operation, order was restored, a democratic system reestablished, and a possible Communist takeover prevented. While all the grievances that triggered the crisis were not redressed in the settlement of 1965—66,[12] the intervention helped set the stage for twenty years of relative peace (if not continuous prosperity) in the Dominican Republic. In a region known for its chronic instability, this is a significant achievement for which the soldiers who took part in Power Pack have expressed pride and satisfaction.

Appendix

Chronology of Crisis Events

1916—24	The United States occupies the Dominican Republic; creates national guard.
1930	The Trujillo dictatorship begins in the Dominican Republic.
1959	Castro comes to power in Cuba.
1960	President Eisenhower wants Castro and Trujillo "sawed off."
	OAS and United States enact economic and diplomatic sanctions against Trujillo regime.
	Kennedy elected president.
Apr 1961	U.S.-backed invasion of Cuba at the Bay of Pigs fails.
May 1961	Trujillo is assassinated.
Summer—Fall, 1961	Kennedy administration prevents Trujillo family from restoring dictatorship.
Jan 1962	OAS and U.S. sanctions against the Dominican Republic lifted as Balaguer promises elections.
Dec 1962	Bosch elected president of Dominican Republic.
Sep 1963	Military coup deposes Bosch.
Nov 1963	President Kennedy assassinated.
Dec 1963	President Johnson recognizes Dominican "Triumvirate."
Early 1965	Rumors of coup against Reid Cabral's "Triumvirate" increase.
24 Apr 1965 (Saturday)	Rebel plotters arrest Dominican chief of staff.
	Military-civilian coup against Reid's regime begins.

24—25 Apr 1965	Rebels arm population; enter Santo Domingo.
25 Apr 1965 (Sunday)	Reid government overthrown.
	Molina sworn in as provisional president of rebel (Constitutionalist) government.
	Loyalist planes attack Presidential Palace, beginning civil war.
	JCS transmits order to move U.S. naval vessels off Dominican shore for use in possible evacuation of Americans from the Dominican Republic.
26 Apr 1965 (Monday)	U.S. naval task group arrives off Dominican shore.
	JCS alerts two battalion combat teams of the 82d Airborne Division for possible deployment to the Dominican Republic.
27 Apr 1965 (Tuesday)	Rebel gang threatens Americans at Hotel Embajador.
	Loyalist troops begin advance on Santo Domingo.
	Evacuation of American and other foreign nationals begins.
	Cable from Rusk outlines U.S. goals: restore law and order, prevent a Communist takeover of the country, and protect American lives.
	Ambassador Bennett returns to Santo Domingo at midday and meets with rebel leaders in the afternoon.
	After meeting with Bennett, moderate rebel political leaders seek asylum; Country Team believes Communists now control rebel movement.
	Constitutionalist movement appears on verge of defeat.
27—28 Apr 1965	Caamaño rallies rebels and plans counterattack against Loyalists.
28 Apr 1965 (Wednesday)	Loyalists form military junta led by Colonel Benoit.
	Rebel counterattack stops Loyalist advance.
	Bennett reports deteriorating situation to Washington; requests communications equipment for Loyalists.
	Bennett recommends landing U.S. marines.
	More than 500 marines come ashore at polo field.
	President Johnson justifies landing of marines as necessary to protect American lives and property.

	Bennett recommends that Washington consider armed intervention to restore order and prevent a Communist takeover.
29 Apr 1965 (Thursday)	3d Brigade (2 BCTs), 82d Airborne Division, receives orders to depart Pope AFB for Ramey AFB in Puerto Rico.
	Vice Admiral Masterson, commander of JTF 122, arrives in Dominican waters.
	More than 1,500 additional marines land; Bennett proposes they establish neutral zone to encompass Hotel Embajador and U.S. Embassy.
	JCS selects Power Pack as code name for Dominican operation.
	3d Brigade, 82d Airborne Division (Power Pack I), en route to Ramey AFB, receives orders to airland at San Isidro airfield in the Dominican Republic; Major General York, the division's commander, is designated land forces commander.
30 Apr 1965 (Friday)	Power Pack I reaches San Isidro at 0215.
	York and Masterson meet aboard *Boxer*; York requests more troops; Masterson relays request to JCS.
	President Johnson meets with advisers to consider further troop deployments to the Dominican Republic; authorizes sending rest of 82d, the 4th Marine Expeditionary Brigade, and, if necessary, the 101st Airborne Division; activates Headquarters, XVIII Airborne Corps.
	U.S. paratroopers move toward Santo Domingo; secure east bank of Ozama River and Duarte bridge; establish a bridgehead on west bank.
	U.S. marines establish International Security Zone.
	OAS Council calls for truce in Dominican civil war.
	Ambassador Martin arrives on presidential mission to negotiate cease-fire.
	Papal nuncio, U.S. officials, Loyalists, and Constitutionalists sign cease-fire agreement.
	Loyalist troops move back to San Isidro, leaving gap between U.S. Marine and Army positions.
1 May 1965 (Saturday)	Lieutenant General Palmer arrives at San Isidro shortly after midnight; confers with York; refuses to recognize cease-fire so long as gap between Marine and Army units exists; calls

	for linkup of Marine and Army patrols later in day.
	Bennett, on Palmer's advice, asks Washington to send more troops.
	President Johnson again meets with advisers to reconsider troop deployments discussed Friday.
	Linkup between Marine and Army patrols occurs; linkup convinces Palmer that corridor between Army and Marine positions can be established.
2 May 1965 (Sunday)	Washington approves establishment of corridor.
	Ambassador Martin reports that revolt under Communist control.
	President Johnson, in television address, reveals anti-Communist motive behind intervention.
3 May 1965 (Monday)	At one minute past midnight, operation to establish corridor (LOC) begins; paratroopers establish corridor in just over an hour; 80 percent of rebel force is now trapped in Ciudad Nueva with no prospect of achieving a military victory.
	U.S. military begins participation in relief programs; launch Operation Green Chopper in interior of country.
3–5 May 1965	U.S. troops expand LOC.
4 May 1965	Rebel "congress" elects Caamaño "president."
5 May 1965	U.S. Special Forces take over Green Chopper mission; relief supplies begin arriving from United States; U.S. PSYWAR unit begins broadcasting.
6 May 1965	OAS meeting of foreign ministers approves resolution to establish an inter-American force for use in the Dominican Republic.
7 May 1965	General Imbert becomes "president" of U.S.-backed Government of National Reconstruction (GNR).
	General Palmer is formally designated Commander, United States Forces, Dominican Republic.
13 May 1965	Bennett and Palmer recommend unilateral U.S. action to clear rebels from northern Santo Domingo.
15 May 1965	Bundy mission arrives in Dominican Republic.
	Imbert's troops begin sweep of northern Santo Domingo.

16 May 1965	Washington instructs Palmer to use U.S. troops to prevent GNR naval and air units from participating in northern sweep.
17 May 1965	U.S. troop buildup in the Dominican Republic reaches its peak of nearly 24,000.
20 May 1965	Fighting in northern Santo Domingo ends in GNR victory; Radio Santo Domingo is captured.
21 May 1965	New cease-fire goes into effect.
29 May 1965	General Alvim of Brazil assumes command of the Inter-American Peace Force (IAPF).
1 Jun 1965	IAPF reaches agreement with Loyalists and Constitutionalists on status of National Palace.
4 Jun 1965	Second OAS Committee arrives in Santo Domingo to negotiate political settlement.
Jun 1965	U.S. marines withdrawn from the Dominican Republic.
15 Jun 1965	Serious fighting breaks out between rebels and IAPF; U.S. troops seize and retain an area of thirty square blocks of rebel territory in Ciudad Nueva.
18 Jun 1965	OAS Committee puts forward general proposal for a political settlement.
30 Aug 1965	Constitutionalists and Loyalists accept OAS-sponsored Act of Reconciliation.
3 Sep 1965	Héctor García-Godoy sworn in as president of Provisional Government.
9 Sep 1965	IAPF stops General Wessin's attempt to overthrow Provisional Government; Wessin leaves country.
13–14 Oct 1965	By agreement, rebels evacuate Ciudad Nueva for the 27th of July barracks.
25 Oct 1965	IAPF moves into Ciudad Nueva.
19–20 Dec 1965	IAPF company rescues and evacuates Caamaño and followers from Hotel Matum in Santiago.
6–8 Jan 1966	García-Godoy announces that his military chiefs and certain Constitutionalist officers will be posted overseas; announcement precipitates a coup attempt by the military chiefs; IAPF negotiates end to crisis.
Jan 1966	Generals Alvim and Palmer leave country to be replaced by Brigadier Generals Alvaro de Silva Brago of Brazil and Robert Linvill, respectively.

Jan—Feb 1966	Caamaño, other prominent Constitutionalists, and military chiefs accept overseas postings.
1 Mar 1966	Presidential election campaign between Bosch and Balaguer begins.
1 Jun 1966	Balaguer defeats Bosch in presidential election.
1 Jul 1966	Balaguer sworn in as president.
21 Sep 1966	Last U.S. units leave the Dominican Republic.

Notes

Author's Preface

1. Roger J. Spiller, *"Not War But Like War": The American Intervention in Lebanon*, Leavenworth Papers no. 3 (Fort Leavenworth, KS: Combat Studies Institute, U.S. Army Command and General Staff College, January 1981).

2. Ibid., vii.

3. Herbert Garrettson Schoonmaker, "United States Military Forces in the Dominican Crisis of 1965" (Ph.D. dissertation, University of Georgia, 1977); and Lawrence M. Greenberg, *United States Army Unilateral and Coalition Operations in the 1965 Dominican Republic Intervention*, Historical Analysis Series (Washington, DC: Analysis Branch, U.S. Army Center of Military History, 1987).

Chapter 1

1. The classic work on U.S. relations with Latin America from American independence into World War II is Samuel Flagg Bemis, *The Latin-American Policy of the United States: An Historical Interpretation* (New York: Harcourt, Brace, 1943). Other works on U.S.-Latin American relations during this period are listed in Richard Dean Burns, ed., *Guide to American Foreign Relations Since 1700* (Santa Barbara, CA: ABC-CLIO, 1983).

2. This brief overview of the Truman administration's relations with Latin America is based on Raymond Estep, *United States Military Aid to Latin America*, Air University Documentary Research Study no. AU-200-65-ASI (Maxwell Air Force Base, AL: Aerospace Studies Institute, Air University, 1966), 20—24; Federico G. Gil, *Latin American-United States Relations* (New York: Harcourt, Brace, Jovanovich, 1971), 189—208; Harold A. Hovey, *United States Military Assistance: A Study of Policies and Practices* (New York: Frederick A. Praeger, 1965), 8—10, 50—55; Richard H. Immerman, *The CIA in Guatemala: The Foreign Policy of Intervention* (Austin: University of Texas Press, 1982), 9—13; Walter LaFeber, *Inevitable Revolutions: The United States in Central America* (New York: W. W. Norton, 1983), 88—109; Lester D. Langley, *The United States and the Caribbean in the Twentieth Century* (Athens: University of Georgia Press, 1982), 187—90; Abraham F. Lowenthal and Albert Fishlow, *Latin America's Emergence: Toward a U.S. Response*, Headline Series 243 (New York: Foreign Policy Association, 1979), 5; John Bartlow Martin, *U.S. Policy in the Caribbean* (Boulder, CO: Westview Press, 1978), 29—30; Chester J. Pach, Jr., "The Containment of U.S. Military Aid to Latin America, 1944—49," *Diplomatic History* 6 (Summer 1982):225—43; and Roger R. Trask, "The Impact of the Cold War on United States-Latin American Relations, 1945—59," *Diplomatic History* 1 (Summer 1977): 271—84.

3. Unless otherwise noted, this brief overview of U.S. relations with Latin America during the Eisenhower administration is based on Stephen E. Ambrose, *Eisenhower*, vol. 2, *The President* (New York: Simon and Schuster, 1984), 477, 504—615 passim; Gil, *Latin American-U.S. Relations*, 209—32; LaFeber, *Inevitable Revolutions*, 109—43; Langley, *U.S. and the Caribbean*, 205—19; Lowenthal and Fishlow, *Latin America's Emergence*, 6—9; Martin, *U.S. Policy*, 31—47; Schoonmaker, "U.S. Military Forces," 6; Jerome N. Slater, "The Dominican Republic, 1961—66," in *Force Without War: U.S. Armed Forces as a Political Instrument*, edited by Barry M. Blechman and Stephen S. Kaplan (Washington, DC: Brookings Institute, 1978), 290—91; Jerome N. Slater, *Intervention and Negotiation: The United States and the Dominican Revolution* (New York: Harper & Row, 1970), 6—8; Richard E. Welch, Jr., *Response to Revolution: The United States and the Cuban Revolution, 1959—1961* (Chapel Hill: University of North Carolina Press, 1985); José Zalaquett, "From Dictatorship to Democracy," *New Republic*, 16 December 1985:18; Wayne S. Smith, *The Closest of Enemies: A Personal and Diplomatic Account of U.S.-Cuban Relations Since 1957* (New York: W. W. Norton, 1987), chapters 1 and 2; and Stephen G. Rabe, *Eisenhower and Latin America: The Foreign Policy of Anticommunism* (Chapel Hill: University of North Carolina Press, 1988).

4. The best work to date on the covert U.S. intervention in Guatemala is Immerman, *The CIA in Guatemala*. See also Stephen Kinzer and Stephen Schlesinger, *Bitter Fruit: The Untold Story of the American Coup in Guatemala* (Garden City, NY: Doubleday, 1981); Cole Blaiser, *The Hovering Giant: U.S. Responses to Revolutionary Change in Latin America* (Pittsburgh, PA: University of Pittsburgh Press, 1976); and Rabe, *Eisenhower*, 42—63.

5. On this point, see Stephen G. Rabe, "The Johnson (Eisenhower?) Doctrine for Latin America," *Diplomatic History* 9 (Winter 1985):95—100.

6. Whether Eisenhower knew of CIA plots to assassinate Castro is uncertain. On this point, see the appropriate sections of U.S. Congress, Senate, Select Committee to Study Governmental Operations with Respect to Intelligence Activities, *Alleged Assassination Plots Involving Foreign Leaders*, Senate Report no. 465, 94th Cong., 1st sess. (Washington, DC: U.S. Government Printing Office, 1975), hereafter cited as Senate, *Alleged Assassination Plots*. A facsimile of the report was published commercially by W. W. Norton in 1976.

7. As in any complex government organization, not every person or agency accepted presidential policy. The American ambassador in Cuba remained a staunch defender of Batista even after the administration had taken punitive steps against the Cuban dictator. Also, as Wayne Smith has noted, CIA agents in planning the invasion of Cuba refused to deal with Manuel Ray, a disillusioned Castroite who by 1961 had organized an effective underground movement in Cuba. When it was suggested to one CIA man that the agency help Ray, he responded, "Absolutely not. Ray is anti-Castro, but he's something of a socialist himself. Why, he says he'd do away with the inheritance of wealth!" Smith, *The Closest of Enemies*, 72.

8. Histories of the country prior to the American intervention of 1916 include Selden Rodman, *Quisqueya: A History of the Dominican Republic* (Seattle: University of Washington Press, 1964); and Sumner Welles, *Naboth's Vineyard: The Dominican Republic, 1844—1924*, 2 vols. (New York: Payton & Clarke, 1928). See also material in Richard W. Mansbach, ed., *Dominican Crisis 1965* (New York: Facts on File, 1971), 7—8; Martin, *U.S. Policy*, 74—75; and Howard J. Wiarda and Michael J. Kryzanek, *The Dominican Republic: A Caribbean Crucible* (Boulder, CO: Westview Press, 1982), 25—33.

9. From 1822 to 1844, the Dominican Republic was dominated by its neighbor Haiti, which occupies the western third of Hispaniola. It was a brutal experience that left many Dominicans willing to relinquish their newly found sovereignty to any country that could hold the Haitians at bay. For a brief time, Spain renewed its rule over the Dominicans. At one point during the presidency of Ulysses S. Grant, the United States also sought to annex the country, but the Senate rejected the treaty in 1870. Aside from this episode

and the U.S. Navy's interest in a naval base at Samaná Bay, America by and large showed little interest in the affairs of Santo Domingo in the nineteenth century.

10. The best book published to date on the U.S. intervention of 1916—24 is Bruce J. Calder, *The Impact of Intervention: The Dominican Republic During the U.S. Occupation of 1916—1924* (Austin: University of Texas Press, 1984). See also Stephen M. Fuller and Graham A. Cosmas, *Marines in the Dominican Republic, 1916—1924* (Washington, DC: History and Museums Division, U.S. Marine Corps, 1974); Lester D. Langley, *The Banana Wars: An Inner History of American Empire, 1900—1934* (Lexington: University Press of Kentucky, 1983), 117—65; Allan R. Millett, *Semper Fidelis: The History of the United States Marine Corps* (New York: Macmillan, 1980), 147—211; Dana G. Munro, *Intervention and Dollar Diplomacy* (Princeton, NJ: Princeton University Press, 1964), passim; and Dana G. Munro, *The United States and the Caribbean Republics, 1921—1934* (Princeton, NJ: Princeton University Press, 1974), 44—70.

11. Two insightful books in English on Trujillo's rule are Robert D. Crassweller, *Trujillo: The Life and Times of a Caribbean Dictator* (New York: Macmillan, 1966); and Howard J. Wiarda, *Dictatorship and Development: The Methods of Control in Trujillo's Dominican Republic* (Gainesville: University of Florida Press, 1970). See also G. Pope Atkins and Larman C. Wilson, *The United States and the Trujillo Regime* (New Brunswick, NJ: Rutgers University Press, 1972); Mansbach, *Dominican Crisis*, 9—10; Martin, *U.S. Policy*, 74—75; Thomas G. Paterson, et al., *American Foreign Policy: A History*, 2d ed. (Lexington, MA: D. C. Heath, 1983), 354—55; Rodman, *Quisqueya*, 128—52; Wiarda and Kryzanek, *Dominican Republic*, 34—38.

12. Roosevelt is quoted in Paterson, et al., *American Foreign Policy*, 355. Robert Pastor, in *Condemned to Repetition: The United States and Nicaragua* (Princeton, NJ: Princeton University Press, 1987), 3, 320, raises doubts that Roosevelt ever uttered this oft-quoted sentiment. Byrnes to Truman, 23 November 1945 and no date [March 1946], both in President's Secretary's Files, Harry S. Truman Library, Independence, Missouri. For the U.S. ambassador to the Dominican Republic's strong feelings against Trujillo, see two reports sent by the ambassador to the State Department in March and May 1954, respectively, in U.S. Department of State, *Foreign Relations of the United States, 1952—1954*, vol. 4, *The American Republics* (Washington, DC: U.S. Government Printing Office, 1983), 946—63.

13. On this point, see Rabe, *Eisenhower*, 157.

14. The "Dracula" statement is quoted in Harold Molineu, *U.S. Policy Toward Latin America: From Regionalism to Globalism* (Boulder, CO: Westview Press, 1986), 75.

15. On U.S. involvement in the events surrounding the attempt to overthrow Trujillo, see U.S. Senate, *Alleged Assassination Plots*, 191—215. See also Memorandum of Conference with the President, 13 May 1960 [written on 16 May], *Declassified Documents Reference System* (Washington, DC: Carrollton Press, 1982), entry and microfiche no. 2473; hereafter citations from this source will be identified by document title, *DDRS*, year of publication, and entry number.

16. A thought-provoking analysis of world affairs as seen from the perspective of the New Frontier can be found in John Lewis Gaddis, *Strategies of Containment: A Critical Appraisal of Postwar American National Security Policy* (New York: Oxford University Press, 1982), 198—236. Kennedy's comment on the "sweep of nationalism" is quoted in Arthur M. Schlesinger, Jr., *Robert Kennedy and His Times* (Boston: Houghton Mifflin, 1976), 418. President Kennedy's observation on the importance of Latin America is recorded in a Memorandum of Conversation, 15 February 1963, *DDRS*, 1983, no. 2563.

17. The best overview and critique of the counterinsurgency doctrine developed by the Kennedy administration remains Douglas Blaufarb, *The Counterinsurgency Era: U.S. Doctrine and Performance, 1950 to the Present* (New York: Free Press, 1977). See also Schlesinger, *Robert Kennedy*, 417—42, 460—67; Arthur M. Schlesinger, Jr., "The Alliance

for Progress: A Retrospective," in *Latin America: The Search for a New International Role*, edited by Ronald G. Hellman and H. Jon Rosenbaum (New York: John Wiley & Sons, 1975), 57—92; John Child, *Unequal Alliance: The Inter-American Military System, 1938—1978* (Boulder, CO: Westview Press, 1980), 143—87; numerous documents in the *DDRS*; Andrew Krepinevich, Jr., *The Army and Vietnam* (Baltimore, MD: Johns Hopkins University Press, 1986), 3—127; and Stephen Lee Bowman, "The Evolution of United States Army Doctrine for Counterinsurgency Warfare: From World War II to the Commitment of Combat Units in Vietnam" (Ph.D. dissertation, Duke University, 1985). On the "progressive" role of the Latin American military, see Willard F. Barber and C. Neale Ronning, *Internal Security and Military Power: Counterinsurgency and Civic Action in Latin America* (Athens: Ohio State University Press, 1966).

18. When Kennedy became president, the Special Forces numbered about 2,000 and had as their principal mission the organization of guerrilla units behind enemy lines during conventional war. By the late 1950s, the Special Force mission had begun to take on certain features of counterinsurgency. Kennedy accelerated this transformation, upgraded the Special Warfare Headquarters at Fort Bragg, North Carolina, to the Special Warfare Center under a brigadier general, authorized the wearing of the green beret, and increased Special Forces strength to about 12,000 by 1963. He also insisted that Green Berets be trained not only in counterguerrilla operations but in civic action, engineering, communications, sanitation, medicine, and a variety of other skills that would win the allegiance of the people in countries requiring Special Forces assistance. The president pushed through these measures over the objections of many U.S. officers who found elite units distasteful and who believed that any well-trained soldier could perform the unconventional tasks assigned the Green Berets. For an insightful, albeit sympathetic account of Special Forces development and activities, see Charles M. Simpson, III, *Inside the Green Berets: The First Thirty Years* (Novato, CA: Presidio Press, 1983). See also, U.S. Army, 1st Special Forces, 8th Special Forces Group (Airborne), *Special Action Force for Latin America: Historical Report* (N.p., n.d.); this document covers the period 1962—65, and a copy is available at the U.S. Army Military History Institute, Carlisle Barracks, Pennsylvania, hereafter cited as USAMHI.

19. On the unified commands, see U.S. Joint Chiefs of Staff, Joint Secretariat, Historical Division, *Special Historical Study: History of the Unified Command Plan* (Washington, DC, 20 December 1977), CONFIDENTIAL study declassified in 1981; U.S. Strike Command, *Strike Command History, 1961—1962* (MacDill Air Force Base, FL, n.d.), unclassified portions; Vernon Pizer, *The United States Army* (New York: Frederick A. Praeger, 1967), 100, 126—28; and Lieutenant General Bruce Palmer, Jr., U.S. Army, "XVIII Airborne Corps—All the Way," *Army Digest* 22 (January 1967):12—14.

20. Unless otherwise noted, the brief overview of events in the Dominican Republic that follows is based on Atkins and Wilson, *U.S. and Trujillo*, 124, 133—41; Audrey Bracey, *Resolution of the Dominican Crisis, 1965: A Study in Mediation* (Washington, DC: Institute for the Study of Diplomacy, 1980), xi—xiv; Center for Strategic Studies, Georgetown University, *Dominican Action—1965: Intervention or Cooperation?*, Special Report series no. 2 (Washington, DC, 1966), 1—13; Abraham F. Lowenthal, *The Dominican Intervention* (Cambridge, MA: Harvard University Press, 1972), 11—17, 26—61; Abraham F. Lowenthal, *The Dominican Republic: The Politics of Chaos*, Reprint 158 (Washington, DC: Brookings Institute, 1969); Slater, "Dominican Republic," 289—306; and Wiarda and Kryzanek, *Dominican Republic*, 20—21, 38—40.

21. Arthur M. Schlesinger, Jr., *A Thousand Days: John F. Kennedy in the White House* (Boston, MA: Houghton Mifflin Co., 1965), 769.

22. Lowenthal, *Dominican Intervention*, 11; Slater, "Dominican Republic," 291—97; Piero Gleijeses, *The Dominican Crisis: The 1965 Constitutionalist Revolt and American Intervention* (Baltimore, MD: Johns Hopkins University Press, 1978), 46—48.

23. Bracey, *Resolution*, xi.

24. George W. Ball, *The Past Has Another Pattern: Memoirs* (New York: W. W. Norton, 1982), 327.

25. Quinten Allen Kelso, "The Dominican Crisis of 1965: A New Appraisal" (Ph.D. dissertation, University of Colorado, 1982), 25.

26. Gleijeses, *Dominican Crisis*, 108.

27. The Alliance had promised more than it could deliver, given (1) the resistance or lukewarm support of Congress, U.S. government bureaucrats, American businessmen and financiers, Latin oligarchs, conservative campesinos, and even the allegedly "progressive" Latin military and middle class; (2) the population explosion in Latin America; (3) the use of aid to repay existing debts or to increase the oligarchs' wealth; (4) North American ethnocentrism and lack of technical expertise in projects relevant to the Third World; and (5) the tenacity with which the *ancién regime* would cling to its power and wealth, often under the guise of democracy and reform. The list goes on. For more detailed analyses of the failure of the Alliance, see Jerome Levinson and Juan de Onís, *The Alliance That Lost Its Way: A Critical Report on the Alliance for Progress*, paperback ed. (Chicago, IL: Quadrangle Books, 1972); Schlesinger, "The Alliance"; Walter LaFeber, "Inevitable Revolutions," *Atlantic Monthly* 249 (June 1982):74–83. LaFeber argues that by failing to deliver on its unrealistic promises to ameliorate unemployment, promote democracy, and bring about land reform and a redistribution of wealth and power, the Alliance helped to create a volatile situation that made the violent revolutions of the 1970s and 1980s inevitable.

Chapter 2

1. Unless otherwise noted, the account of events leading up to 24 April 1965 is based on Slater, "Dominican Republic," 303–5; Slater, *Intervention*, 1–17; Lowenthal, *Dominican Intervention*, 42–61; Gleijeses, *Dominican Crisis*, 107–74; and Kelso, "Dominican Crisis," 28–29, 31–50.

2. Lowenthal, *Dominican Republic*, passim; and Lowenthal, *Dominican Intervention*, 33.

3. On the 1J4's rebuffs of "limited overtures" by one wing of the *PRD*, see Gleijeses, *Dominican Crisis*, 380 n. 258. Gleijeses argues that the 1J4's public appeals for a united front with moderate parties were calculated to embarrass the *PRD*, which, it was assumed, would reject making common cause with the Communists. When the *PRD* privately explored the possibility of a united front, the 1J4 rejected the overture out of hand.

4. On the Dominican military's dislike of American civic action programs, Lieutenant Colonel Paul E. Smith wrote in 1968, "Conscious of their dominant military role, and as they are generally unresponsive to the needs of the people, the Dominican military leaders have felt no need to improve their 'image' among the people. *They accept a civic action program as a distasteful job, at the urging of the United States, as one of the conditions for receiving U.S. military assistance and equipment.*" Lieutenant Colonel Paul E. Smith, U.S. Army, "The United States Military Assistance Program in the Dominican Republic, 1953–1965: A Lesson Learned?" (Student essay, U.S. Army War College, Carlisle Barracks, Pennsylvania, 18 January 1968), 11 [italics in original]. The essay is located in the Army War College archives at USAMHI.

5. Ambassador (ret.) W. Tapley Bennett, Jr., interview with author, Washington, DC, 12 November 1986.

6. Dominican officer, interview with author. By April 1965, the Dominican armed forces and police numbered nearly 28,000. The air force contained 3,700 officers and enlisted men and sported 30 F-51 fighter aircraft and 12 Vampire jets. The navy totaled 3,370 personnel and 35 "poorly manned and poorly maintained" vessels. Two destroyers and three destroyer escorts represented the "pride" of its fleet. The army rolls contained between

8,000 and 9,000 men. Membership in the national police neared 10,000 men, 3,000 of whom were stationed in Santo Domingo. *CEFA's* 2,000 men made up the remainder. What gave *CEFA* the advantage over the other military and paramilitary groups was its monopoly on tanks and recoilless cannon, its updated equipment, its superior training, and its being collocated with the air force base. This was by far the largest concentration of troops and weaponry in the country as well as its most effective force. Wessin's control over the *conjunto* was not seriously challenged until January 1965 when Colonel Juan de los Santos, a "man with his own mind," was given the temporary rank of brigadier general and made chief of staff of the air force. Wessin's influence over the 19th of November air base diminished as a result, but only slightly. Gleijeses, *Dominican Crisis*, 128—30; and Smith, "U.S. Military Assistance Program," 13—14. Smith concludes that the United States produced few "positive results" with the MAP. By 1965, the military "was still far from being a professional apolitical force." With the crisis of April 1965, the Dominican armed forces virtually disintegrated. Smith blames this poor performance primarily on political factors. Smith, "U.S. Military Assistance Program," 13—14.

7. Gleijeses, *Dominican Crisis*, 129.

8. Lowenthal, *Dominican Intervention*, 48.

9. The CIA station chief argued for accommodation with Balaguer. Ibid., 48—49. The station chief soon stepped down for medical reasons. His replacement, David Atlee Phillips, was told by his superior that the Dominican Republic "is sick, Reid is ailing politically, and we need a doctor."After reviewing the files on the country, Phillips informed his superior, "I'm afraid you don't need a doctor in Santo Domingo. You need an undertaker." David Atlee Phillips, *The Night Watch: 25 Years of Peculiar Service* (New York: Atheneum, 1977), 146.

10. Lowenthal, *Dominican Intervention*, 47.

11. Gleijeses, *Dominican Crisis*, 160.

12. Telegram, CRITIC ONE, AmEmbassy, Santo Domingo, to DIRNSA, 24 April 1965, U.S. National Security Council History of Dominican Intervention, Lyndon B. Johnson Library, Austin, Texas, hereafter cited as NSC History. Further references to the Johnson Library will be cited as LBJL. Kelso indicates that Connett telephoned the State Department to report rumors of a coup over an hour before sending this cable. Kelso, "Dominican Crisis," 56—57.

13. Telegrams, CRITIC ONE, CRITIC NO. 2, and no. 1037, AmEmbassy, Santo Domingo, to Secretary of State, 24 April 1965, NSC History.

14. Gleijeses, *Dominican Crisis*, 173—74; Telegram nos. 1039 and 1040, AmEmbassy, Santo Domingo, to Secretary of State, 25 April 1965, both in *Crises in Panama and the Dominican Republic: National Security Files and NSC Histories*, edited by Paul Kesaris (Frederick, MD: University Publications of America, 1982), microfilm reel no. 5, hereafter cited as *Crises*; Center for Strategic Studies, *Dominican Action*, 14—16; Lowenthal, *Dominican Intervention*, 69; Jack K. Ringler and Henry I. Shaw, Jr., *U.S. Marine Corps Operations in the Dominican Republic, April—June 1965* (U) (Washington, DC: Historical Division, U.S. Marine Corps, 1970), declassified document, 20; and Kelso, "Dominican Crisis," 61—64.

Despradel's declaration of neutrality came Saturday afternoon. U.S. Embassy officials, apparently unaware of this, grew concerned about police inaction. No one seems to have challenged Despradel's assurances to the Embassy that he stood behind Reid but could not challenge the tanks and bazookas of the rebels. That the rebels had no tanks at that time, and few if any bazookas, apparently did not occur to U.S. officials receiving this information. Despradel's neutrality and the willingness of General de los Santos to meet with rebel officers Sunday morning left Hernando's forces free to enter Santo Domingo Saturday night and Sunday morning. Kelso, "Dominican Crisis," 56, 58—60.

15. Gleijeses, *Dominican Crisis*, 168—70; Telegram, CRITIC ONE, and Telegram no. 1034, AmEmbassy, Santo Domingo, to Secretary of State, 24 April 1965, both in NSC History; Telegram nos. 1035 and 1036, 24 April 1965, and Telegram nos. 1038—1040, AmEmbassy, Santo Domingo, to Secretary of State, 25 April 1965, all in *Crises*, reel no. 5; entries for Sunday morning, 25 April 1965, "Chronology of Dominican Crisis—1965," undated document in NSC History, hereafter cited as "Chronology"; Lowenthal, *Dominican Intervention*, 64—66, 68—69; Center for Strategic Studies, *Dominican Action*, 11—16.

16. Lowenthal, *Dominican Intervention*, 70—74; Center for Strategic Studies, *Dominican Action*, 16—19, 22; entries for Sunday morning, 25 April 1965, "Chronology"; Telegram no. 633, Department of State to AmEmbassy, Santo Domingo, 25 April 1965, NSC History; and Telegram no. 1042, AmEmbassy, Santo Domingo, to Secretary of State, 25 April 1965, in *Crises*, reel no. 5. While he still occupied the Presidential Palace, Reid had asked the U.S. naval attaché about the possibility of U.S. military intervention. The attaché informed Connett of the request, but when Connett met with Reid that morning, the Dominican leader's comments on the military situation dealt exclusively with concerns over the loyalty of Dominican units. After Reid was arrested, a mob gathered at the Palace demanding his execution. Rather than let Reid fall into the hands of the mob, Caamaño allowed the deposed leader to "escape." Officials at the U.S. Embassy refused Reid asylum for fear it would compromise their officially proclaimed "neutrality," deemed essential if the United States hoped to effect a favorable outcome to the crisis. Reid consequently took refuge in the home of a friend.

17. Telegram no. 1051, AmEmbassy, Santo Domingo, to Secretary of State, 25 April 1965, NSC History.

18. Lowenthal, *Dominican Intervention*, 81—82. Loyalist naval units joined in the attack on the Palace. At one point, an errant shell blew open an armory door, thus making more weapons available to the rebels. Kelso, "Dominican Crisis," 64.

19. Telegram no. 1051; and Lowenthal, *Dominican Intervention*, 80—81. Lowenthal states that some accounts claim that a U.S. military attaché ordered the Loyalist attacks. Lowenthal himself could find no evidence to substantiate the charge. Ibid., 202 n. 13.

20. Entry for Saturday, 24 April 1965, "Chronology"; Lyndon Baines Johnson, *The Vantage Point: Perspectives of the Presidency, 1963—1969* (New York: Holt, Rinehart and Winston, 1971), 187—88; Schoonmaker, "U.S. Military Forces," 21—23; Kelso, "Dominican Crisis," 40; and Bennett interview.

21. Entry for 25 April 1965, in *Daily Diary of President Johnson (1963—1969)*, edited by Paul Kesaris (Frederick, MD: University Publications of America, 1980), microfilm reel no. 4, hereafter cited as *Daily Diary*.

22. According to Kelso, Richard Lippincott, State's deputy director of the Office of Caribbean Affairs, arrived at the department at 0615. "He was soon joined by the Director of Caribbean Affairs, Kennedy Crockett, by the Dominican desk officer, Harry Shlaudeman, and by Acting Assistant Secretary of State Robert M. Sayre. Among their first actions was the organization of a task force within the Operations Center, ..." Kelso, "Dominican Crisis," 60. See also Telegram no. 1039; and Lowenthal, *Dominican Intervention*, 68—70. Except where noted, the discussion of the crisis management system in this section is based on Schoonmaker, "U.S. Military Forces," 22—23, 25, 29, 67 n. 21, 74—83.

23. Phillips, *Night Watch*, 146—47.

24. LBJ's assessment of Castro's designs on the Dominican Republic are in Johnson, *Vantage Point*, 188. Reference to the infiltration of Communist agents into the Dominican Republic can be found in U.S. Forces, Dominican Republic, "Report of Stability Operations in the Dominican Republic" (Santo Domingo, 31 August 1965), pt. 1, vol. I, chap. 1, 4, hereafter cited as U.S.F.D.R., "Stability Operations." Johnson's statement linking Vietnam and the Dominican Republic is quoted in John Bartlow Martin, *Overtaken by Events: The*

Dominican Crisis from the Fall of Trujillo to the Civil War (Garden City, NY: Doubleday & Co., 1966), 661. On the argument that U.S. intervention in Vietnam was necessary to demonstrate American resolve and credibility as an ally, see Warren I. Cohen, *Dean Rusk, The American Secretaries of State and Their Diplomacy*, vol. 19 (Totowa, NJ: Cooper Square, 1980), 244—46; and Gaddis, *Strategies of Containment*, 201—2, 206, 212—13.

25. Ball, *The Past*, 329.

26. On the then-current theories of limited war and the military's perception of its role in international crises, see Richard K. Betts, *Soldiers, Statesmen, and Cold War Crises* (Cambridge, MA: Harvard University Press, 1977), 8—15; and Stephen Peter Rosen, "Vietnam and the American Theory of Limited War," *International Security* 7 (Fall 1982):83—113. Rosen critiques the seminal works on limited war theory by such academicians as Robert Osgood and Thomas Schelling. He includes the following observations in summarizing their views. "The object of [limited] war is political, to be obtained by negotiation and compromise, and not military, involving the physical destruction of the enemy.... Military problems had no proper place in a theory of limited war. This was because limited war was, essentially, a diplomatic instrument, a tool for bargaining with the enemy.... If limited war is to be a diplomatic tool, it must be centrally directed by the political leadership. The special needs of the military should not affect the conduct of the war.... If war is just another form of coercive diplomacy, then it should be run by the political leadership in Washington, not by the generals in the field.... Neither 'limited war' nor 'the strategy of conflict' are about war, but about diplomacy and bargaining. The conference table and not the battlefield is the center of the action." Rosen concludes his critique by arguing that the "military should *not* be given a free hand, but they must be allowed the freedom to solve the military problem within the limits set for them." For its part, the civilian leadership needs to learn "enough about military problems to set meaningful missions for the military."

On LBJ's reliance on McNamara, see Betts, *Soldiers*, 8; on not meeting with Wheeler until the 29th, see entry for 29 April 1965 in *Daily Diary*, reel no. 4.

Chapter 3

1. Telegram no. 1051.

2. Lowenthal, *Dominican Intervention*, 70; Kelso, "Dominican Crisis," 60—61; Telegram no. 1056, AmEmbassy, Santo Domingo, to Secretary of State, 25 April 1965; Telegram no. 633; and Telegram, JCS to CINCLANT, 1432Z 25 April 1965, all in NSC History. Telegram no. 1053, AmEmbassy, Santo Domingo, to Secretary of State, 25 April 1965, in *Crises*, reel no. 5; and entries for Sunday, 25 April 1965, in "Chronology."

3. Ringler and Shaw, *Marine Corps Operations*, 91—92; Major General R. McC. Tompkins, U.S. Marine Corps, "Ubique," *Marine Corps Gazette* 49 (September 1965):34; Captain James A. Dare, U.S. Navy, "Dominican Diary," *U.S. Naval Institute Proceedings*, 91 (December 1965):37—38; and Schoonmaker, "U.S. Military Forces," 26—28. As described by Schoonmaker, the six ships in Task Group 44.9 were "the *Boxer*, an amphibious assault ship equipped with helicopters, the *Raleigh*, an amphibious transport accommodating helicopters, landing craft, tanks, and assault troops, the *Ruchamkin*, a high-speed troop transport, the *Fort Snelling*, a landing ship carrying helicopters, landing craft and tanks; the *Rankin*, an attack cargo ship, and the *Wood County*, a tank landing ship." Schoonmaker, "U.S. Military Forces," 27. The 6th MEU was composed of "the 3rd Battalion of the Sixth Marines, Marine Medium Helicopter Squadron 264, the headquarters of the Marine Expeditionary Unit, a provisional Marine air group, and some force and division attached units...." Dare, "Dominican Diary," 37. For additional information on Marine Corps force structure and weaponry in the mid-1960s, see James A. Donovan, Jr., *The United States Marine Corps* (New York: Frederick A. Praeger, 1967), 75—107, 146—69.

4. Dare, "Dominican Diary," 38—39; and Ringler and Shaw, *Marine Corps Operations*, 92.

5. Dare, "Dominican Diary," 39; and Ringler and Shaw, *Marine Corps Operations*, 20—21.

6. Kelso, "Dominican Crisis," 71—72.

7. Kelso, "Dominican Crisis," 72—73; Lowenthal, *Dominican Intervention*, 83—84, 86—87; and Center for Strategic Studies, *Dominican Action*, 21, 24. As early as 1800 Sunday, a delegation of *PRD* moderates arrived at the Embassy and asked U.S. assistance in ending the air force attacks. U.S. officials refused to interfere in the matter but offered to arrange talks with the "legitimate military hierarchy," that is, the Loyalist officers. The *PRD* leaders demurred.

8. Dare, Dominican Diary, 40; Center for Strategic Studies, *Dominican Action*, 24; and Tompkins, "Ubique," 34. Telegram nos. 1080, 1091, 1095, and 1097, AmEmbassy, Santo Domingo, to Secretary of State, 26 April 1965; Telegram nos. 1102, 1105, 1108, and 1109, AmEmbassy, Santo Domingo, to Secretary of State, 27 April 1965; Telegram nos. 634 and 641, State Department to AmEmbassy, Santo Domingo, 26 April 1965; and Telegram no. 643, State Department to AmEmbassy, Santo Domingo, 27 April 1965; all in NSC History.

9. Lowenthal, *Dominican Intervention*, 85—90; and entries for Tuesday, 27 April 1965, in "Chronology."

10. Ringler and Shaw, *Marine Corps Operations*, 92—93; Tompkins, "Ubique," 34; Lowenthal, *Dominican Intervention*, 90; Center for Strategic Studies, *Dominican Action*, 26; entries for Tuesday, 27 April 1965, in "Chronology"; and Johnson, *Vantage Point*, 191—92.

11. For details of the evacuation, see entries for Tuesday, 27 April 1965, in "Chronology"; Dare, "Dominican Diary," 40—42; Tompkins, "Ubique," 34; and Ringler and Shaw, *Marine Corps Operations*, 22—24, 92—94.

12. Lowenthal, *Dominican Intervention*, 90, 92—93; and Kelso, "Dominican Crisis," 74—75, 78—79.

13. Telegram no. 1118, AmEmbassy, Santo Domingo, to Secretary of State, 27 April 1965, in NSC History; Kelso, "Dominican Crisis," 79—80; Lowenthal, *Dominican Intervention*, 90—93; and Center for Strategic Studies, *Dominican Action*, 24, 27—28.

14. Telegram nos. 1118, 1120, and 1121, AmEmbassy, Santo Domingo, to Secretary of State, 27 April 1965, in NSC History; Kelso, "Dominican Crisis," 78—79; and Dare, "Dominican Diary," 41.

15. On the issue of mediation, Bennett told the author, "Mediation is a very precise thing, and once you mediate, you take on yourself the responsibility for the settlement. Those were not my instructions, so I said I had no instructions to mediate." Bennett interview. See also Kelso, "Dominican Crisis," 82, 106 n. 54.

16. Telegram no. 1128, AmEmbassy, Santo Domingo, to Secretary of State, 27 April 1965, in NSC History; Lowenthal, *Dominican Intervention*, 90; and Johnson, *Vantage Point*, 193.

17. Lowenthal, *Dominican Intervention*, 94—96. Telegram no. 1125, AmEmbassy, Santo Domingo, to Secretary of State, 27 April 1965; and Telegram no. 653, Department of State to AmEmbassy, Santo Domingo, 27 April 1965; both in NSC History. Entry for 1015, 28 April 1965, "Chronology"; and Schoonmaker, "U.S. Military Forces," 37.

18. Center for Strategic Studies, *Dominican Action*, 29, 31; Lowenthal, *Dominican Intervention*, 96—98; and Schoonmaker, "U.S. Military Forces," 48.

19. Bennett apparently reported to Washington that the Palace was seized not by General Montas but by General Antonio Imbert Barreras acting independently with his own group of armed men. Entry for 1015, 28 April 1965, in "Chronology."

20. Kelso, "Dominican Crisis," 75.

21. Telegram no. 1136, AmEmbassy, Santo Domingo, to Secretary of State, 28 April 1965, in

NSC History; Lowenthal, *Dominican Intervention*, 98; and Center for Strategic Studies, *Dominican Action*, 31—32.

22. Telegram no. 1143, AmEmbassy, Santo Domingo, to Secretary of State, 28 April 1965, in *Crises*, reel no. 5.

23. Telegram no. 1144, AmEmbassy, Santo Domingo, to Secretary of State, 28 April 1965, in *Crisis*, reel no. 5; Tad Szulc, *Dominican Diary* (New York: Delacorte Press, 1965), 41—42; and Telegram nos. 1146 and 1147, AmEmbassy, Santo Domingo, to Secretary of State, 28 April 1965, in NSC History.

24. Lowenthal, *Dominican Intervention*, 100; and Telegram no. 1149, AmEmbassy, Santo Domingo, to Secretary of State, 28 April 1965, in NSC History.

25. Lowenthal, *Dominican Intervention*, 101; and Kelso, "Dominican Crisis," 88—90.

26. Telegrams, CRITIC FOUR and CRITIC FIVE, AmEmbassy, Santo Domingo, to DIRNSA, 28 April 1965, both in NSC History.

27. Lowenthal, *Dominican Intervention*, 103—4; Johnson, *Vantage Point*, 195; and Telegram CINCLANTFLT to COMCARIBSEAFRON and to CTG 44.9, 2146Z 28 April 1965, in NSC History. Apparently, Mann informed Wheeler of the president's decision to send in marines, while McNamara followed up by authorizing the JCS chairman to issue the necessary "execute orders." See Kelso, "Dominican Crisis," 79—80.

28. Lowenthal, *Dominican Intervention*, 102, 105; and U.S. Department of State, "The Dominican Republic," in State Department Administrative History, 1965, LBJL.

29. Telegram, CRITIC SIX, AmEmbassy, Santo Domingo, to DIRNSA, 28 April 1965, in NSC History; and Center for Strategic Studies, *Dominican Action*, 40. A cable containing Benoit's addendum did not arrive at the State Department until 0120 on the 29th. Telegram no. 1163, AmEmbassy, Santo Domingo, to Secretary of State, 29 April 1965, in NSC History.

30. On the communication and coordination problems that arose during the landing of the first wave of marines on the 28th, see Ringler and Shaw, *Marine Corps Operations*, 24—25; Dare, "Dominican Diary," 42; and "Military Operations in the Dominican Republic," no date, teleconference between the Department of State and American Embassy, Santo Domingo, 28 April 1965, hereafter cited as Teleconference, 28 April 1965; Telegram, CRITIC SIX; and Telegram nos. 1155 and 1156, AmEmbassy, Santo Domingo, to Secretary of State, 28 April 1965, all in NSC History.

31. Dare, "Dominican Diary," 42; Ringler and Shaw, *Marine Corps Operations*, 25—26; and Teleconference, 28 April 1965.

32. "Alerting, Movement, and Execution Orders Directed by JCS" and Daily Report, 28 April 1965, both in NSC History; and *New York Times*, 29 April 1965:1, 14.

33. Szulc, *Dominican Diary*, 56—59.

Chapter 4

1. Telegram no. 1155; and Kelso, "Dominican Crisis," 117.

2. "Alerting, Movement, and Execution Orders," in NSC History; John W. Ault, "Dominican Republic Crisis: Causes, Intervention, Lessons Learned" (Research paper, Air Command and Staff College, Air University, Maxwell Air Force Base, Alabama, 1970), 30; Palmer, "XVIII Airborne Corps," 16; U.S.F.D.R., "Stability Operations," pt. 1, vol. I, chap. 4, 1, and vol. II, IV-A-1. For a more detailed discussion of the force structure of pentomic and ROAD divisions and the transition from one to the other, see Robert A. Doughty, *The Evolution of US Army Tactical Doctrine, 1946—76*, Leavenworth Papers no. 1 (Fort

Leavenworth, KS: Combat Studies Institute, U.S. Army Command and General Staff College, 1979), 17—23.

3. Ringler and Shaw, *Marine Corps Operations*, 15—18; U.S.F.D.R., "Stability Operations," pt. 1, vol. II, III-B-1; Colonel John J. Costa, U.S. Army, telephone interview with author, 12 February 1988; and Lieutenant Colonel Earl E. Bechtold, U.S. Army, interview with author, Fort Leavenworth, Kansas, 29 October 1987. The Tactical Air Command's unclassified report on the Dominican intervention refers to the benefits of Quick Kick VII but, unlike the Army and Marine histories, argues that the "cons" of the exercise outweighed the "pros" in that forces were still being reconstituted and consumables replaced when the crisis in Santo Domingo began. U.S. Department of the Air Force, *The Tactical Air Command in the Dominican Crisis, 1965* (Langley Air Force Base, VA: Office of TAC History, May 1977), 9—10.

4. Robert P. Haffa, Jr., *The Half War: Planning U.S. Rapid Deployment Forces to Meet a Limited Contingency, 1960—1983*, Westview Replica ed. (Boulder, CO: Westview Press, 1984), 94.

5. U.S.F.D.R., "Stability Operations," pt. 1, vol. II, IV-A-1; David W. Gray, *The U.S. Intervention in Lebanon, 1958: A Commander's Reminiscence* (Fort Leavenworth, KS: Combat Studies Institute, U.S. Army Command and General Staff College, August 1984), 43; and Greenberg, *Dominican Republic Intervention*, 36—37.

6. "U.S. Strike Command," *Army Information Digest* 17 (May 1962):19—23; "USARSTRIKE: Ready to Go," *Army Information Digest* 20 (October 1965):12—15; and General Paul D. Adams, U.S. Army, Oral history, 33—34, USAMHI. The Navy had opposed the creation of STRICOM from its conception in 1961, one reason, perhaps, why CINCLANT sought to bypass the unified command during the Dominican crisis. As a further hindrance to cooperation, there were officers in STRICOM who believed that the Caribbean should become their area of operational responsibility, not LANTCOM's. After the crisis, Adams and CINCLANT Admiral Thomas Moorer attempted to work out their joint operational problems. A tentative agreement was reached but, according to Adams, was scuttled by Moorer's superiors. Adams, Oral history, 40—42; and Haffa, *Half War*, 136 n. 77.

7. Schoonmaker, "U.S. Military Forces," 86, 96 n. 39; U.S.F.D.R., "Stability Operations," pt. 1, vol. II, III-B-1; and Ringler and Shaw, *Marine Corps Operations*, 30.

8. U.S.F.D.R., "Stability Operations," pt. 1, vol. II, III-A-1, E-15; J. D. Yates, "The Dominican Crisis," Mitre Working Paper (Bedford, MA: Mitre Corporation, 1973), 14; U.S. Air Force, 464th Troop Carrier Wing, "History of the 464th Troop Carrier Wing, Pope Air Force Base, North Carolina, January 1965—June 1965" (N.p., 1965), Narrative, vol. 1, 36 (this document is available at the Albert F. Simpson Historical Research Center, Maxwell Air Force Base, Alabama); U.S. Department of the Air Force, "Case Studies of Airpower: The Dominican Republic Crisis of 1965," Aerospace Studies Institute Project no. AU-434-66-ASI (Maxwell Air Force Base, AL: Air University, 1966), 13; and Lieutenant General Eugene Forrester, U.S. Army, ret., interview with author, Washington, DC, 11 November 1986.

9. Planning for the deployment of the designated Army and Air Force units was accomplished at Fort Bragg and Pope Air Force Base by staff officers from the XVIII Airborne Corps, the 82d Airborne Division, the Nineteenth Air Force, and the 464th Troop Carrier Wing. As noted in the text, CINCSTRIKE also sent staff officers to assist in the planning. Because the text does not provide a detailed account of the planning activities of these officers, readers might wish to consult Schoonmaker, "U.S. Military Forces," passim; U.S.F.D.R., "Stability Operations," pt. 1, vol. II, secs. III and IV; USAF, "History of the 464th," 35—36; USAF, "Case Studies of Airpower," 9—12, 17—19; USAF, 9th Air Force, Airlift Task Force Tactical Operations, "Final Report on Power Pack" (Shaw Air Force Base, SC, 24 May 1965), copy at the Simpson Research Center, Maxwell Air Force Base, Alabama; and USAF, *TAC in the Dominican Crisis*, 3—8.

10. On the disruptive effects of Blue Chip V, see U.S.F.D.R., "Stability Operations," pt. 1, vol. II, III-B-2 to III-B-4, IV-A-7 to IV-A-8; USAF, *TAC in the Dominican Crisis*, 10—11;

Major General William E. Klein, U.S. Army, interview with author, MacDill Air Force Base, Florida, 4 November 1986; and Forrester interview.

11. See references in note 9. Also see the Klein interview.

12. U.S.F.D.R., "Stability Operations," pt. 1, vol. II, IV-A-2; and USAF, *TAC in the Dominican Crisis*, 5, 8.

13. Intelligence problems during this early phase are discussed in U.S.F.D.R., "Stability Operations," pt. 1, vol. II, I-3, II-3, III-C-1, IV-A-5, VI-3 to VI-4, and pt. 1, vol. I, C-19, C-20, D-1. Yates, "Dominican Crisis," 14; Schoonmaker, "U.S. Military Forces," 91; and Lieutenant Colonel Steven Butler, U.S. Army, interview with author, Fort Leavenworth, Kansas, 21 March 1986.

14. U.S.F.D.R., "Stability Operations," pt. 1, vol. II, III-A-2; Colonel Eldredge R. Long, U.S. Army, ret., interview with author, Washington, DC, 5 November 1985; and Greenberg, *Dominican Republic Intervention*, 37.

15. Ringler and Shaw, *Marine Corps Operations*, 27, 97—98. Telegram, CTG 44.9 to CINCLANTFLT, 0152Z 29 April 1965; and Telegram no. 1167, AmEmbassy, Santo Domingo, to Secretary of State, 29 April 1965; both in NSC History.

16. Kelso, "Dominican Crisis," 113—16. Telegram nos. 1160 and 1161, AmEmbassy, Santo Domingo, to Secretary of State, 28 April 1965; Telegram nos. 1173 and 1178, AmEmbassy, Santo Domingo, to Secretary of State, 29 April 1965; all in NSC History. Dare, "Dominican Diary," 45; and Center for Strategic Studies, *Dominican Action*, 42.

17. Lowenthal, *Dominican Intervention*, 107, 110—11; and Schoonmaker, "U.S. Military Forces," 70 n. 47.

18. Telegram, CRITIC SEVEN, AmEmbassy, Santo Domingo, to DIRNSA, 29 April 1965; and Telegram no. 1137, AmEmbassy, Santo Domingo, to Secretary of State, 29 April 1965; both in NSC History.

19. Telegram no. 1137; and Kelso, "Dominican Crisis," 126—27.

20. Dare, "Dominican Diary," 44—45; and Ringler and Shaw, *Marine Corps Operations*, 27—28.

21. At 1514 EDT, the JCS ordered the initial assault force of the 82d to proceed to Ramey Air Force Base. At 1630 EDT, CINCLANT relayed the order verbally to TAC and CONARC. The sources do not agree as to exactly when the first C-130s left Pope Air Force Base. Schoonmaker, "U.S. Military Forces," 99, puts the time at 1900 EDT; Ringler and Shaw, *Marine Corps Operations*, 99, and previously cited Air Force histories put it at 1911 EDT; while the 82d Airborne's report in U.S.F.D.R., "Stability Operations," pt. 1, vol. II, IV-B-1, places it one and one-half hours later, at 2054 EDT.

22. Even though the departure of the first (and subsequent) echelons of Power Pack from Pope AFB suffered delays for a variety of reasons, troops, once they were marshaled by the aircraft, could not always use the additional time to their advantage. Thus, among the first-echelon troops, several departed Pope with A bags but not B bags. (The A bags contained minimal essential clothing, while the B bags contained additional clothing and articles.) For security reasons, troops were not able to use the extra time caused by delays to notify family members of the 82d's imminent departure. This resulted in numerous problems, ranging from inconvenience to desperation. Paratroopers had no time to give their wives paychecks, PX and commissary cards, car keys, or even to notify spouses and next of kin that the 82d was being deployed overseas. Consequently, many families who were left behind at Fort Bragg had no money for food or rent and no readily available transportation. To ease the plight of these families, wives and friends not afflicted by such problems pooled resources and offered assistance. Uncoordinated efforts soon acquired organizational status and became the forerunner of the Army Community Services. Bechtold interview; and Mrs. Hugh Cunningham, telephone interview with author, 29 March 1985. (Mrs. Cunningham's husband was, in 1965, the 82d's chief of staff.)

23. Greenberg, *Dominican Republic Intervention*, 37–38.

24. Ibid.; and Tomkins, "Ubique," 36.

25. On the decision to airland at San Isidro and the condition of the area proposed for an airdrop, see U.S.F.D.R., "Stability Operations," pt. 1, vol. II, IV-B-1 and IV-B-2; and Forrester and Klein interviews.

26. Greenberg, *Dominican Republic Intervention*, 39.

27. Schoonmaker, "U.S. Military Forces," 101; and U.S.F.D.R., "Stability Operations," pt. 1, vol. II, II-5.

28. U.S.F.D.R., "Stability Operations," pt. 1, vol. II, IV-B-3 to IV-B-4; Schoonmaker, "U.S. Military Forces," 101–2; and Colonel Orlando Rodríguez Alvarez, U.S. Army, interview with author, MacDill Air Force Base, Florida, 5 November 1986.

Chapter 5

1. Bowman, "U.S. Army Doctrine for Counterinsurgency Warfare," 129–30; and General Harold K. Johnson, U.S. Army, "Landpower Missions Unlimited," *Army* 15 (November 1964):41.

2. Lieutenant General Bruce Palmer, Jr., "Lessons to Be Learned from the Dominican Republic," Speech given 26 October 1966, Bruce Palmer, Jr., Papers, USAMHI.

3. General Bruce Palmer, Jr., interview with Senior Officer Debriefing Program, USAMHI, 161, hereafter cited as Palmer MHI interview.

4. It is misleading to depict the conflict between military tradition and political control of military operations simply in terms of military officers versus civilian policymakers. The Dominican case study itself offers a more complex pattern in which personalities and perspectives more than careers often determined which side one took on a particular issue. U.S. diplomats in Santo Domingo, for example, often sided with military officers who desired a freer hand in confronting the rebels militarily, while among U.S. officers there was no unanimity on this question, as demonstrated by the differences of opinion that emerged between Palmer and York.

5. By 30 April, the administration was beginning to prepare the American people for an announcement proclaiming the anti-Communist motive behind the intervention. On that date, President Johnson issued a statement in which he revealed that "there are signs that people trained outside the Dominican Republic are seeking to gain control.... The United States,... will never depart from its commitment to the preservation of the right of all of the free people of this hemisphere to choose their own course without falling prey to international conspiracy from any quarter." "Statement by President Johnson, April 30," *Department of State Bulletin*, 17 May 1965:742–43.

6. Telegram no. 1187, AmEmbassy, Santo Domingo, to Secretary of State, 29 April 1965; Telegram, JCS to CINCLANT, 0056Z 30 April 1965; Telegram no. 1196, AmEmbassy, Santo Domingo, to Secretary of State, 30 April 1965; Telegram no. 693, State Department to AmEmbassy, Santo Domingo, 30 April 1965; all in NSC History. Various entries in "Chronology"; and Johnson, *Vantage Point*, 200–201.

7. Telegram nos. 1196 and 693; and Telegram, JCS to CJTF 122, 0527Z 30 April 1965; all in NSC History.

8. Telegram nos. 675 and 689, State Department to AmEmbassy, Santo Domingo, 29 April 1965, both in NSC History; and Slater, "Dominican Republic," 311.

9. U.S.F.D.R., "Stability Operations," pt. 1, vol. II, II-5 to II-7, IV-C-2 to IV-C-3.

10. Ibid., II-5 to II-7, IV-B-3, IV-C-2 to IV-C-3. Telegram, CJTF 122 to CINCLANT [for JCS], 0608Z 30 April 1965; and Telegram, CJTF 122 to CINCLANT, 1440Z 30 April 1965; both in NSC History. Ringler and Shaw, *Marine Corps Operations*, 32.

11. Telegram no. 675; Johnson, *Vantage Point*, 200; Martin, *Overtaken by Events*, 661—62; and Lowenthal, *Dominican Intervention*, 115—16.

12. Lowenthal, *Dominican Intervention*, 115—17; and Martin, *Overtaken by Events*, 660—62.

13. Telegram no. 695 [sanitized], State Department to AmEmbassy, Santo Domingo, 30 April 1965, in NSC History; and Lowenthal, *Dominican Intervention*, 118.

14. Telegram, CJTF 1122 to CINCLANT [for JCS], 0608Z 30 April 1965; and Ringler and Shaw, *Marine Corps Operations*, 100.

15. Telegram no. 1208, AmEmbassy, Santo Domingo, to Secretary of State, 30 April 1965, in NSC History; U.S.F.D.R., "Stability Operations," pt. 1, vol. II, II-7, IV-B-6; and Ringler and Shaw, *Marine Corps Operations*, 33.

16. The account of the 82d's operations on 30 April is based on U.S.F.D.R., "Stability Operations," pt. 1, vol. II, IV-B-4 to IV-B-10; Robert F. Barry, ed., *POWER-PACK* (Portsmouth, VA: Messenger Printing Co., 1965), 21, 24, 29, 34; Lieutenant Colonel Eldredge R. Long, U.S. Army, "The Dominican Crisis 1965: An Experiment in International Peace Keeping" (Thesis, School of Naval Warfare, U.S. Naval College, Newport, Rhode Island, 1967), 39—40; Long interview; and Schoonmaker, "U.S. Military Forces," 123. On the question of the withdrawal of Loyalist forces to San Isidro, at least one study by a battalion commander indicates that the action was taken by agreement between Loyalist and U.S. officers on the spot, perhaps unaware that York and Masterson had other plans for those troops. Lieutenant Colonel Elbert E. Legg, U.S. Army, "The US Military Role in Coping with a Sudden Revolt in the Dominican Republic" (Course essay, U.S. Army War College, Carlisle Barracks, Pennsylvania, 1968), 6.

17. Szulc, *Dominican Diary*, 78.

18. Except where otherwise noted, the account of Marine operations on 30 April is taken from Ringler and Shaw, *Marine Corps Operations*, 33—36.

19. Szulc, *Dominican Diary*, 79—80.

20. The 82d's report on the cease-fire meeting implies that York merely *witnessed* the signing of the document; Bennett's report to State indicates that York *signed* the document. The difference in these two positions would become a matter of some significance the next day. U.S.F.D.R., "Stability Operations," pt. 1, vol. II, IV-B-9; and Telegram no. 1217, AmEmbassy, Santo Domingo, to Secretary of State, 30 April 1965, in NSC History.

21. Telegram no. 1217; Martin, *Overtaken by Events*, 662—64; and Lowenthal, *Dominican Intervention*, 121—22.

22. Ringler and Shaw, *Marine Corps Operations*, 37, 104.

23. Long, "Dominican Crisis," 40—41.

24. U.S.F.D.R., "Stability Operations," pt. 1, vol. II, IV-B-10; Telegram no. 1217; Slater, "Dominican Republic," 311; and Lowenthal, *Dominican Intervention*, 121.

25. Martin, *Overtaken by Events*, 668—71; Tompkins, "Ubique," 38; and Ringler and Shaw, *Marine Corps Operations*, 48.

26. Lowenthal, *Dominican Intervention*, 116; General Bruce Palmer, Jr., U.S. Army ret., interview with author, Washington, DC, 4 November 1985; U.S.F.D.R., "Stability Operations," pt. 1, vol. I, chap. 2, 2; Palmer MHI interview, 152, 154—55, 160; and General Bruce Palmer, Jr., U.S. Army ret., to Dr. Roger Spiller, 15 November 1983, attached to letter of 16 November 1983, copies in author's possession with General Palmer's permission

to cite. In his letter to Spiller, Palmer alleges that Wheeler told him that "once the situation was stabilized in the Dominican Republic, he intended to have the commander there report directly to Washington and to place CINCLANT in a supporting role. This was never carried out because of the strenuous objections of the Navy and Marines, as well as Moorer, and so CINCLANT remained nominally in the chain of command for the duration. The Secretary of Defense, however, directed that communications from my headquarters in Santo Domingo be transmitted for information to Washington at the same time they were sent to Norfolk." It should also be noted that Wheeler circumvented the chain of command in giving Palmer his instructions directly instead of going through General Harold K. Johnson, the chief of staff of the Army, primarily because Johnson was "in a dentist's chair" and Wheeler needed to talk to Palmer immediately. Palmer, in fact, left for Bragg that afternoon without having time to tell his wife he was leaving.

27. Palmer MHI interview, 156—57, 165, 170—71; and Klein and Forrester interviews.

28. Palmer MHI interview, 165—67; U.S.F.D.R., "Stability Operations," pt. 1, vol. I, chap. 2, 7, 9; and Lowenthal, *Dominican Intervention*, 209 n. 8.

29. Telegram, COMLAN [Palmer] to JCS, 0720Z 1 May 1965; Telegram no. 1234, AmEmbassy, Santo Domingo, to Secretary of State, 1 May 1965; "Alerting, Movement, and Execution Orders"; and entries for 1 May 1965 in "Chronology"; all in NSC History. U.S.F.D.R., "Stability Operations," pt. 1, vol. I, chap. 2, 7, 9; Lowenthal, *Dominican Intervention*, 124—25; and Palmer, "XVIII Airborne Corps," 14.

30. U.S.F.D.R., "Stability Operations," pt. 1, vol. II, IV-C-1 to IV-C-2; Ringler and Shaw, *Marine Corps Operations*, 37; Barry, ed., *POWER-PACK*, 24; Rodríguez Alvarez and Long interviews; and Lowenthal, *Dominican Intervention*, 127.

31. Telegram no. 718, State Department to AmEmbassy, Santo Domingo, 1 May 1965; and Telegram nos. 1242, 1243, 1245, and 1249, AmEmbassy, Santo Domingo, to Secretary of State, 1 May 1965; all in NSC History.

32. "Alerting, Movement, and Execution Orders"; Telegrams, CINCAFLANT Command Post to CINCLANT, 0929Z 30 April 1965; CINCLANT to CINCSTRIKE, 1252Z 30 April 1965; and JCS to CINCLANT, 1310Z, 1559Z, 1602Z, 1628Z, and 1804Z 30 April 1965; all in NSC History.

33. Telegram, JCS to CINCLANT, 0026Z 1 May 1965, NSC History. U.S.F.D.R., "Stability Operations," pt. 1, vol. I, enclosure 2 to chap. 4, 12; chap. 4, 4; and vol. II, II-19 to II-20.

34. Telegram, COMLAN to JCS, 0720Z 1 May 1965, NSC History. U.S.F.D.R., "Stability Operations," pt. 1, vol. I, chap. 4, 12, 14, and vol. II, IV-A-12. On the early insertion of medical units into the airlift, the 82d Airborne's report covering this development reads as follows: ". . . higher headquarters ordered major elements of the 15th Field Hospital and two ambulance platoons flown into the objective area early in the operation. Given the fact that early divisional build up included 2 clearing companies and 56 front line ambulances, the strategic air evacuation capability and the very short evacuation routes involved, it appears that the 400 bed capacity and the 24 panel ambulances were most wasteful of airlift. To compound the inefficiency, the Air Force flew in additional panel ambulances to discharge its responsibility for movement of patient to aircraft. Further, an Army helicopter evacuation platoon(-) was deployed although there was no real requirement for this unit. In fact, early in the operation it was decided that helicopter evacuation would not be used in view of the short distances and the paucity of landing areas in the city. The Marines already had adequate helicopters in the area to handle their evacuation needs." U.S.F.D.R., "Stability Operations," vol. II, II-23.

35. Entry for 1 May 1965, "Chronology"; Major Lawrence M. Greenberg, U.S. Army, "The Army in Support of Political Initiatives: The 1965 Dominican Republic Intervention" (Paper presented at the Missouri Valley History Conference, Omaha, Nebraska, March 1987), 7—8; and Lowenthal, *Dominican Intervention*, 120—25.

36. Lowenthal, *Dominican Intervention*, 127—28.

37. Ibid., 128—29; Telegram, CJTF 122 to CINCLANT, JCS, 0418Z 2 May 1965, in NSC History; entries for 1 and 2 May 1965 in "Chronology"; and entry for 0432 2 May 1965, in *Daily Diary*, reel no. 4.

38. Telegram, JCS to CINCLANT, 2340Z 1 May 1965; and Telegram, CJTF 122 to JCS, 0714Z 2 May 1965; both in NSC History. U.S.F.D.R., "Stability Operations," pt. 1, vol. I, chap. 2, 9—10.

39. Telegram nos. 1267, 1283, and 1284, AmEmbassy, Santo Domingo, to Secretary of State, 2 May 1965; Telegrams, CJTF 122 to JCS, 0714Z and 0818Z 2 May 1965; all in NSC History. Martin, *Overtaken by Events*, 676.

40. Entries for 2 May 1965 in "Chronology"; and "Statement by President Johnson, May 2," *Department of State Bulletin*, 17 May 1965:744—48.

41. Palmer MHI interview, 171; Telegram no. 742; and U.S.F.D.R., "Stability Operations," pt. 1, vol. I, chap. 2, 9. The reasons for leaving Radio Santo Domingo outside the U.S. corridor are not clear. Lowenthal argues that the troops sent to establish the LOC took a wrong turn south before they came to the station. Lowenthal, *Dominican Intervention*, 131. Palmer has argued that the ESSO map used to plan the route simply failed to show the station and that those who knew about it failed to bring it up in a conversation concerned primarily with finding the safest route. Palmer interview.

42. Ringler and Shaw, *Marine Corps Operations*, 38.

43. U.S.F.D.R., "Stability Operations," pt. 1, vol. I, chap. 2, 9—10, and vol. II, IV-D-1, IV-E-4; Lieutenant General Bruce Palmer, Jr., U.S. Army, "The Army in the Dominican Republic," *Army* 15 (November 1965):44; and Brigadier General James R. Ellis, U.S. Army, interview with author, Fort Leavenworth, Kansas, 7 July 1987.

44. Palmer, "Dominican Republic," 44.

45. Ellis interview.

46. U.S.F.D.R., "Stability Operations," pt. 1, vol. I, chap. 2, 8—9; chap. 4, 15; and vol. II, II-16.

Chapter 6

1. Telegram, JCS to CINCLANT, 2205Z 1 May 1965, in NSC History; and USAF, "Case Studies of Airpower," 9—10, 18—20, 27—29.

2. USAF, *TAC in the Dominican Crisis*, 20.

3. U.S.F.D.R., "Stability Operations," pt. 1, vol. I, chap. 4, 13, and vol. II, II-19 to II-24, II-26. Entries for 30 April and 1 May 1965, in "Alerting, Movement, and Execution Orders."

4. Costa interview. U.S.F.D.R., "Stability Operations," pt. 1, vol. I, chap. 2, 19; chap. 3, 7; chap. 4, 5, 12—13; and vol. II, II-22, IV-C-4. York was also critical of the number of headquarters that became involved in the airlift by issuing oral and written messages, many of which contradicted one another or were ambiguous and confusing. His recommended solution was to establish direct communications between the ground commander and the Department of Defense or Department of the Army and to prohibit all intermediate headquarters from interpreting guidance between the top and the bottom. Ibid., vol. II, II-20. The Air Force had its own complaints about the airlift, beginning with the enormous problems created by last-minute changes to mission requirements that did not allow enough time for changing plans and disseminating procedural instructions to operating elements. Furthermore, the decision to send the 82d to the Dominican Republic overwhelmed the control and support capabilities at the crowded and ill-lit Pope Air Force

Base, an installation usually limited to the support of only one Troop Carrier Wing (twenty-nine C-130s). One Air Force study criticized the Army units for aggravating the overcrowded situation at Pope by delivering massive amounts of equipment, often incompletely configured and out of proper load sequence, to the runway aprons. The large numbers of aircraft returning from San Isidro in clusters also added to the problems at Pope. USAF, "Case Studies of Airpower," 35—39, 41.

5. U.S.F.D.R., "Stability Operations," pt. 1, vol. I, chap. 4, 13—14, and vol. II, II-21 and II-27; and Long interview.

6. In some cases, elements of the 82d relieved Marine units on a temporary basis, pending arrival of the IAPF. For further discussion of the IAPF, see chapter 8.

7. U.S.F.D.R., "Stability Operations," pt. 1, vol. II, IV-E-1 to IV-E-2.

8. Szulc, *Dominican Diary*, 113, 124. My interviews with several U.S. soldiers who served in the Dominican intervention confirm these feelings toward the rebels.

9. Barry, ed., *POWER-PACK*, 34; U.S.F.D.R., "Stability Operations," pt. 1, vol. I, chap. 3, 2—3, 9, and vol. II, II-6, VI-4 to VI-9; and MI officer, interview with author.

10. MI officer interview; Sanford J. Unger, *FBI* (Boston, MA: Little, Brown and Co., 1976), 241; and Phillips, *Night Watch*, 150, 155—56, 160. Phillips recounts how the chief of the FBI team, a close friend, confided to him that his agents lacked experience in gathering political intelligence, whereupon the two men worked out a plan to coordinate their efforts, even though in some ways this violated the rules prohibiting one federal agency from identifying its informants to another. Phillips, *Night Watch*, 160.

11. U.S.F.D.R., "Stability Operations," pt. 1, vol. I, chap. 3, 2—4, 6, and vol. II, VI-7, VI-9; and Butler interview.

12. U.S.F.D.R., "Stability Operations," pt. 1, vol. I, chap. 3, 3—4, and vol. II, VI-7, IX-1; and MI officer interview.

13. MI officer interviews. While many U.S. troops in the Dominican Republic harbored personal doubts about the wisdom or morality of backing the Loyalists, most who entertained such doubts refused to dwell on the matter. Their view was that they were professional soldiers who had a job to do and that the moral issue was hardly so clear as to require them to challenge U.S. policy. Only a few soldiers became so disenchanted (or enamored of local conditions) as to "go native."

14. U.S.F.D.R., "Stability Operations," pt. 1, vol. I, chap. 3, 7, and previously cited interviews of U.S. officers, e.g., Palmer, Long, Butler. The impact of the shortages in Spanish-speaking intelligence personnel, civilian clothing, and an in-country capability to produce false documentation are discussed in U.S.F.D.R., "Stability Operations," pt. 2, chap. 2, enclosure 1, "Clandestine Collection Effort," 1—3, 6. The report, for example, states that the failure "to deploy personnel with adequate civilian clothing and documentation to support its wear has severely restricted contacts with agents and unnecessarily exposed agents to possible hostile surveillance where knowledge that source is even contacting U.S. Army personnel could jeopardize both the agent's success and his personal safety."

The CIA, of course, had been running its own agents and informants for some time. As to the delicacy of such operations, Phillips gives an account of how a classified report from the CIA to the Voice of America was inadvertently read over the air, the result being that a CIA deep-cover agent was on the verge of being compromised. Only a middle-of-the-night phone call to Carl Rowen, director of the U.S. Information Agency, made it possible to counteract the blunder and save the agent's credibility, not to mention his life. Phillips, *Night Watch*, 150—51, 58.

15. Barry, ed., *POWER-PACK*, 78; USAF, "Case Studies of Airpower," 29—31; and U.S.F.D.R., "Stability Operations," pt. 1, vol. I, chap. 3, 5—6, and vol. II, VI-10 to VI-11.

16. After the contending parties reached a tentative political settlement in September, the intelligence mission changed to one of collecting "little other than purely political information, or information with definite political overtones." U.S.F.D.R., "Stability Operations," pt. 2, chap. 2, enclosure 1, 1.

17. Ibid., pt. 1, vol. I, chap. 3, 3, and vol. II, VI-9; and Butler interview.

18. Phillips, *Night Watch*, 148—50.

19. Telegram JCS to CINCLANT, 2010Z 1 May 1965; and Telegram nos. 1265 and 1284, AmEmbassy, Santo Domingo, to Secretary of State, 2 May 1965; all in NSC History.

20. U.S.F.D.R., "Stability Operations," pt. 1, vol. I, chap. 3, 3. The most detailed, unclassified account of the Green Chopper operation is contained in pt. 1, volume III, of "Stability Operations," which is devoted exclusively to Special Forces operations. Annex D to this volume pertains to highly classified Special Forces operations and has been removed from the report. Palmer's report places the number of towns visited under Green Chopper at thirty-four; the Special Forces report says that the Green Berets visited forty-one towns but does not indicate if this number includes the seven visited prior to their assuming the mission. That the cover stories broke down is reported in U.S.F.D.R., "Stability Operations," pt. 2, chap. 7, enclosure 2.

21. This account of the command and control problems that plagued Palmer during his first week in the Dominican Republic is based on Roger Spiller to General Wallace Nutting, Memorandum, 30 September 1983, in author's possession; Palmer to Spiller, 16 November 1983; Palmer MHI interview, 158—60, 169—70; General Bruce Palmer, Jr., interview with Captain Richard S. Switzer, U.S. Air Force, 20 August 1974, 21, in Richard Switzer Collection, Hoover Institution Archives, Stanford, California; U.S.F.D.R., "Stability Operations," pt. 1, vol. I, chap. 2, 7—8, and chap. 4, 7—8; U.S. Army, Chief of Staff, *Challenge: Compendium of Army Accomplishment—A Report by the Chief of Staff* (Washington, DC: Department of the Army, July 1964—April 1968), 39—40, copy located in Archives, USAMHI.

    Tactical communications also were substandard during the early phase of the intervention. Several 82d units had PRC-10 radios, which as one participant put it, "couldn't communicate across the street." The arrival of PRC-25 radios provided much better tactical communication. Bechtold interview.

22. For a more thorough discussion of political developments from 4 May to 7 May, see various entries in "Chronology"; and Martin, *Overtaken by Events*, 680—84.

23. Various entries, 4—14 May 1965, in "Chronology." Telegram no. 1576, AmEmbassy, Santo Domingo, to Secretary of State, 10 May 1965; Telegram nos. 1626 and 1644, AmEmbassy, Santo Domingo, to Secretary of State, 12 May 1965; all in NSC History. Martin, *Overtaken by Events*, 685—94.

24. Telegram no. 1690, AmEmbassy, Santo Domingo, to Secretary of State, 14 May 1965; and Telegram no. 1644; both in NSC History.

25. Telegram no. 1561, AmEmbassy, Santo Domingo, to Secretary of State, 10 May 1965; Telegram nos. 1644 and 1656, AmEmbassy, Santo Domingo, to Secretary of State, 12 May 1965; and Telegram, USCOMDOMREP to CINCLANT, 0645Z 13 May 1965; all in NSC History.

26. Telegram no. 1682, AmEmbassy, Santo Domingo, to Secretary of State, 13 May 1965; and Telegram no. 1697, AmEmbassy, Santo Domingo, to Secretary of State, 14 May 1965; both in NSC History.

27. Slater, "Dominican Republic," 322; and U.S.F.D.R., "Stability Operations," pt. 1, vol. I, chap. 2, 4, 19.

28. Slater, "Dominican Republic," 322—23; Martin, *Overtaken by Events*, 694; Szulc, *Dominican Diary*, 218, 228—30, 235, 244, 254—55; U.S.F.D.R., "Stability Operations," pt. 1, vol. I, chap. 2, 14; and Palmer and Long interviews. On an evening newscast, CBS showed footage of what was purportedly truckloads of GNR troops crossing the LOC during the northern offensive. Upon close examination of the report, however, it became apparent from changes in the height of stacked sandbags passed by the trucks that the footage had been spliced from pictures taken of national police crossing the LOC over a period of days prior to the offensive. A senior CBS correspondent in the Dominican Republic later offered a personal apology to Palmer for what the correspondent admitted was deplorable journalism on the part of CBS executives who handled the footage in New York. Palmer and Long interviews.

29. Martin, *Overtaken by Events*, 694; Szulc, *Dominican Diary*, 228, 242; Slater, "Dominican Republic," 323; and U.S.F.D.R., "Stability Operations," pt. 1, vol. I, chap. 2, 15.

30. Slater, "Dominican Republic," 323—24; and U.S.F.D.R., "Stability Operations," pt. 1, vol. I, chap. 2, 14, and vol. II, XIII-B-2.

31. U.S.F.D.R., "Stability Operations," pt. 1, vol. I, chap. 2, 13—14.

Chapter 7

1. The author is indebted to Professor Richard Millett for providing copies of various fact sheets distributed to U.S. troops entering the Dominican Republic.

2. Schoonmaker, "U.S. Military Forces," 91—92. The best published account of the lessons learned from urban combat in the Dominican Republic is Major William E. Klein, U.S. Army, "Stability Operations in Santo Domingo," *Infantry* 56 (May—June 1966):35—39.

3. Sergeant Kenneth White, U.S. Army, ret., interviews with the author, Fort Leavenworth, Kansas, 14 and 16 May 1985.

4. Barry, ed., *POWER-PACK*, passim; Klein, "Santo Domingo," passim; and Long and White interviews.

5. Long interview.

6. Klein, "Santo Domingo," 38; Colonel Stephen Silvasy, U.S. Army, interview with author, Fort Bragg, North Carolina, 29 March 1985; Peter T. Chew, "On a Lonely Point," *Army* 15 (June 1965):94; U.S.F.D.R., "Stability Operations," pt. 1, vol. III, C-6-1 to C-6-3; and Telegram, CJTF 122 to CINCLANT, 0245Z 6 May 1965, in NSC History. One day before the ship *Santo Domingo* was sunk, the State Department informed the Embassy that a JCS situation report contained an item about an "unidentified ship tied up at Santo Domingo [that] may have been used to bring in weapons which were distributed to Rebels during *early stages* [of the] revolt." [Italics mine.] State requested that the ship be searched, if need be, by the Dominican Navy. It would be interesting to know if the "unidentified ship" was indeed the *Santo Domingo*. If it were, then it might have been targeted by the 82d unit that sank it—not because paratroopers witnessed it unloading arms but because they had received the report that it *might* have brought weapons to the rebels. Telegram no. 766, State to AmEmbassy, Santo Domingo, 3 May 1965, in NSC History.

7. Klein, "Santo Domingo," 38—39. The author's interviews with several persons who participated in the intervention for the most part confirm the weapon assessment offered in the text.

8. Silvasy interview; Klein, "Santo Domingo," 38; and Colonel Herbert J. Lloyd, U.S. Army, telephone interview with author, 13 July 1987.

9. Klein, "Santo Domingo," 38.

10. White interview.

11. Long and White interviews; and U.S.F.D.R., "Stability Operations," pt. 1, vol. II, IX, and vol. IV, chap. 12, and pt. 2, chap. 1, 47.

12. U.S.F.D.R., "Stability Operations," pt. 1, vol. IV, chap. 12, 5—6; and Barry, ed., *POWER-PACK*, 86.

13. Silvasy and Long interviews; Barry, ed., *POWER-PACK*, 86; and U.S.F.D.R., "Stability Operations," pt. 1, vol. III, 3, and pt. 2, chap. 1, 47.

14. Ellis interview; and U.S.F.D.R., "Stability Operations," pt. 1, vol. III, 3.

15. U.S.F.D.R., "Stability Operations," pt. 1, vol. I, chap. 2, 11, and vol. II, II-24; Long interview; and Phillips, *Night Watch*, 152—53.

16. U.S.F.D.R., "Stability Operations," pt. 1, vol. I, chap. 2, 11—12, 21, vol. II, II-9, and vol. III, 2, C-3-1-1 to C-3-2-1; and Ringler and Shaw, *Marine Corps Operations*, 56. Telegram no. 821, Secretary of State to AmEmbassy, Santo Domingo, 5 May 1965; and Telegram, USCOMDOMREP to CINCLANT, 0645Z 13 May 1965; both in NSC History.

    In a commander's summary covering the period 31 May 1965 to 25 October 1965, Palmer offered his impressions of the role of Special Forces in stability operations. "Special Forces demonstrated their versatility and skill in a clear-cut manner," he began. "They were profitably employed in a great variety of tasks, generally of a covert nature. I am convinced that the unconventional warfare field is their forte and that this is where they can make their most valuable contributions. However, by the very nature of their organization, equipment and operating methods, they cannot perform the hard-core role that combat forces play in stability operations, but rather they are invaluable adjuncts who can perform particularly sensitive and difficult tasks with skill and finesse. It was always reassuring to have this superb asset ready at hand for specially tough missions." U.S.F.D.R., "Stability Operations," pt. 2, chap. 1, 46.

17. U.S.F.D.R., "Stability Operations," pt. 1, vol. III, C-7-4-1.

18. Unless otherwise noted, the discussion of the civic action-civil affairs programs is based on documents provided the author by Major Michael A. Dobry while he was assigned to the civil affairs section of the John F. Kennedy Special Warfare Center, Fort Bragg, North Carolina. The efforts of Major Dobry prevented these documents, mainly situation updates, from being destroyed. Also consulted were Schoonmaker, "U.S. Military Forces," 152—54; Barry, ed., *POWER-PACK*, 38, 65, 74; Klein, "Santo Domingo," 36; Long interview; Ringler and Shaw, *Marine Corps Operations*, 48—49; and U.S.F.D.R., "Stability Operations," pt. 1, vol. I, chap. 2, 3, 13, vol. II, XIII-C-4, and vol. IV, chap. 10.

19. Telegram no. 712, State to AmEmbassy, Santo Domingo, 30 April 1965, in NSC History.

20. Unless otherwise noted, the discussion of psychological warfare operations in the Dominican Republic is based on U.S.F.D.R., "Stability Operations," pt. 1, vol. IV, chap. 11; Lieutenant Colonel Wallace J. Moulis, U.S. Army, and Major Richard M. Brown, U.S. Army, "Key to a Crisis," *Military Review* 46 (February 1966):9—14; and Bert H. Cooper, Jr., "Teamwork in Santo Domingo," in *Military Propaganda: Psychological Warfare and Operations*, edited by Ron D. McLaurin (New York: Praeger, 1982), 282—85.

21. Telegram no. 732, State to AmEmbassy, Santo Domingo, 1 May 1965, in NSC History; and U.S.F.D.R., "Stability Operations," pt. 1, vol. I, chap. 2, 3.

22. Telegram nos. 1301 and 1304, AmEmbassy, Santo Domingo, to Secretary of State, 3 May 1965; and Telegram no. 1286, AmEmbassy, Santo Domingo, to Secretary of State, 2 [4?] May 1965; all in NSC History.

23. U.S.F.D.R., "Stability Operations," pt. 2, chap. 1, 45; and Palmer interview with Switzer.

24. Butler interview.

25. One fact sheet, titled "Your Duty in the Dominican Republic," warned U.S. soldiers arriving in the country that "many Dominican citizens are not pleased by the presence in their country of foreign troops...," although "the farther we come from the early days of violence and bloodshed that marked the revolution, the more reasonable the Dominican people will become in their attitude toward us." To hasten that transformation, the sheet urged "very correct" contacts with the people based on "our American sense of justice and fair play." Soldiers were to be friendly, but not ostentatiously so, when the occasion warranted and were to learn Spanish, or at least enough words "to help bring about a better understanding between the nations of the hemisphere that are represented here." If taunted by "unruly elements," soldiers were to "ignore it." They were also to "keep quiet" when Dominicans engaged in political discussions in their presence, and above all, they were to be "modest in talking to local people. The bragging Yankee does more harm than good and certainly is not respected." Professor Richard Millett provided the author a copy of this fact sheet.

26. U.S.F.D.R., "Stability Operations," pt. 1, vol. II, XIII-C-3; Schoonmaker, "U.S. Military Forces," 154; White, Silvasy, and Long interviews; and Telegram, SUB JIB AmEmbassy, Santo Domingo, to CINCLANT, et al., 0031Z 11 May 1965, in NSC History.

27. Charles C. Moskos, Jr., "Grace Under Pressure: The U.S. Soldier in the Dominican Republic," *Army* 16 (September 1966):42, 44.

28. Training programs abounded and included artillery firing, airmobile exercises, parachute jumps, jungle exercises (in preparation for Vietnam), and testing the Checkerboard concept developed by Colonel Harry Emerson of the Army War College for fighting guerrillas.

29. Palmer MHI interview, 161. A discussion and partial list of the rules of engagement can be found in U.S.F.D.R., "Stability Operations," pt. 1, vol. II, XIII-A-1 to XIII-A-6.

30. Author's interviews with several veterans of the Dominican intervention, e.g., Long and Silvasy.

31. Harold K. Johnson to Colonel Frank Linvell, 15 May 1965, Harold K. Johnson Papers, USAMHI.

32. Barry, ed., *POWER-PACK*, 34.

Chapter 8

1. Telegram no. 1543, AmEmbassy, Santo Domingo, to Secretary of State, 9 May 1965, in NSC History; and U.S.F.D.R., "Stability Operations," pt. 1, vol. I, chap. 2, 16, and vol. IV, chap. 17, 1.

2. U.S.F.D.R., "Stability Operations," pt. 1, vol. I, chap. 2, 5, 16, and vol. IV, chap. 17, 1.

3. Child, *Unequal Alliance*, 164—65.

4. Entries for 1—3 May 1965, in "Chronology." As part of the lobbying campaign, Bennett was instructed to persuade the first OAS Commission, then in Santo Domingo, to recommend passage of the resolution. At first, the commission seemed reluctant to do so because, in Bennett's opinion, the deployment of Latin American troops would be construed as an "endorsement of our military intervention." But the commission's fear of a Communist takeover in the Dominican Republic outweighed their reservations, and it made the desired recommendation in its report to the OAS. Entries for 2—6 May 1965, in "Chronology." Telegram no. 744, State to AmEmbassy, Santo Domingo, 2 May 1965; Telegram no. 788, State to AmEmbassy, Santo Domingo, 3 May 1965; and Telegram nos. 1338, 1350, 1359, AmEmbassy, Santo Domingo, to Secretary of State, 4 May 1965; all in NSC History.

5. At the time, the acronym for the Commander in Chief, Southern Command, was CINCSO. Given the later use of the same acronym in reference to another unified command, I have chosen to use CINCSOUTH when referring to the CINC of the Southern Command. Telegram, CINCSOUTH to JCS, 1918Z 5 May 1965; Circular no. 2174, State Department to all ARA diplomatic posts (except Kingston, Port-au-Prince, and Port-of-Spain), 8 May 1965; Circular no. 2178, State Department to all ARA diplomatic posts (except Kingston, Port-au-Prince, and Port-of-Spain), 9 May 1965; and Telegram, CINCSOUTH to JCS, 2146 13 May 1965; all in NSC History. Greenberg, *Dominican Republic Intervention*, 67, 69; and U.S.F.D.R., "Stability Operations," pt. 1, vol. IV, chap. 16, 1. Given the historical animosity between the Dominican Republic and its neighbor on the island of Hispaniola, the Johnson administration judged it prudent not to request a troop contribution from Haiti.

6. U.S.F.D.R., "Stability Operations," pt. 1, vol. IV, chap. 16, 1-2, 5-6, Enclosures 2 and 3. Telegrams, JCS to CINCLANT, 2046Z 12 May 1965 and 0038Z 13 May 1965; and Telegram, U.S. Army Military Attaché, Honduras, to Department of the Army, 1538Z 14 May 1965; all in NSC History. Greenberg, *Dominican Republic Intervention*, 71.

7. Telegram no. 856, State [Joint State-Defense Message] to AmEmbassy, Santo Domingo, 6 May 1965, in NSC History.

8. Telegram no. 1526, AmEmbassy, Santo Domingo, to Secretary of State, 9 May 1965, in NSC History; and U.S.F.D.R., "Stability Operations," pt. 1, vol. IV, chap. 16, 1.

9. Telegram no. 1526.

10. U.S.F.D.R., "Stability Operations," pt. 1, vol. IV, chap. 16, 1; Greenberg, *Dominican Republic Intervention*, 71; and entries for late May and early June 1965, in "Chronology."

11. Circular no. 2328, State to all ARA diplomatic posts (except Kingston and Port-of-Spain), 24 May 1965, in NSC History.

12. U.S.F.D.R., "Stability Operations," pt. 1, vol. IV, chap. 16, 4—5; Greenberg, *Dominican Republic Intervention*, 70—71, 73; and Lieutenant Colonel Frederick C. Turner, Jr., U.S. Army, "Experiment in Inter-American Peace-Keeping," *Army* 17 (June 1967):35.

13. In formulating the force regulations, Alvim used a draft prepared by the U.S. State Department. The Defense Department provided recommendations on several points, including the authority of the IAPF deputy commander, who, it argued, at minimum should be considered "the alter ego of the Commander and shall have full power and authority to act for the Commander and to exercise the powers of the Commander upon any and all matters concerning which the Commander is authorized to act pursuant to the Act Establishing the Inter-American Force and these Regulations." Defense also suggested, as an alternative to the above, wording that bestowed upon the deputy commander the appointment of "Commander, Ground Forces," with "operational control over ground operations subject to the policy guidance of the Commander." Telegram, Secretary of Defense to AmEmbassy, Santo Domingo, 1400Z 27 May 1965, in NSC History.

14. Greenberg, *Dominican Republic Intervention*, 73—74; and Palmer to Spiller, 16 November 1983.

15. Greenberg, *Dominican Republic Intervention*, 74. In a television interview that stirred some controversy, General Palmer declared that if he had to choose between obeying an order issued by Alvim and one by the president, he would be bound by oath to obey the latter.

16. U.S.F.D.R., "Stability Operations," pt. 1, vol. I, chap. 2, 15—16, and vol. IV, chap. 16, 5, and pt. 2, chap. 3, 4, 8—9.

17. U.S.F.D.R., "Stability Operations," pt. 1, vol. I, chap. 2, 16, and vol. IV, chap. 16, 4—6. One might note for the record that on at least one occasion, that of the U.S. intervention in northern Russia from 1918 to 1919, U.S. troops were placed under the direct command of a British general for the purpose of carrying out combat missions.

18. U.S.F.D.R., "Stability Operations," pt. 1, vol. IV, chap. 16, 3; pt. 2, chap. 1, 3; pt. 2, chap. 3, 5, 6—8; and pt. 2, chap. 16, 4. Schoonmaker, "U.S. Military Forces," 172. The Inter-American Commission on Human Rights, invited into the country by Dr. Mora, also investigated atrocities while becoming involved, as well, in such matters as the treatment and exchange of political prisoners and alleged violations of human rights. For a discussion of the commission's activities, see Anna P. Schreiber and Philippe S. E. Schreiber, "The Inter-American Commission on Human Rights in the Dominican Crisis," *International Organization* 22 (Spring 1968):508—28.

19. U.S.F.D.R., "Stability Operations," pt. 2, chap. 1, 3.

20. Telegram no. 888, State to AmEmbassy, Santo Domingo, and CJTF-120, 7 May 1965, in NSC History; and U.S.F.D.R., "Stability Operations," pt. 2, chap. 3, 1, and chap. 16, 5.

21. Long interview; Telegram, USCOMDOMREP to CINCLANT, 2311Z 14 May 1965, in NSC History; and entry for 10 June 1965, in "Chronology."

22. Entry for 14 June 1965, in "Chronology."

23. The account of the fighting on 15—16 June is based on the Palmer, Long, Forrester, Klein, and Butler interviews; Barry, ed., *POWER-PACK*, 25, 35, 66; entry for 15 June 1965, in "Chronology"; and Mansbach, *Dominican Crisis*, 91—92. U.S.F.D.R., "Stability Operations," pt. 1, vol. I, chap. 2, 17, pt. 2, chap. 2, and pt. 2, chap. 3, 2.

24. U.S.F.D.R., "Stability Operations," pt. 2, chap. 16, 5, 8; Mansbach, *Dominican Crisis*, 91—92; and Forrester, Klein, and Palmer interviews.

25. U.S.F.D.R., "Stability Operations," pt. 1, vol. I, chap. 2, 17.

26. Ibid., pt. 2, chap. 3, 3, and chap. 6, 2; Slater, "Dominican Republic," 324; and entries for June and July in "Chronology."

27. U.S.F.D.R., "Stability Operations," pt. 2, chap. 3, 6—7.

28. The extent of rebel atrocities did not become apparent until late October when the IAPF cleared Ciudad Nueva.

29. U.S.F.D.R., "Stability Operations," pt. 2, chap. 1, 8—10; and Phillips, *Night Watch*, 166—67.

30. U.S.F.D.R., "Stability Operations," pt. 2, chap. 1, 5; Bracey, *Resolution*, 1—2; Palmer interview; and Phillips, *Night Watch*, 161.

31. U.S.F.D.R., "Stability Operations," pt. 2, chap. 1, 5—6, and chap. 16, 11; and Palmer interview.

32. U.S.F.D.R., "Stability Operations," pt. 2, chap. 1, 11—12, and chap. 3, 8.

33. Slater, "Dominican Republic," 326—27; and U.S.F.D.R., "Stability Operations," pt. 2, chap. 1, 10.

34. The Wessin affair is recounted in U.S.F.D.R., "Stability Operations," pt. 2, chap. 1, 14—16; and Palmer MHI interview. Alvim, Palmer, and the others had been preceded by the CIA station chief, who, in a similar visit to Wessin's home, had failed to persuade the general to resign. Phillips, *Night Watch*, 169.

35. Bracey, *Dominican Crisis*, 32; and U.S.F.D.R., "Stability Operations," pt. 2, chap. 1, 19—24.

36. U.S.F.D.R., "Stability Operations," pt. 2, chap. 1, 26—28.

37. Ibid., 29, 31.

38. The account of the Hotel Matum affair is based on ibid., 16; Butler and Costa interviews; Slater, "Dominican Republic," 327; and Bracey, *Dominican Crisis*, 36—37. Bracey raises the question of "why it took the IAPF so long [five to eight hours] to get to the scene to aid Caamaño." Some speculated that García-Godoy deliberately held up sending the IAPF in hopes that the military in Santiago would eliminate Caamaño and the "remaining

constitutionalist hierarchy." This explanation, as Bracey indicates, suffers from ignoring the close relationship between García-Godoy and Caamaño. "The delay," Bracey concludes, "appears to have occurred for reasons internal to the IAPF itself." Another explanation would take into account the time between the beginning of the firefight, the time at which the military intelligence officer made contact with XVIII Airborne Corps, and the time it takes to mount a rescue operation. The MI officer on the scene observed the situation develop before phoning the Marine Guard at the U.S. Embassy and, then, USFORDOMREP. More time elapsed while García-Godoy was notified, a decision made, and authorization passed down the chain of command to Costa. Once Costa was told to send a company to Santiago, the troops had to marshal at the Polo Grounds and at San Isidro. Flying time to Santiago airfield was less than an hour. After the troops arrived in Santiago, Costa had to be briefed and the troops had to march to the hotel. Given these activities, an interval of between five to six hours between the beginning of the firefight and the arrival of IAPF troops at the hotel does not necessarily connote political mischief.

39. Phillips recounts how, as CIA chief of station, he met with García-Godoy, who told him, "I am having real problems holding my government together.... It is essential that I broaden the political base of the provisional cabinet and my subministers. To do that I plan several new appointments. Some will not please your government.... I realize that I cannot keep this flimsy government together without American support, but I must have some young people of the left in my camp. Otherwise it will not work." Phillips was sympathetic and, in a deal arranged by circumlocution and inference, ended up bending CIA rules by screening certain prospective appointees to see if their Leftist ties were strong enough to sound alarm bells in Washington. Phillips, *Night Watch*, 172—73.

40. Bracey, *Dominican Crisis*, 34, 37; and U.S.F.D.R., "Stability Operations," pt. 2, chap. 1, 17—19, 24—25, 35—36.

41. Slater, "Dominican Republic," 327—28; Bracey, *Dominican Crisis*, 37—38; and entries for 6—8 January 1966 in "Chronology." Caamaño was killed in 1973 when he tried to reenter the Dominican Republic with a guerrilla force. As for Wessin, Imbert, Bosch, Balaguer, and other prominent Dominicans involved in the 1965 crisis, they are, as of this writing, still involved in Dominican politics and government.

42. Slater, "Dominican Republic," 328—29; and U.S.F.D.R., "Stability Operations," pt. 2, chap. 1, 36—37, 40.

43. Bracey, *Dominican Crisis*, 39; and Palmer MHI interview.

Chapter 9

1. *New York Times*, 1 May 1985:2.

2. Ibid.

3. Abraham F. Lowenthal, "The Dominican Intervention in Retrospect," *Public Policy* 18 (Fall 1969):140—41.

4. Ibid., 141. Several policymakers and scholars have suggested that the failure of President Jimmy Carter's administration to persuade the OAS to form a peace force for the purpose of intervening in Nicaragua to prevent the Sandinistas from coming to power can be traced, in part, to the reluctance of Latin American leaders to repeat the IAPF experiment in the Dominican Republic. On this point, see, for example, Pastor, *Condemned to Repetition*, 145.

5. Telegram no. 753, State to AmEmbassy, Santo Domingo, 2 May 1965, in NSC History. For additional information on the credibility gap that developed between the military and some correspondents in Santo Domingo, see Szulc, *Dominican Diary*, passim; and Kelso, "Dominican Crisis," 139—47.

6. One officer from the 82d remembers another example of television journalists deliberately distorting an event. After an anti-American rally had ended, the journalists in question asked several of the demonstrators to re-create the effect of the demonstration for the benefit of the television cameras. The journalists provided stage directions for what would be described to U.S. television audiences as a spontaneous event. Costa interview.

7. U.S.F.D.R., "Stability Operations," pt. 1, vol. I, chap. 2, 6, 20; and Szulc, *Dominican Diary*, passim.

8. U.S. Department of the Army, FM 57-10, *Army Forces in Joint Airborne Operations* (Washington, DC, March 1962), 11.

9. U.S.F.D.R., "Stability Operations," pt. 1, vol. II, II-20.

10. U.S.F.D.R., "Stability Operations," pt. 1, vol. I, chap. 2, 2.

11. The quotation on Wheeler's speech is taken from Betts, *Soldiers*, 11.

12. *New York Times*, 1 May 1985:2.

Glossary

AID	Agency for International Development
ALTF	airlift task force
BCT	battalion combat team
BLT	battalion landing team
CEFA	*Centro de Entrenamiento de las Fuerzas Armadas* (Armed Forces Training Center)
CIA	Central Intelligence Agency
CINCAFLANT	Commander in Chief, U.S. Air Forces, Atlantic Command
CINCAFSTRIKE	Commander in Chief, U.S. Air Forces, Strike Command
CINCARLANT	Commander in Chief, U.S. Army Forces, Atlantic Command
CINCARSTRIKE	Commander in Chief, U.S. Army Forces, Strike Command
CINCLANT	Commander in Chief, Atlantic Command
CINCLANTFLT	Commander in Chief, Atlantic Fleet
CINCSOUTH	Commander in Chief, U.S. Southern Command
CINCSTRIKE	Commander in Chief, U.S. Strike Command
CJTF	commander, joint task force
COMCARIBSEAFRON	Commander, Caribbean Sea Frontier
CTG	commander, task group
DA	Department of the Army
DCSOPS	Deputy Chief of Staff for Operations and Plans

DEFCON	defense readiness condition
DOD	Department of Defense
DRF	division ready force
GNR	Government of National Reconstruction
HUMINT	human intelligence (the intelligence collection function that uses human beings as both sources and collectors)
IAAF	Inter-American Armed Force
IAF	Inter-American Force
IAPF	Inter-American Peace Force
ISZ	International Security Zone
JCS	Joint Chiefs of Staff
JTF	joint task force
LANTCOM	(See USLANTCOM)
LBJL	Lyndon B. Johnson Library
LOC	lines of communication
LVT	landing vehicle, tracked
MAAG	Military Assistance Advisory Group
MAP	Military Assistance Program
MEB	Marine expeditionary brigade
MEU	Marine expeditionary unit
MTT	mobile training team
NMCC	National Military Command Center
NSC	National Security Council
OAS	Organization of American States
OES	*Organización de Estados Americanos* (Organization of American States)
OPLAN	operation plan
PR	*Partido Reformista* (Reform Party)
PRD	*Partido Revolucionario Dominicano* (Dominican Revolutionary Party)
PSYWAR	psychological warfare
ROAD	Reorganization Objective Army Divisions
RSD	Radio Santo Domingo
SEAL	sea-air-land team
SOUTHCOM	(See USSOUTHCOM)
TAC	Tactical Air Command

TF	task force
TG	task group
TOE	table(s) of organization and equipment
USAF	U.S. Air Force
USCOMDOMREP	Commander, U.S. Forces, Dominican Republic
USCONARC	U.S. Continental Army Command
USFORDOMREP	U.S. Forces, Dominican Republic
USIA	U.S. Information Agency
USIS	U.S. Information Service
USLANTCOM (or LANTCOM)	U.S. Atlantic Command
USMC	U.S. Marine Corps
USSOUTHCOM (or SOUTHCOM)	U.S. Southern Command
USSTRICOM (or STRICOM)	U.S. Strike Command

Bibliography

Primary Sources

Published and Unpublished Collections

Declassified Documents Reference System. Washington, DC: Carrollton Press, 1976—. This source is still being published.

Johnson, Harold K., General, U.S. Army. Papers. U.S. Army Military History Institute, Carlisle Barracks, Pennsylvania.

Kesaris, Paul, ed. *Crises in Panama and the Dominican Republic: National Security Files and NSC Histories.* Frederick, MD: University Publications of America, 1982. Microfilm.

———. *Daily Diary of President Johnson (1963—1969).* Frederick, MD: University Publications of America, 1980. Microfilm.

Palmer, Bruce, Jr., General, U.S. Army. Papers. U.S. Army Military History Institute, Carlisle Barracks, Pennsylvania.

President's Secretary's Files. Harry S. Truman Library, Independence, Missouri.

U.S. National Security Council. History of Dominican Intervention. Lyndon B. Johnson Library, Austin, Texas.

Individual Memoirs, Studies, Reports, Etc.

Barry, Robert F., ed. *POWER-PACK.* Portsmouth, VA: Messenger Printing Co., 1965.

Estep, Raymond. *United States Military Aid to Latin America.* Air University Documentary Research Study no. AU-200-65-ASI. Maxwell Air Force Base, AL: Aerospace Studies Institute, Air University, 1966.

Gray, David M., General, U.S. Army ret. *The U.S. Intervention in Lebanon, 1958: A Commander's Reminiscence.* Fort Leavenworth, KS: Combat Studies Institute, U.S. Army Command and General Staff College, August 1984.

Johnson, Lyndon Baines. *The Vantage Point: Perspectives of the Presidency, 1963—1969.* New York: Holt, Rinehart and Winston, 1971.

Legg, Elbert E., Lieutenant Colonel, U.S. Army. "The US Military Role in Coping with a Sudden Revolt in the Dominican Republic." Course essay, U.S. Army War College, Carlisle Barracks, Pennsylvania, 1968.

Long, Eldredge R., Lieutenant Colonel, U.S. Army. "The Dominican Crisis 1965: An Experiment in International Peace Keeping." Thesis, School of Naval Warfare, U.S. Naval War College, Newport, Rhode Island, 1967.

Phillips, David Atlee. *The Night Watch: 25 Years of Peculiar Service.* New York: Atheneum, 1977.

Szulc, Tad. *Dominican Diary.* New York: Delacorte Press, 1965.

U.S. Air Force. 9th Air Force. Airlift Task Force Tactical Operations. "Final Report on Power Pack." Shaw Air Force Base, SC, 24 May 1965. Copy at the Albert F. Simpson Historical Research Center, Maxwell Air Force Base, Alabama.

U.S. Air Force. 464th Troop Carrier Wing. "History of the 464th Troop Carrier Wing, Pope Air Force Base, North Carolina, January 1965—June 1965." N.p., 1965. This document is available at the Albert F. Simpson Historical Research Center, Maxwell Air Force Base, Alabama.

U.S. Army. Chief of Staff. *Challenge: Compendium of Army Accomplishment—A Report by the Chief of Staff.* Washington, DC: Department of the Army, July 1964—April 1968. In Archives, U.S. Army Military History Institute, Carlisle Barracks, Pennsylvania.

U.S. Army. 1st Special Forces. 8th Special Forces Group (Airborne). *Special Action Force for Latin America: Historical Report.* N.p., n.d. Available at the U.S. Army Military History Institute, Carlisle Barracks, Pennsylvania.

U.S. Department of State. *Foreign Relations of the United States.* Vol. 4. *The American Republics, 1952—54.* Washington, DC: U.S. Government Printing Office, 1983.

U.S. Department of the Army. FM 57-10. *Army Forces in Joint Airborne Operations.* Washington, DC, March 1962.

U.S. Forces, Dominican Republic. "Report of Stability Operations in the Dominican Republic." 2 parts. Santo Domingo, 1965.

U.S. Strike Command. *Strike Command History, 1961—1962.* MacDill Air Force Base, FL, n.d. Unclassified portions.

Interviews and Oral Histories

Adams, Paul D., General, U.S. Army. Oral history. U.S. Army Military History Institute, Carlisle Barracks, Pennsylvania.

Bechtold, Earl E., Lieutenant Colonel, U.S. Army. Interview with author, Fort Leavenworth, Kansas, 29 October 1987.

Bennett, W. Tapley, Jr., Ambassador (ret.). Interview with author, Washington, DC, 12 November 1986.

Butler, Steven, Lieutenant Colonel, U.S. Army. Interview with author, Fort Leavenworth, Kansas, 21 March 1986.

Costa, John J., Colonel, U.S. Army. Telephone interview with author, 12 February 1988.

Cunningham, Mrs. Hugh. Telephone interview with author, 29 March 1985. Mrs. Cunningham is the wife of General Hugh Cunningham, who in 1965 was the chief of staff of the 82d Airborne Division.

Dominican officer. Interview with author.

Ellis, James R., Brigadier General, U.S. Army. Interview with author, Fort Leavenworth, Kansas, 7 July 1987.

Forrester, Eugene, Lieutenant General, U.S. Army, ret. Interview with author, Washington, DC, 11 November 1986.

Klein, William E., Major General, U.S. Army. Interview with author, MacDill Air Force Base, Florida, 4 November 1985.

Lloyd, Herbert J., Colonel, U.S. Army, telephone interview with author, 13 July 1987.

Long, Eldredge R., Colonel, U.S. Army ret. Interview with author, Washington, DC, 5 November 1985.

Military intelligence officers. Interviews with author.

Palmer, Bruce, Jr., General, U.S. Army ret. Interview with author, Washington, DC, 4 November 1985.

―――――. Interview with Captain Richard S. Switzer, U.S. Air Force, 20 August 1974. Richard S. Switzer Collection, Hoover Institution Archives, Stanford, California.

―――――. Interview with Senior Officer Debriefing Program, U.S. Army Military History Institute, Carlisle Barracks, Pennsylvania, 1976.

Rodríguez Alvarez, Orlando, Colonel, U.S. Army. Interview with author, MacDill Air Force Base, Florida, 5 November 1986.

Silvasy, Stephen, Colonel, U.S. Army. Interview with author, Fort Bragg, North Carolina, 29 March 1985.

White, Kenneth, Sergeant, U.S. Army ret. Interview with author, Fort Leavenworth, Kansas, 16 May 1985.

Correspondence

Palmer, Bruce, Jr., General, U.S. Army ret., to Dr. Roger Spiller, 15 November 1983.

Palmer, Bruce, Jr., General, U.S. Army ret., to Dr. Roger Spiller, 16 November 1983.

Spiller, Roger, to General Wallace Nutting, U.S. Army, Memorandum, 30 September 1983.

Articles

Chew, Peter T. "On a Lonely Point." *Army* 15 (June 1965):92—94.

Dare, James A., Captain, U.S. Navy. "Dominican Diary." *U.S. Naval Institute Proceedings* 91 (December 1965):37—45.

Johnson, Harold K., General, U.S. Army. "Landpower Missions Unlimited." *Army* 15 (November 1964):41—42.

Klein, William E., Major, U.S. Army. "Stability Operations in Santo Domingo." *Infantry* 56 (May—June 1966):35—39.

New York Times, 29 April 1965 and 1 May 1985.

Palmer, Bruce, Jr., Lieutenant General, U.S. Army. "XVIII Airborne Corps—All the Way." *Army Digest* 22 (January 1967):12—18.

―――. "The Army in the Dominican Republic." *Army* 15 (November 1965):43—44, 136, 138.

"Statement by President Johnson, April 30." *Department of State Bulletin*, 17 May 1965:742—43.

"Statement by President Johnson, May 2." *Department of State Bulletin*, 17 May 1965:744—48.

Tompkins, R. McC., Major General, U.S. Marine Corps. "Ubique." *Marine Corps Gazette* 49 (September 1965):32—39.

"USARSTRIKE: Ready to Go." *Army Information Digest* 20 (October 1965):12—15.

"U.S. Strike Command." *Army Information Digest* 17 (May 1962):18—23.

Other Sources

Published Monographs

Ambrose, Stephen E. *Eisenhower*. Vol. 2. *The President*. New York: Simon and Schuster, 1984.

Atkins, G. Pope, and Larman C. Wilson. *The United States and the Trujillo Regime*. New Brunswick, NJ: Rutgers University Press, 1972.

Ball, George W. *The Past Has Another Pattern: Memoirs*. New York: W. W. Norton, 1982.

Barber, Willard F., and C. Neale Ronning. *Internal Security and Military Power: Counterinsurgency and Civic Action in Latin America*. Athens: Ohio State University Press, 1966.

Bemis, Samuel Flagg. *The Latin-American Policy of the United States: An Historical Interpretation*. New York: Harcourt, Brace, 1943.

Betts, Richard K. *Soldiers, Statesmen, and Cold War Crises*. Cambridge, MA: Harvard University Press, 1977.

Blaiser, Cole. *The Hovering Giant: U.S. Responses to Revolutionary Change in Latin America*. Pittsburgh, PA: University of Pittsburgh Press, 1976.

Blaufarb, Douglas. *The Counterinsurgency Era: U.S. Doctrine and Performance, 1950 to the Present.* New York: Free Press, 1977.

Bracey, Audrey. *Resolution of the Dominican Crisis, 1965: A Study in Mediation.* Washington, DC: Institute for the Study of Diplomacy, 1980.

Burns, Richard Dean, ed. *Guide to American Foreign Relations Since 1700.* Santa Barbara, CA: ABC-CLIO, 1983.

Calder, Bruce J. *The Impact of Intervention: The Dominican Republic During the U.S. Occupation of 1916—1924.* Austin: University of Texas Press, 1984.

Center for Strategic Studies, Georgetown University. *Dominican Action— 1965: Intervention or Cooperation?* Special Report Series no. 2. Washington, DC, 1966.

Child, John. *Unequal Alliance: The Inter-American Military System, 1938— 1978.* Boulder, CO: Westview Press, 1980.

Cohen, Warren I. *Dean Rusk.* The American Secretaries of State and Their Diplomacy, vol. 19. Totowa, NJ: Cooper Square, 1980.

Crassweller, Robert D. *Trujillo: The Life and Times of a Caribbean Dictator.* New York: Macmillan, 1966.

Donovan, James A., Jr. *The United States Marine Corps.* New York: Frederick A. Praeger, 1967.

Doughty, Robert A. *The Evolution of US Army Tactical Doctrine, 1946—76.* Leavenworth Papers no. 1. Fort Leavenworth, KS: Combat Studies Institute, U.S. Army Command and General Staff College, 1979.

Fuller, Stephen M., and Graham A. Cosmas. *Marines in the Dominican Republic, 1916—1924.* Washington, DC: History and Museums Division, U.S. Marine Corps, 1974.

Gaddis, John Lewis. *Strategies of Containment: A Critical Appraisal of Postwar American National Security Policy.* New York: Oxford University Press, 1982.

Gil, Federico G. *Latin American-United States Relations.* New York: Harcourt, Brace, Jovanovich, 1971.

Gleijeses, Piero. *The Dominican Crisis: The 1965 Constitutionalist Revolt and American Intervention.* Baltimore, MD: Johns Hopkins University Press, 1978.

Greenberg, Lawrence M. *United States Army Unilateral and Coalition Operations in the 1965 Dominican Republic Intervention.* Historical Analysis Series. Washington, DC: Analysis Branch, U.S. Army Center of Military History, 1987.

Haffa, Robert P., Jr. *The Half War: Planning U.S. Rapid Deployment Forces to Meet a Limited Contingency, 1960—1983.* Westview Replica ed. Boulder, CO: Westview Press, 1984.

Hovey, Harold A. *United States Military Assistance: A Study of Policies and Practices*. New York: Frederick A. Praeger, 1965.

Immerman, Richard H. *The CIA in Guatemala: The Foreign Policy of Intervention*. Austin: University of Texas Press, 1982.

Kinzer, Stephen, and Stephen Schlesinger. *Bitter Fruit: The Untold Story of the American Coup in Guatemala*. Garden City, NY: Doubleday, 1981.

Krepinevich, Andrew, Jr. *The Army and Vietnam*. Baltimore, MD: Johns Hopkins University Press, 1986.

LaFeber, Walter. *Inevitable Revolutions: The United States in Central America*. New York: W. W. Norton, 1983.

Langley, Lester D. *The Banana Wars: An Inner History of American Empire, 1900–1934*. Lexington: University Press of Kentucky, 1983.

————. *The United States and the Caribbean in the Twentieth Century*. Athens: University of Georgia Press, 1982.

Levinson, Jerome, and Juan de Onís. *The Alliance That Lost Its Way: A Critical Report on the Alliance for Progress*. Paperback ed. Chicago, IL: Quadrangle Books, 1972.

Lowenthal, Abraham F. *The Dominican Intervention*. Cambridge, MA: Harvard University Press, 1972.

————. *The Dominican Republic: The Politics of Chaos*. Reprint 158. Washington, DC: Brookings Institute, 1969.

Lowenthal, Abraham F., and Albert Fishlow. *Latin America's Emergence: Toward a U.S. Response*. Headline Series 243. New York: Foreign Policy Association, 1979.

Mansbach, Richard W., ed. *Dominican Crisis 1965*. New York: Facts on File, 1971.

Martin, John Bartlow. *Overtaken by Events: The Dominican Crisis from the Fall of Trujillo to the Civil War*. Garden City, NY: Doubleday & Co., 1966.

————. *U.S. Policy in the Caribbean*. Boulder, CO: Westview Press, 1978.

Millett, Allan R. *Semper Fidelis: The History of the United States Marine Corps*. New York: Macmillan, 1980.

Munro, Dana G. *Intervention and Dollar Diplomacy, 1900–1921*. Princeton, NJ: Princeton University Press, 1964.

————. *The United States and the Caribbean Republics, 1921–1934*. Princeton, NJ: Princeton University Press, 1974.

Molineu, Harold. *U.S. Policy Toward Latin America: From Regionalism to Globalism*. Boulder, CO: Westview Press, 1986.

Pastor, Robert A. *Condemned to Repetition: The United States and Nicaragua*. Princeton, NJ: Princeton University Press, 1987.

Paterson, Thomas G., et al. *Amerian Foreign Policy: A History*. 2d ed. Lexington, MA: D. C. Heath, 1983.

Pizer, Vernon. *The United States Army*. New York: Frederick A. Praeger, 1967.

Rabe, Stephen G. *Eisenhower and Latin America: The Foreign Policy of Anticommunism*. Chapel Hill: University of North Carolina Press, 1988.

Ringler, Jack K., Major, and Henry I. Shaw, Jr. *U.S. Marine Corps Operations in the Dominican Republic, April—June 1965*. (U). Washington, DC: Historical Division, U.S. Marine Corps, 1970. Unclassified monograph.

Rodman, Selden. *Quisqueya: A History of the Dominican Republic*. Seattle: University of Washington Press, 1964.

Schlesinger, Arthur M., Jr. *A Thousand Days: John F. Kennedy in the White House*. Boston, MA: Houghton Mifflin Co., 1965.

———. *Robert Kennedy and His Times*. Boston: Houghton Mifflin, 1976.

Simpson, Charles M., III. *Inside the Green Berets: The First Thirty Years*. Novato, CA: Presidio Press, 1983.

Slater, Jerome N. *Intervention and Negotiation: The United States and the Dominican Revolution*. New York: Harper & Row, 1970.

Smith, Wayne S. *The Closest of Enemies: A Personal and Diplomatic Account of U.S.-Cuban Relations Since 1957*. New York: W. W. Norton, 1987.

Spiller, Roger J. *"Not War But Like War": The American Intervention in Lebanon*. Leavenworth Papers no. 3. Fort Leavenworth, KS: Combat Studies Institute, U.S. Army Command and General Staff College, January 1981.

Unger, Sanford. *FBI*. Boston, MA: Little, Brown and Co., 1976.

U.S. Congress. Senate. Select Committee to Study Governmental Operations with Respect to Intelligence Activities. *Alleged Assassination Plots Involving Foreign Leaders*. Senate Report no. 465. 94th Cong., 1st sess. Washington, DC: U.S. Government Printing Office, 1975.

U.S. Department of the Air Force. *The Tactical Air Command in the Dominican Crisis, 1965*. Langley Air Force Base, VA: Office of TAC History, May 1977.

U.S. Joint Chiefs of Staff. Joint Secretariat. Historical Division. *Special Historical Study: History of the Unified Command Plan*. Washington, DC, 20 December 1977. Confidential, declassified in 1981.

Welch, Richard E., Jr. *Response to Revolution: The United States and the Cuban Revolution, 1959—1961*. Chapel Hill: University of North Carolina Press, 1985.

Welles, Sumner. *Naboth's Vineyard: The Dominican Republic, 1844—1924*. 2 vols. New York: Payton & Clarke, 1928.

Wiarda, Howard J. *Dictatorship and Development: The Methods of Control in Trujillo's Dominican Republic*. Gainesville: University of Florida Press, 1970.

Wiarda, Howard J., and Michael J. Kryzanek. *The Dominican Republic: A Caribbean Crucible*. Boulder, CO: Westview Press, 1982.

Articles

Cooper, Bert H., Jr. "Teamwork in Santo Domingo." In *Military Propaganda: Psychological Warfare and Operations*, edited by Ron D. McLaurin. New York: Praeger, 1982.

LaFeber, Walter. "Inevitable Revolutions." *Atlantic Monthly* 249 (June 1982):74—83.

Lowenthal, Abraham F. "The Dominican Intervention in Retrospect." *Public Policy* 18 (Fall 1969):133—48.

Moskos, Charles C., Jr. "Grace Under Pressure: The U.S. Soldier in the Dominican Republic." *Army* 16 (September 1966):41—44.

Moulis, Wallace J., Lieutenant Colonel, U.S. Army, and Major Richard M. Brown, U.S. Army. "Key to a Crisis." *Military Review* 46 (February 1966):9—14.

Pach, Chester J., Jr. "The Containment of U.S. Military Aid to Latin America, 1944—49." *Diplomatic History* 6 (Summer 1982): 225—43.

Rabe, Stephen G. "The Johnson (Eisenhower?) Doctrine for Latin America." *Diplomatic History* 9 (Winter 1985):95—100.

Rosen, Stephen Peter. "Vietnam and the American Theory of Limited War." *International Security* 7 (Fall 1982):83—113.

Schlesinger, Arthur M., Jr. "The Alliance for Progress: A Retrospective." In *Latin America: The Search for a New International Role*, edited by Ronald G. Hellman and H. Jon Rosenbaum. New York: John Wiley & Sons, 1975.

Schreiber, Anna P., and Philippe S. E. Schreiber. "The Inter-American Commissions on Human Rights in the Dominican Crisis." *International Organization* 22 (Spring 1968):508—28.

Slater, Jerome N. "The Dominican Republic, 1961—66." In *Force Without War: U.S. Armed Forces as a Political Instrument*, edited by Barry M. Blechman and Stephen S. Kaplan. Washington, DC: Brookings Institute, 1978.

Trask, Roger R. "The Impact of the Cold War on United States-Latin American Relations, 1945—1949." *Diplomatic History* 1 (Summer 1977):271—84.

Turner, Frederick C., Jr., Lieutenant Colonel, U.S. Army. "Experiment in Inter-American Peace-Keeping." *Army* 17 (June 1967):34—39.

Zalaquett, José. "From Dictatorship to Democracy." *New Republic*, 16 December 1985:17—21.

Unpublished Materials

Ault, John W., Jr., Major, U.S. Army. "Dominican Republic Crisis: Causes, Intervention, Lessons Learned." Research paper, Air Command and Staff College, Air University, Maxwell Air Force Base, Alabama, 1970.

Bowman, Stephen Lee. "The Evolution of United States Army Doctrine for Counterinsurgency Warfare: From World War II to the Commitment of Combat Units in Vietnam." Ph.D. dissertation, Duke University, 1985.

Greenberg, Lawrence M., Major, U.S. Army. "The Army in Support of Political Initiatives: The 1965 Dominican Republic Intervention." Paper presented at the Missouri Valley History Conference, Omaha, Nebraska, March 1987.

Kelso, Quinten Allen. "The Dominican Crisis of 1965: A New Appraisal." Ph.D. dissertation, University of Colorado, 1982.

Schoonmaker, Herbert Garrettson. "United States Military Forces in the Dominican Crisis of 1965." Ph.D. dissertation, University of Georgia, 1977.

Smith, Paul E., Lieutenant Colonel, U.S. Army. "The United States Military Assistance Program in the Dominican Republic, 1953—1965: A Lesson Learned?" Student essay, U.S. Army War College, Carlisle Barracks, Pennsylvania, 18 January 1968; now located in the Army War College archives in the U.S. Army Military History Institute, Carlisle Barracks.

U.S. Department of the Air Force. "Case Studies of Airpower: The Dominican Republic Crisis of 1965." Aerospace Studies Institute Project no. AU-434-66-ASI. Maxwell Air Force Base, AL: Air University, 1966.

Yates, J. D. "The Dominican Crisis." Mitre Working Paper. Bedford, MA: Mitre Corporation, 1973.

LEAVENWORTH PAPERS

1. *The Evolution of U.S. Army Tactical Doctrine, 1946—76*, by Major Robert A. Doughty
2. *Nomonhan: Japanese-Soviet Tactical Combat, 1939*, by Dr. Edward J. Drea
3. *"Not War But Like War": The American Intervention in Lebanon*, by Dr. Roger J. Spiller
4. *The Dynamics of Doctrine: The Changes in German Tactical Doctrine During the First World War*, by Captain Timothy T. Lupfer
5. *Fighting the Russians in Winter: Three Case Studies*, by Dr. Allen F. Chew
6. *Soviet Night Operations in World War II*, by Major Claude R. Sasso
7. *August Storm: The Soviet 1945 Strategic Offensive in Manchuria*, by Lieutenant Colonel David M. Glantz
8. *August Storm: Soviet Tactical and Operational Combat in Manchuria, 1945*, by Lieutenant Colonel David M. Glantz
9. *Defending the Driniumor: Covering Force Operations in New Guinea, 1944*, by Dr. Edward J. Drea
10. *Chemical Warfare in World War I: The American Experience, 1917—1918*, by Major Charles E. Heller, USAR
11. *Rangers: Selected Combat Operations in World War II*, by Dr. Michael J. King
12. *Seek, Strike, and Destroy: U.S. Army Tank Destroyer Doctrine in World War II*, by Dr. Christopher R. Gabel
13. *Counterattack on the Naktong, 1950*, by Dr. William Glenn Robertson
14. *Dragon Operations: Hostage Rescues in the Congo, 1964—1965*, by Major Thomas P. Odom

RESEARCH SURVEYS

1. *Amicicide: The Problem of Friendly Fire in Modern War*, by Lieutenant Colonel Charles R. Shrader
2. *Toward Combined Arms Warfare: A Survey of 20th-Century Tactics, Doctrine, and Organization*, by Captain Jonathan M. House
3. *Rapid Deployment Logistics: Lebanon, 1958*, by Lieutenant Colonel Gary H. Wade
4. *The Soviet Airborne Experience*, by Lieutenant Colonel David M. Glantz
5. *Standing Fast: German Defensive Doctrine on the Russian Front During World War II*, by Major Timothy A. Wray
6. *A Historical Perspective on Light Infantry*, by Major Scott R. McMichael

STUDIES IN PROGRESS

Deciding What Has to Be Done: General William E. DePuy and the 1976 Edition of FM 100-5, Operations

•

Petsamo-Kirkenes Operation, October 1944

•

Huai Hai Campaign: Chinese People's Liberation Army Performance at the Operational Level of War

•

Busting the Bocage: U.S. Combined Operations in France, 6 June—31 July 1944

•

Japan's Okinawa, April—June 1945

•

The Struggle for Decisive Terrain in the Sinai: The Battles of Abu Ageila in 1957 and 1967

•

The Russian-Soviet Experiences in Unconventional Warfare in Asia Since 1801

•

Brazilian Internal Security and Defense Measures, 1964—1984

•

U.S. Army World War II Corps Commanders' Profile

•

Lam Son 719

•

Battles in the Support Area (Rear Area Operations During the Korean War)

•

Operations of Third U.S. Army Against the German First Army, France, August 1944

•

An Assessment of Soviet Military Historiography

•

Pastel: Deception in the Invasion of Japan